# Experience

"*Experience* is not so much criticism or polemic as it is a guide to living one's life inside and outside of poetry, and of making that life consonant with one's art."

—Susan M. Schultz, author of *A Poetics of Impasse in Modern and Contemporary Poetry* and editor of *The Tribe of John: Ashbery and Contemporary Poetry*

"Norman Fischer's essays constitute a rare reminder that criticism should be inspiring. Reading them, I often feel the impulse to jump up off the page I'm on and go to that other where a poem is waiting for me to write it—a sign of how exciting Fischer's prose can be. Then again, there is the reward in continually attending to Fischer's thought, so clear, exacting, and pertinent as to bolster Wittgenstein's assertion that the right expression for the miracle of existence is the miracle of language itself."

—Bill Berkson, author of *Expect Delays* and *Portrait and Dream: New and Selected Poems*

"Reading *Experience* might be likened to sitting on a piano bench with Norman Fischer—beloved poet/sage—while listening in on his beguiling and most learned ontological array of personal abiding in the very action of insight. Told with uncommon intimacy, honesty and radical presence, here is an immensely moving and embodied richness of being probing our imputational natures, recreation and its silent spring. A prodigious work to be held close."

—Lissa Wolsak, author of *Of Beings Alone: The Eigenface* and *Squeezed Light: Collected Poems 1994–2005*

"It is a profound pleasure learning from *Experience*, Norman Fischer's collection of writing from the last few decades. These essays, reviews, interviews, and poems range widely, but their focus is always singular: the present moment. Under Fischer's scrutiny, that moment widens to encompass the avant-garde poetic tradition and a millennia-wide range of reading—St. Augustine, Dogen, Gerard Manley Hopkins, Paul Celan, Philip Whalen, Leslie Scalapino—and as well as a thorough grounding in the intricacies of Zen historical development. Fischer is an extraordinary poet and a deeply respected Zen religious teacher, and *Experience* contains a wealth of intricate, accurate teaching. But its best quality, to my mind, is its continuous demonstration of beginner's mind: open, non-expert, vulnerable, buffeted by the storms of ordinary experience, sane."

—Bob Perelman, author of *Iflife* and *The Future of Memory*

"Norman Fischer's writing on writing inspires me to write. In the years since I first read them, the essays in this collection have led me to think and not think about writing. They've moved me to ponder words, language, literature, mind, emotion, experience. They've shown me how to live writing as my life. For better or for worse, I would not be the writer I am today without them."

—Ruth Ozeki, author of *A Tale for the Time Being*

# MODERN & CONTEMPORARY POETICS

# Experience

## THINKING,

## WRITING,

## LANGUAGE

## & RELIGION

NORMAN FISCHER

*for Karin, Gunnar,*

*Yours,*

*Norman Fischer*

*Dharma Field      3/26/16*

The University of Alabama Press
Tuscaloosa, Alabama 35487–0380
uapress.ua.edu

Typeface: Janson Text

Manufactured in the United States of America
Cover photograph: courtesty of the author
Cover and interior design: Michele Myatt Quinn

∞

The paper on which this book is printed meets the
minimum requirements of American National Standard
for Information Sciences—Permanence of Paper for
Printed Library Materials, ANSI Z39.48–1984.

Cataloging-in-Publication data is available from the
Library of Congress.
ISBN: 978–0–8173–5828–0
E-ISBN: 978–0–8173–8852–2

This book is for my wife, Kathie Fischer, and for my many colleagues and close friends in the writing world, too many to mention—you know who you are.

# Contents

## ❧ I Early Takes ❧

## ❧ II Are You Writing? ❧

## ❧ III Beyond Thinking ❧

## ❧ IV Experience ❧

# Preface

Assembling this collection has been an experience. Representing work written over a period of thirty or so years (including forgotten early typescript material found in a crumpled folder when I was cleaning out my study in the summer of 2013), this volume is a life. Some of its essays were written by an expansive young man, possibly foolhardy about the prospects for writing; others by an older man sobered by life's brevity and sorrows. Finding, rereading, pondering, and polishing this material has been instructive and fun; writing it kept me going for a long while. It is good to see it now gathered here.

I remember being asked by one of my sons, when he was in his early twenties, "Well, Dad, what was your plan, what did you think you'd be doing when you were forty or fifty?" and his being astonished when I told him, "I had no plan. I never thought about it." I was not alone in this—it was so for many of us who came of age in the 1960s. We were determinedly doing what we were doing, with full commitment, and there was no tomorrow. For me, the determination was writing, impractical though that was, and writing not as a profession or an act of literature, but as a whole life. Somehow my college short stories had won me admission to the University of Iowa Writers' Workshop, where I had the vague expectation of becoming a famous novelist like Hemingway—the same preposterous expectation Philip Whalen had had as a young writer. It turned out that this was as impossible for me as it was for him (although he actually did write a few really good published novels). I spent my two years at Iowa bewildered by the ambitions of my fellow students, who, unlike me, understood well that you enroll at a place like Iowa to make connections, find agents and publishers. Alienated from my prose-writing classmates, I found community among the poets. Ted Berrigan and Anselm Hollo headed up the poetry section at that time; Alice Notley and Barrett Watten (among many others of note) were students, and they and other friends I met through them become lifelong colleagues and companions along the writing way. At Iowa I also met Alan Lew, who later—through a series of coincidences—became a well-known rabbi as well as my inspiration and collaborator in the Jewish meditation movement.

Leaving Iowa, I had no idea what to do. Despair, confusion, and philosophical and religious interest led me to Zen practice as a survival strategy. The intensity of the practice matched the intensity of my life at the time, and the alternative of getting an honest job and settling into a reasonable life seemed impossible. I met Philip Whalen at the San Francisco Zen Center, where, thanks to his being there, I lived for decades. I had already discovered—and been thunderstruck by—Philip's work at Iowa. My long friendship with him was crucial and formative.

All this autobiography is to indicate the contradictory impulses that stand behind the works in this volume. Throughout my adult life I have been seriously involved in Zen Buddhist practice, Jewish meditation practice, and poetry. I have been an ordained Zen priest since 1980. I have been an abbot of a major Western Zen Center, have founded a network of Zen communities and a Jewish Meditation Center that I still direct, and, simultaneously, have been active in poetry. For a poet to be involved in an occupation that has nothing to do with poetry is not unusual—or at least wasn't when I came of age. Williams and Stevens, both important to me, were models. But for a poet to be seriously involved as a religious professional is unusual—or has been for the last hundred and fifty years or so. In our time, the two occupations/interests/impulses have seemed to be mutually exclusive, and throughout my "career" (such as it is), people interested in my work in Zen have been completely baffled by my poetry, while those interested in my poetry seemed slightly embarrassed by my involvement in Zen, although they were generous enough to ignore it. This, anyway, seemed to me to be generally the case from 1980 or so until about 2000. Gradually, it became less taboo for writers to have religious or spiritual concerns. And I began to recognize the extent to which my writing and my spiritual practice came from the same root.

The works in this volume, therefore, do, I hope, cohere, though they were written for different audiences. Many of them were published in

Buddhist magazines read by an audience more or less uninterested in literary matters (many Buddhists, of course, are interested in poetry, but probably not in the sort of poetry I practice and read, and not in poetics). Others appeared in poetry journals for an audience of innovative or avant-garde poets and critics. Some readers of these latter journals noticed, over the years, what I was doing and appreciated it, Charles Bernstein and Hank Lazer chief among them. Charles and Hank have been close friends and collaborators, and I have followed and been influenced by their work for many years. It was their idea to collect the essays in the present volume, and my confidence in their sense of the importance of my doing so provided the impulse for me to get it done.

A word on Zen meditation and Buddhism in general for those readers who may not be familiar with them: Zazen, Zen meditation, is a simple but profound practice of sitting still and paying attention to the sensations of the body, and to breathing, while remaining aware of what comes and goes in the mind, without directly engaging in shaping that material. It is not "meditation" in the sense of making the mind tranquil or thought-free. Rather it is a practice of being aware of radical presence, being oneself, and whatever arises within or as that. It differs from ordinary mental activity in that rather than thinking in a ruminative, discursive, or problem-solving mode, the practitioner focuses on what is coming and going in the present. The connection of this sort of practice to much of the theory that goes with avant-garde art practice, which is so open to the improvised, uncontrolled, and irrational, will be clear to most readers. As for Buddhism, the influence of its discourse on contemporary Western philosophy and psychology is pretty well known by now. Buddhist thought proposes a radical redefinition and recontextualizing of the idea of self or person, seeing the self as an ideological phenomenon rather than a fixed, truly existing entity, and the actual person as being impossible outside the radical interconnection of everything with and as everything else. This idea, too, has many parallels with developments in postmodern thought. Self and person are concepts—inherently self-contradictory, and therefore painful (painful, that is, unless recognized as concepts). The application of these notions to writing and poetry as I have practiced and understood them is the overarching subject of these essays.

There is, as I have said, a variety of styles, tones, and intentions in the pieces in this volume. This comes not only from the several audiences for which they were written, but also from the fact that they were written over such a long time span (early 1980s through 2013). While I have done a certain amount of polishing and rewriting, I have left the original impulses and ideas intact, even when I no longer agree with them. "Part I: Early Takes" consists of material written before or around 1990. While themes in that writing seem to be consistent with what I have been writing since, the style, tone, and feeling for the historical period are so strong it seemed best to give the work its own place. "Part II: Are You Writing?" includes pieces about the process of writing. "Part III: Beyond Thinking" emphasizes Buddhism and spirituality, and includes comments on some writers who have been important to me. "Part IV: Experience" includes interviews and recently written pieces on topics (like "Imagination" and "Experience") that I have been thinking about for many decades. I supply brief introductory notes to the pieces, to give context and publication information.

# Acknowledgments

Much of this material was published in magazines over the years. I would like to thanks the editors of *Jacket, Jacket2, Sibila*, the *Poetry Project Newsletter, Tyonomi, Enough, Tricycle, Buddhadharma, Shambhala Sun, Jimmy and Lucy's House of K., Talisman, Poetics Journal, Facture, Religion and Literature, Five Fingers Review, Inquiring Mind, The Argoist Online, Dharma Life,* and *Zen Monster* for their support of my writing. I would also like to thank Stephen Paul Miller and Daniel Morris, editors of *Radical Poetics and Secular Jewish Culture* (a volume in this series from the University of Alabama Press), for their publications of the essay "Light(silence)word."

Hank Lazer, Susan Schultz and Lissa Wolsak read early drafts of this manuscript and offered enormous support and helpful suggestions. I especially want to thank Hank and Charles Bernstein, the general editors of the Poetics Series, not only for suggesting this collection but for decades of generous support of my work. They have been friends and companions in the writing life, and I would have been lonely without them. This goes for Susan and Lissa as well. One is lucky to have such astute friends and amazed when they appreciate what you do.

I want to remember the late Philip Whalen and Leslie Scalapino, who were both mentors and inspirations to me. As was the late Rabbi Alan Lew, who encouraged me to undertake a serious study of Judaism, which has had a major impact on my writing and thinking.

The late Gil Ott, who founded Singing Horse Press, and Paul Naylor, who took it over from him, have been invaluable in their support, and several of the pieces in this volume wouldn't have been written without their urging. This goes as well for Melvin McCloud, editor of *Shambhala Sun*, who often suggests that I write something on this or that.

Dan Waterman, editor in chief at the University of Alabama Press, has been delightful to work with, as have been managing editor Vanessa Rusch and copy editor Bethany Startin. Being used to informal and easy-going writing, I was worried about preparing this volume, but they made it easy.

I am also grateful to the San Francisco Zen Center and Everyday Zen communities for supporting me these many years to do full-time Zen practice and part-time writing. And to my wife Kathie for graciously putting up with it all.

—Norman Fischer, Muir Bach, California. March, 2015

# Experience

# I

# Early Takes

# Manifesto on Writing

*Going through notebooks from the 1970s, I found a mimeographed one-page form letter from Bruce Andrews and Charles Bernstein, postmarked November 9, 1977, inviting me to submit to L=A=N=G=U=A=G=E magazine, which was about to start the following February. It included a handwritten note from Bruce with some suggestions about what I might send. I also found two typed pages, undated and unsigned, that I now assume I must have written in response to Bruce's request, but apparently never sent. I am not sure if this is so; I am not even sure this is my writing, though it more or less sounds like me, and more or less sounds like what I would have thought at the time. Retyping this manifesto on a computer, I am impressed most of all by the unconscious assumption that there is an intense and crucial relationship between writing and action, living, and, toward the end of the piece, the breath. And that the characteristic of it should be "warmth." This seems very true to me, and very interesting, though I had no idea that I had such notions in 1977. Also, it seems this manifesto contains ideas about writing that are quite different from those typically associated with the Language School; I am not sure if I would have known that in 1977, when I was intensely interested in Language writing, aspiring to it, close friends with its main proponents, and probably misinformed as to its tenets.*

The basic point is: *to be in a position to write.*

Next: what is writing made of.

Writing is not scientific—narrowly defined, objectified, founded on method, of limited scope, of limited end. Nor is writing an art—full of the sense of its own importance and overflowing with the feelings and sense of the one who is doing the writing. Stories are no longer told—all stories are now known, everyone does anything. Mental states interpenetrate physical space, the physical object—hence words' meanings gain immeasurably, their exactitudes become momentary—*what they refer to* is certain only in the moment of writing and reading.

Writing must be *clear*, it must be *vivid*. If it is not, the resultant confusion is wholly mental and blocks action. One goes around and around in the same place. Not good. For the writing. Which must always be new. We know now there is nobody there: anywhere. It is in our body, this fact at this time. No need then to break apart what we know is broken. With clarity and vividness we evoke the life. So experience is vivid if language is vivid. Otherwise we are approaching life from behind a screen of words. This assumes there are "words," there is "life."

And writing must be *sincere*. It must connect to warm accuracy of perception, of simultaneous action. After all, no one's writing is a particular thing—if so, what is it and what makes it more than what it seems to say? It is, as they've said, that poetry springs up fully made out of life—in the spaces between, perhaps, the moments—that is, the moments themselves supercharged with meaning. To focus in on time that way—lovingly, warmly—is sincerity—it must be in action, perception, and such must be the mental state in the act of writing—otherwise, despite what skill one may possess, the writing falls flat—"oh it is good enough but so what." Mouth to mouth, hand to hand. Otherwise writing is specialized out of existence. Otherwise language stands aside, in its own slot, and thought is destroyed forever. And with thought, action.

And writing is not an *object*. If we say writing is to convey meaning—"my insights about life"/"the troubles I have known"—how foolish we are! The words slip beyond us. Form is gone, or is so simple it is not nice, no longer gives an open feeling—as cruising an empty stretch of road in a car—to where? Too much meaning holds it back. Form, the shape of it, is it, if writing is architecture, and it is. So we are tempted to say writing is an object— we place it over there, in its form, an object now, made of glass? This contains an exact inaccuracy. For in this meaning is affixed more solidly than ever and consciousness is blotted out. Writing is not an object. Far from it—it is the final subjectivity. So much so it doesn't appear as such. May appear as an object. Is, in fact, an *action*, a *gesture*. This way meanings are exact and momentary, form moves. It is a dance—or a strong arm slinging paint with spirit—the result of a momentary impulse fixed for all time. Or as long as it lasts. And it cannot.

What makes the form in writing. *Breath* makes the form. The breath in, the breath out. These two make it in its dance—as speech does, in and out, as anything goes in and out, pain, relief of it; sun and dark; love and hate. Any shape in words is shaped by breath. If we know the breath, we know what we say and how to say it.

AND THESE ARE THE CHARACTERISTICS OF WRITING WHICH ARE INTERESTING.

# The Poetics of Emptiness

*In April 1987, with Gary Snyder and others, I organized a public event at Green Gulch Farm Zen Center called "The Poetics of Emptiness: A Collaborative Gathering of Poets Who Meditate." The final issue of the magazine* Jimmy and Lucy's House of "K" *(January 1989), edited by Andrew Schelling and Benjamin Friedlander, was devoted to transcripts and other writing from the event. Below I reproduce two of my own pieces for the magazine: my introduction to the issue and my "poetics statement" (which was later reproduced in the anthology* Beneath a Single Moon, Buddhism in Contemporary American Poetry, *edited by Kent Johnson and Craig Paulenich, Shambhala, 1990). Also below is the text of my "The Birth of the Buddha" poem, which has been performed annually at Green Gulch Zen Center since I wrote it in 1988 as a response to conversations about traditional Buddhist pageantry at our "Poetics of Emptiness" event. Words in brackets are notes added in 2012.*

I've been doing zazen for almost twenty years and have been writing for longer than that, but until I began doing zazen, I couldn't get the feel of writing. When I finally did get the feel of it, inevitably that feel had everything to do with zazen. I had to have a way of writing that put me into the world rather than out of it looking at it and describing it.

In 1985, while I was living and practicing Zen in New York City, I decided to start talking about all of this, so I organized an event called "Beyond Words and Phrases? A Symposium on Language and Meditation." It was held at Greyston Seminary, Zen Community of New York, in Riverdale, the Bronx, and included ten poets/practitioners of meditation, among them the poets Jackson MacLow; Alan Davies; Charles Bernstein [who is proud to be a nonmeditator, but somehow was included]; Nick Piombino, who is a poet and theoretician coming from a background in psychotherapy; Lou Nordstrom, a Zen priest and philosophy PhD; myself; and some others [including, I now remember, Armand Schwerner and Charles Stein]. The event was organized as a presentation/discussion, very serious, not much of an audience or publicity, a working situation. We had a pretty lively day of it, and as I recall, the main point of controversy, and it was a hot one, was whether the poem is on the page or in the mind.

Returning to California, I wanted to see what it would be like to do this again, on another coast, where I anticipated we'd have a very different sort of discussion. I began talking with Gary Snyder about my idea, and soon the thing took quite a different shape: we'd have a large, public event, the centerpiece of which would be not discussion but demonstration of how poetry and meditation work together.

So in April 1987, we held "The Poetics of Emptiness: A Collaborative Gathering of Poets Who Meditate," a full weekend at Green Gulch Farm Zen Center, where I live and work as a Zen priest. About thirty people joined Gary and me, including Phil Whalen, Anne Waldman, Jane Hirshfield, Gail Sher, Steve Benson, Andrew Schelling, and Will Staple. They stayed for the whole weekend, which included, as the New York event had not, zazen, meals, Zen talks, and hanging around time, and was capped by what we called a "Buddhist Poetical Performance and Meditation Event" in the Meditation Hall, which was attended by probably three hundred people. This performance was truly memorable. It involved many events, word- as well as music-based, including one that I produced: a droning reading of the phantasmagorical Avatamsaka Sutra from a corner of the room while the audience, given strips of paper with my one-line poems on them, spontaneously performed the poems as the sutra was being read. The most powerful part of the program, in my memory now, was the chanting of En Mei Jikku Kannon Gyo—the brief Kannon Sutra—that went on for a very, very long time, repeating and repeating. Memorable for me because I was playing the big Fish Drum during the chanting, which sped up as it went, and I lost all sense of time and physicality as the drum went on playing itself long past my ability to play it, and then it stopped abruptly, and there was the sort of intensely present silence that you can only experience out in the country, far from traffic. This silence lasted for what seemed quite a long time—no stirring whatsoever from the audience—until suddenly a frog from the pond behind the zendo began to croak. Immediately a second frog responded, and within five seconds there were what sounded to be ten thousand more frogs croaking—and then roars of laughter from the audience. With this, and nothing more, the performers left the stage and the evening ended.

It was, I think, an extraordinary event, and I am very grateful that *Jimmy and Lucy's* is devoting this issue to publication of the proceedings. I believe that there is a great deal to be said and understood about this subject of meditation and poetry and that we are only now beginning to think about it after many years, collectively, of practicing these disciplines here on this continent. It has been a notion of mine for many years that began, I think, early on with my appreciation of Williams and Olson, that what we are about here is a writing that is not the same as European writing but rather comes out of this wide landscape and experience of mixing of peoples in a democratic way. And I am convinced still as I have been for many years that the transmission of the meditative traditions of Buddhism are central to the making of this writing. [From the standpoint of the present this seems impossibly Whitmanesque.]

Since 1987, I have been continuing. In the spring of 1988, I led a workshop at Green Gulch that combined again time on the sitting cushion with time behind a pen; in April 1988, for Buddha's Birthday, we held a "passion play" here, based on a poem by me, with masks and theatrical direction by Annie Hallat, a direct outgrowth of some of our discussions during the weekend of the 1987 event.

Unquestionably, the work will continue. I do not think we will have spectacular results or even terribly noticeable results. But very steadily and gradually and clearly I think it becomes more and more impossible not to think of our minds our bodies our hearts and our words as of a piece.

## Poetics Statement: On Meditation and Poetry

At their best, both of them, meditation and poetry, are ways of being honest with ourselves. Only by honesty can we see anything because honesty opens the eyes or cleans them. Without it we'd see what we'd like to see, or what we think we'd like to see, or what someone else would like us to see.

Meditation is when you sit down, let's say that, and don't do anything.

Poetry is when you get up and do something.

I don't think there is any escape from these activities: all of us have to do both of them. And both of them are involved with the imagination, that human faculty that creates, envisions, or transforms a world.

Somewhere we've developed the misconception that poetry is self-expression, and that meditation is going inward. Actually, poetry has nothing to do with self-expression; it is a way to be free, finally, of self-expression, to go much deeper than that. And meditation is not a form of thought or reflection; it is a looking at or an awareness of what is there, equally inside and outside, and then it doesn't make sense anymore to mention inside or outside.

Experience, I think, is a never-ending adjustment.

Practically speaking, I would say that meditation gets you used to failure and gives you great familiarity with the mind's excitement, to the point of boredom, and so much so that there is a great acceptance of all experience, and there is no wish to favor one kind of experience over another. It is all pretty remarkable. This attitude is an aid to poetry.

So you are not interested in "poetic" experience or in "poetic" language. These seem unnecessary exaggerations. Only that you know, as a human, that you live intimately, intensely, with language, honestly with it, in it, as it, and it is necessary to keep that up, to clarify and deepen it.

That is why some aspects of poetic form are not helpful. And that is why, with your eye on the main purpose of the poem, you feel compelled at first to challenge poetic form, and then later to simply do away with it (by which I mean to stop being concerned with it terribly).

How do you do this? Practically speaking, I think meditation offers a feeling for or sense of experience, very broadly, that allows us to find a way to do this. The grip on self can very naturally loosen, the grip on meaning loosens, and there is the possibility of entering wholeheartedly into a dark or unknown territory. That, and talent, a little, familiarity with poetic form, a little more, courage, and luck. An interesting footnote is that it is not a struggle; it is the release from struggle.

I imagine that no really amusing (a word Ted Berrigan [a mentor, teacher, supporter, and friend of my early years] insisted on, and I understand, as "from the muse") literary work was ever conceived without meditation. Without an insistent, intent, single-minded holding in mind of a single object until it dissolves. I am convinced every poem involves this process, at least narrowly conceived. And the broader we make our meditation, the more implications it has for our poetry.

Do not imagine that I am advocating a particular approach or that, even worse, I am suggesting a "meditative" verse modeled on the Oriental or Occidental [*sic*] poetry written in previous centuries by meditators or contemplatives. I read and learn from this poetry but much of it I do not like very much.

No, I am talking about a life in which we can be radically simple. And out of this great simplicity or honesty, one does what one can.

I think if meditation can show you that there is really no such thing as, nor would one want, a poetic voice, then it is already worthwhile.

If I am recommending one thing that can be clearly understood, I suppose it must be an unerring sense of humor.

Text of my poem performed annually at Green Gulch for the Buddha's Birthday celebration:

## THE BIRTH OF THE BUDDHA

1.
Listen to the story of the birth of the Buddha, a story that is always told
Whenever beings gather together to work or to play
And even when they fight or shout
The story of the birth of the Buddha is told on every breath in and out

2.
There was a king of the mighty Shakya tribe, Suddodhana by name
Whose purity of conduct and grace of manner
Caused him to be loved by his people
As pens love paper, flowers love the spring

3.
His queen was Mahamaya whose splendor bounced from the clouds to
    the earth
And she was like the earth in her abundant solidity
In her beauty like a great blue heron or like a mass of willow trees at
    dawn
Seen from a distance from a truck

4.
This great king and splendid queen in dallying
Spread open happiness like a picnic basket in May

And without any ants or spilled wine extruded the vine-like fruit of a
    gestating babe
As concentration and mindfulness together gently produced the winds
    of the wisdom gone beyond

5.
Queen Maya before conceiving saw in her sleep a great white lord of an
    elephant
Emerge from a cave and come close to her envelop her incorporate her
Into his all-embracing comprehension
Like a nation state a political movement a trance or a soothing bath

6.
This lord of elephants with the Queen dissolved into a pure melody
And so she sought in all purity, piety, and joy, without illusion, a place in
    the sin-free forest
A valley among trees by the sea
A place suitably arrayed for the practice of meditation and birth, called
    Lumbini

7.
Here the queen aware of the stirrings of beginnings and endings
Amid the welcome of thousands of waiting women
On her couch covered over with awnings and leaves gave birth without
    pain from out of her side
To a son born for the weal of the world from out of her vows

8.
Forth he came yet not from earth or cloud or spirit but as if from out of
    the empty sky
Pure of being as the breath itself long or short without beginning or end
    fully aware
And like a brilliant sun in the summer sky
His beautiful gaze held all eyes like a full moon in Autumn

9.
For like the sun he awakened all life on earth the trees and children deer
    and little fish
He woke up stars in the night that whispered to one another

He woke up seas and breezes, the tall mountains that nail the universe
   shut
And the streams in the mountains that flow to the rivers like tongues

10.
And standing up straight like a mountain attending above and below
He took seven silver steps his feet lifted up unwavering and straight
The strides spanning earth and heaven
ONE...TWO...THREE...FOUR...FIVE...SIX...SEVEN

11.
And like a lion in charge of the jungle
Like an elephant ruling the grounds
Proclaimed the truth and sang,
"I am born for enlightenment, for the weal of all beings!"

12.
Hot and cold running water like jewels from the sky poured forth for his
   refreshment
The softest couch appeared bedecked with pears and apples flowers
   potatoes lettuce and pets
The invisible dwellers in the heavens
Shielded him with their giant umbrellas

13.
And the dragons of the earth and air flew and blew the air for him
And the dragons of the seas tipped the purple waves with points of silver
And the dragons of the houses flapped the houses
Like nightgowns bedsheets or banners

14.
And animals stopped eating one another to take a look—
And people stopped killing one another to take a look—
And noxious creatures and ghosts stopped haunting one another to take
   a look
They all looked and wept with unconsidered joy

15.
For he will give up his kingdom to be a light removing darkness from all
   beings

And he will be a boat to carry the beings up from the ocean of suffering
O'erspread with the foam of disease and the waves of old age and the
flood of death
And the world will drink of the stream of his Law to slake the ageless
thirst born of affliction

16.
People are lost in the desert baked and blistered—he will show them a
trail out
People are sweltering in the humidity of desire—he will rain the cool
rain of Dharma down
People are locked up in themselves
He will offer the key of Awakening to open up the doors

17.
He will cool us with the tractors of concentration
He will make us solid with precepts like pine trees
He will cause us to dance with the joy
Of the ducks of deepest vows

18.
And so in this world and in the worlds beyond in time and space and out
of time and space
The baby's steps and song ended struggles that had no end
And all beings were permanently disordered
With delight

# On Difficulty in Writing

*I found this piece and the one that follows it—"The Name"—in the folder of typescripts. Both pieces appear to have been written in the mid-1980s, but I have no record of their publication.*

I find language a tremendous perplexity. Certainly there is no escape from it. There is nowhere else to go. Nowhere but more deeply inside it. And you find that on the one hand it brings you into intimate relation to what is in front of you, and there is no way you can face anything without language; and that on the other hand it pushes what is in front of you away. The fact is that there isn't anything in front of you; whatever it is, in its coming to face you, in your absorption in it, it is brought to life and you are brought to life in the same moment (and here the attempt to speak about this already defeats me). Out of the intimacy of this "bringing together" comes naming. And then naming has its own momentum. It becomes a form of control. We name something out of love. And our naming of it immediately becomes a way to control it. And we can't control it. Consider naming a child as one example of what I am speaking of.

I believe that evidence of this perplexing, this agonizing, situation can be seen all around us. In speaking and thinking, it is easy to miss it. But in the act of writing, when language is not produced automatically but is always consciously confronted, I do not think it is possible to avoid working out a way of dealing with this knot that is essentially what language is.

Suppose you don't notice this problem either in language or in the human world that is, after all, essentially a product of language. Then there is no problem for you about writing, and the world can go on and on as it is and has been. Everything makes sense.

But if you can appreciate this problem, then you have, of course, a big problem with writing, and you can neither accept the given situation of the world around you nor can you write or think while taking anything for granted. You are forced to write at the edge of what you know, to write at the edge of what language seems to be, to use language, that is to say, to surpass language, to wake you up to what language does beneath its seductively reasonable surface. Contemporary criticism (structuralist, deconstructionist, etc.) sees this and tries to work with it.

Writing thus becomes a struggle with language, a pressing up against language, and this makes writing difficult. I do not mean difficult in the sense of unpleasant for the writer (because such writing may come quite freely, even joyfully) but difficult for the reader (who can also be the writer after the act of writing has passed). Because there is a barrier to understanding that must be gotten through in order to enter into the world of the text. This is the source of the difficulty. Once that barrier has been passed through, there can certainly be and usually is a great deal of pleasure in the reading. You feel as if you are going somewhere, as if you are engaged in an experience that is somehow real, more real in a way than ordinary life is real. I think this has always been the pleasure of really good writing. Really good writing is always in this sense difficult. The newspaper is not difficult.

Lately my thinking on this subject (because I am trying to think it through over again) has started at this point. From here another kind of problem arises: you get stuck in difficulty or you get stuck in this revolving door of language's possibilities/limitations. The difficulty itself becomes the experience produced and its relation to a world actually lived in becomes confused, cut off. Going deeply into language as language you forget that language is always about the world or if you remember that you remember it only in terms of language. So that even though you are writing about a world, that world slowly recedes into the distance of language and bears no longer any relation to actually lived experience. What do I mean by "actually lived experience"? I mean experience that is grounded in silence as much as it is grounded in language. Experience that understands language itself as fundamentally a form of silence. Experience, to make this clearer, that knows "this is language and language is primarily not a thing in itself but a relation." Without a grounding in such experience, there is less and less communication, less and less warmth in the writing, and more and more pain in the process of writing. And, not incidentally, more and more pain in the process of living. Difficulty opens language, but it can also shut it tight.

What I am saying is that difficulty in writing, insofar as it arises as a result of the confrontation with the deepest thing that language is, is necessary for good writing. But when difficulty itself becomes a value in writing or a mode of writing, writing becomes irrelevant. In this latter case, difficulty becomes a way of hiding, of avoiding what in the end cannot be avoided.

# The Name

When a literary work is presented, the name of the author of the work is always included, what about that? Is it because we want to know who to praise or blame? But why do we need to praise or blame anyone? Such considerations certainly only detract from the experience of our reading of the work; if we want only to find out what is being said, we don't need the name. Yet, of course, if we leave out the name, it seems volubly to beg the question; for the absence of the name would create a strong feeling in us: why did this author not furnish his or her name; what is being communicated in this refusal of identification? No, the name is a powerful word that is certainly an integral part of a literary work. It needs to have a name on it. It demands this kind of word. ("Anonymous" is also a name.) Expressions like, "She is a big name," or, "You can make a name for yourself," are quite intelligent because the name is an important and powerful word in a literary work that is not the same at all as the person who wrote that work, and it doesn't have much to do after all with praise or blame. Think about it. The name has the significant effect of tying together a great many disparate works into really what amounts to a single work, and then all the parts of the single work modify each other. Imagine rearranging names, cutting and splicing life lists of works, mixing up the lists and the names. You could change completely the meaning of the works. You could change the world that way. Ted Berrigan thought that an interesting experiment was to type one of your poems and type "Robert Creeley" at the bottom, or to type a Robert Creeley poem and type your name at the bottom. Sometimes I type other people's work without including the name and put them in folders that contain my own works with no name and later I have forgotten which are which. This is also an interesting thing to do.

In my mind there are many considerations, myriad contradictions; I have found nearly everything that can be thought and felt; and I am sure that if I look still longer, I will find much more; but when I say hello to you, you can identify that it is me; not only by the look and sound my body makes, but also because my actions now seem consistent with my actions then; this still is different from "Norman Fischer" as a powerful word that conditions a literary work or group of works; what that word means is clearly socially defined, having far less to do with myself in any way I can understand myself than with the collective self of those people who have created it (readers). I have many times had the clear experience of receiving a definition of that word from a person who knew clearly what it meant, and yet I could neither understand the meaning nor recognize in it anything of what I'd intended in the literary work to which the word was attached. The name is over and over again repeated in the same way; everything that swirls around the name, mental, physical, literary, keeps changing, is different always. The name is like a lens, a powerful thick piece of glass, clearly transparent, with no content, that transmits something that is swirling on one side of the lens to something that swirls on the other side; and neither of these swirling things (I mean the author and the reader) can be pinned down precisely (since the author as part of the process of authorship is a reader of the text, and reader as reader must author the text to some extent in order to comprehend it). The reader and author exist in place only because the medium, the text, brings them to life, defines them. (The same argument can also be made for the world and the people in it.) And the name is repeated over and over the same. It is as if we could eliminate the works, we don't need them, only the names: Herman Melville. Emily Dickinson. Shakespeare. This seems to be in the end where the real power lies; this is the world as we know it; it is why we feel always there is so much at stake in our literary arguments and productions. Think about it.

I am always interested in knowing of an author particularly how he or she earns a living because I believe the author's economic relation to society powerfully conditions not only the content but also the form of the work produced. Steve Benson once wrote me, "The only difference between me and John Keats is that I have a job." This has always struck me as essentially true and essentially profound; it is a fact that I have happily embraced because I have always loved while I have always mistrusted the possibility of art because it provides access to depth in living, and it has always been the province of the privileged few. I think our generation (the generation formed by the 1960s) has had this problem very deeply: artists, not pop artists, nor commercial artists, we have been wedged tightly between consideration of, need for, uncompromised art, and a politics that can't stomach the elitism that this kind of art has always entailed. This distaste is not just ideological: it is ingrained in our very personalities, in our philosophical and psychological approaches to life. We are not patronized, do not sell, we work for a living (most of us not for the successor to the old patronage system, the academy [a true statement at the time of this writing; not true now]), this fact has conditioned the forms and entirely the nature of our projects. Works that come directly out of an involvement with the repeated day in day out commerce with ordinary people; being a poet is no excuse for anything; if my poetry is neither read by nor understood by "ordinary" people (and I would hope that this could be as little the case as possible) yet I myself must be; I am not going to suffer and die of alcoholism or madness because of my brilliance: my life as a writer justifies nothing.

I have a need to consider the implications of what I write, the effects of what I write, even though I cannot know them. It is not that I search for the truth: I do not want to be bound by the truth, one truth is not identifiable. Rather I have the obligation (the joy of) coming ever closer to the world around me; writing out of but also into this relation. I reject what is unconcerned and unconsidered by writing not only because it is cruel or fruitless: formally also it doesn't satisfy. Aesthetics is ethics: I think we have come to this.

None of what I have said considers "audience," which is quite different from the "reader." The reader receives the text alone and intimately; the audience receives the text in the marketplace. I myself have had little experience with the audience; dimly I am aware that the audience exists, that it manifests materially (books, magazines, reviews, grants, events, reputations, etc.) and I do not want to be naive about it, or ungrateful for the psychological (if not economic) sustenance it provides me, but because of the nature of my own project in writing, and the isolated or at least non-ordinary relationship to the society it places me in, I have not really dealt straightforwardly with the audience and do not know much about it. My sense of it is that, like most human activities, it is based on fear and greed. I try to recognize this but not increase the quantity of fear and greed already produced; why I, why all of us, I believe, take up the practice of writing is for reasons wholly otherwise.

# For *Tyuonyi*

*This piece was written for* Tyuonyi, *a literary magazine of the 1980s, at the request of the editors, Philip Fosse and Charles Bernstein (Issue 6/7, 1980). The online description of the issue says: "This issue poses several questions about the nature of poetry to dozens of writers including Michael Palmer, Hannah Weiner, Ronald Johnson, Johanna Drucker and dozens more."*

I have a sense of culture's narrowing to a needle's eye these last decades, approaching the end of progress, the end of history. Perhaps people have imagined in the past such a thing; this time I think it's the truth. It seems that developments in poetry over the last twenty-five years (in the direction of a more open poetry, less emphasis on the subjectivity of the poet, more on the objectivity inherent in language making, seeing the poem as a field in which a variety of responses occur, seeing the text as a negotiation between reader and writer and culture) have returned poetry in a way to its most primitive state by a strange and marvelous route, one that does not try to avoid the changes of the last century and return to the good old days, but rather through the use of and by the playing out of the implications of those changes come to a place finally of real possibility. In a sense infinite possibility. Exactly because there is no next step possible, as ordinarily conceived.

I think the nature of this cultural narrowing is linguistic: our concepts of reality, our descriptions of reality, our words, don't fit anymore. I really think that mixed-up language is the key to every difficulty we find ourselves in, and so I think there is a tremendous importance for the work of the poet now, but not in the way, say, of Pound and Olson, who felt, magnificently, that they as poets could figure the thing out. In trying to do this, they were caught in the trap of mixed-up language. Rather by way of jumping into language, feet hands and head, with love and honesty, communally and cooperatively. With this kind of shared effort there is little by little a clarifying of language and therefore, finally, a righting of culture, producing the accuracy necessary to sail right through the needle's eye without smashing into the cold steel.

This is theoretical but I mean it practically. It's time for the poets, like they did in old China, to move on into the give and take of the world, to use their skills with language to help run the world. This means the creation of institutions, either alternative institutions (my own involvement is with Buddhist institutions, and there are also many other alternative institutions, including businesses) or the creation of new frameworks within existing institutions. It means also bringing the work of poetry into relationships, personal, familial, societal. It seems to me at this moment that the universities are not lively places for these transformations; but things change rather quickly now. Ten years is enough time for a complete reversal, and they tell me that the 1990s are going to be quite different in the universities.

Oddly, I never think about what I'll be doing ten years from now. I assume that my objective circumstances will be completely changed but that essentially I'll be doing just what I'm doing now: trying to clarify my life on a daily basis through language and through the multitudinous implications of language.

# Zen / Poetry

*In the 1980s, I began giving workshops at Green Gulch Farm Zen Center on poetry and meditation. I would often write short essays to be read and discussed at those events. This one, dated January 1989, appears to be one of them.*

There has always been a strong relationship between the practice of Buddhism, especially Zen, and poetry. From the Buddhist side, it is clear from the later philosophical texts and the early sutras that the issue of language, of human conceptualizations of reality and how such conceptualizations create delusion and alienation, has been central to the problem of human life as seen by practitioners through the ages; and from the Zen standpoint (which is to say, Buddhism as reinterpreted through the filter of Chinese thought), all of this has been redone within the medium of poetry, since the Zen or "sudden" approach replaces exhaustive philosophical analysis with flashes of poetic insight which are produced within the context of meditation practice.

It is interesting that these issues, very ancient in Buddhist studies, are the same issues that are being raised by the most crucial poets of our own period, and so my work has found its inspiration and teacher not necessarily in Buddhist writers of the past (although in these, too) but in the work of twentieth-century Western poets and of my own American contemporaries, notably those writers who are called, often with a degree of scorn, "Language Poets."

The scorn arises, I think, because these writers or at least the tendency they represent are seen as excessively theoretical, hyper-intellectual, unfriendly, and worse, anti-poetic. This may be so, or this may be the way it looks from the outside, but at closer range one can see that their concerns (which are my own concerns and, I believe, the concerns of Buddhism) are humane and basic: that the self be clarified and therefore liberated from the grip of wrongheaded views that create suffering; and that the unexamined language by which society, through someone's or no one's particular fault and to someone's or no one's particular advantage, manipulates and alienates individuals.

For a practitioner of Buddhism, the central issue is, of course, the self. As is well known. Buddhism starts with the certainty that there is in fact "no self," which is to say the notion of self conventionally held—that I am over here, you are over there, I see this say this or think this and it is mine in such and such a way and it is not yours—is untenable and furthermore dangerous, productive of suffering for one's self and others.

This is a great problem for the poet, whose job, we are taught in the writing workshop, is to "express himself" or "express herself," to make precious "his" or "her" presumed "experience," and then to tell the "reader" what that is so as to instruct.

It is a problem because meditation practice makes it very soon clear that none of the words in scare quotes in the preceding paragraph fit their usual denotations and connotations. Great and unfounded assumptions are being made.

So there has to be another way to approach poetry if one is not to remain silent; and it is also clear to the meditator that there is no way to remain silent.

I often wonder why this situation, which seems so manifestly clear as an implication of Buddhist thought, did not erupt in previous periods as it does now. And I think the answer is historical: that language was fresher and more differentiated then than it is now, less frayed at the edges than it is now; social forms likewise had not played out their implications of vastly helpful and vastly destructive potential as they have now. The Buddha himself within his social context was clearly a revolutionary, and there have been other periods throughout the history of the tradition that were also revolutionary. Perhaps it is simply a matter of that revolutionary tendency within Dharma practice coming round again in our own time. Certainly Dharma represents the human possibility for peace among people and openness and clarity for individuals; it is precisely in our own time that these possibilities achingly suggest themselves, and that to work on them in a serious way does, I believe, necessitate a cracking open of, if not an attack on, the underlying basis on which society opposes them: language. This is because language in our time has been multiplied, beamed everywhere, bought, sold, and turned more or less into noise.

This is fifty percent of my poetics; the other fifty percent has to do with friendliness.

It is frightening to realize that in order to solve the problems we're in, to solve the problems that are us, a taking apart of everything personally and socially is necessary. This taking apart, if done in fear, is really horrifying and will lead to worse horrors than those of the present; but if it is done in a friendly way and with humor, it may not be so bad. Life and death is not such a big deal, or at least one can understand it that way, and this is helpful, and also, incidentally, effective.

This is the simple case: language creates thought and thought creates action; but the totality of action as we find it creates language. My language is a given that precedes and creates me, and so the notion of my own expression as if I were an isolated individual apart from all of that is really a false and pernicious notion. Poetry is a communal process, a process of sharing.

These simple facts completely do away with all our notions of who the poet is and how he or she writes.

The case is the same in Dharma practice, especially I think in Zen, where practice is a group effort and the Buddha is not an individual but is precisely that appearance which arises as an expression of all of us as a result of all of us, which is to say any one of us and each of us. The one who knows this through and through is our teacher.

What does this mean for poetry? How are we going to judge a poem, put a price tag on and incorporate the great poems? And yet there are, of course, standards. There are great discussions to be held.

The poetry that I want to see made and that I am trying to make and will never quite succeed in making will take all of this into account and will itself be a force in the world as real and as plain as a chair and as useful; it will not be a polite comment on what is happening (as if one could comment without the comment itself being what is happening at the time it is made) nor will it be an expression of individual anguish or joy. We are all in this together and there is no other way accurately to speak or that is worth the expensive paper on which we'd speak it. The old Zen teachers knew this.

None of this that I am saying is an ideology and none of it comes from books [sic!]. It is just concretely the case as I live and breathe and write, and furthermore it gives me a great deal of pleasure to live and to write in this way; any other way would just not please me.

# Explanations About My Poetry
# for Kenyon College Students

*The Headlands Institute for the Arts is not far from Green Gulch Zen Center, where I lived from 1981 until 2000. Artists in residence there would often find their way to Green Gulch to say hello. That's how I first met Gil Ott, poet and publisher of Singing Horse Press, and Lewis Hyde, poet, scholar, and author of the famous and essential* The Gift. *Lewis had recently been appointed to the faculty of Kenyon College and invited me for a visit there to talk to his students about poetry. This piece was written for them in response to questions they proposed. The word "explanations" in the title of the piece seems to be drenched with irony.*

I say poetry and meditation are about honesty, and I mean a deeper honesty than the one anyone usually means. (The usual one involves a point of view that comes immediately to mind, about which one can dissemble or not. But I think that in meditation you can see that that point of view is strikingly arbitrary and likely false. It comes up like smoke over and over again, and it conditions the way you see things. If you can see that conditioning, and think a little harder, and let it melt away, as it naturally will, then you can be what I would call honest. To take something simple, like the word "honest," and to let it lie there, and then to turn it also completely different, is one of the main techniques in my poetry.) So I don't profess to be discovering anything in particular in my poems. I am only trying to be present with this kind of honesty, moment by moment. In a way, my writing is an extended improvisation. I try to stay as free as possible to go where it takes me. I try not to have any preconceptions beginning middle or end.

It doesn't mean that "anything goes" or that there is absolute formlessness (though I am not necessarily against these). I do always try to go deeper than just what I happen to think or feel about anything, in the faith that if I can go deeper than that, there will be something worthwhile coming. Just as there are stupid garbage dreams you have at night, and there are deeper dreams that seem to have some sense of discovery to them. (But "deeper" might just as well be "more superficial" because it is not a question of depth or surface; I mean simply "not as usual.") But you don't know what they mean. If you stick with them for a while, eventually you know. Or anyway, you know something that will last for a certain amount of time. After that you need to dream a new dream.

This is how you unknow yourself: you see what's there, all of it, the stupid stuff especially, and you stay with it, letting it come and go, and then you see beyond it, and you then let that go, too. You keep being present and surprised, knowing how little you know, and you persist in that. You don't become disoriented; at least I don't think so. But you do develop, I hope, a sense of true humility and an ultimate kind of fearlessness, which is also friendliness.

I would hope my poetry exhibits, expresses, this in the doing of it. It doesn't exactly say it because you can't say it. Of course you can say it, but that would only be saying it, which doesn't matter that much. You need to do it, and do it all the time. I do or try to do this in my poetry and I think a satisfied reader of my work is one who himself or herself also comes close to doing this.

An important experience for me many years ago was reading the poetry of Philip Whalen. I made me realize directly as I never had before that poetry was right where one was; one didn't have to go elsewhere for it. I felt fully affirmed to be who I was and make that the locus of writing. I would aspire also to produce that effect for readers, if there were any effect in my poetry. I am not trying to make an argument that there is no self-expression in my poetry when I say things like "poetry has nothing to do with self-expression." Of course there will be self-expression and certainly usually one can identify a piece of work by me as by me (though I do write in several different styles). What I am speaking about when I say this is the intention with which one writes: preferably intending to get down there to where you and I and everyone are pretty much the same. I don't need to tell you about how wonderful or terrible I am or what I had for lunch or what I am thinking. These things are all just vehicles. That is what I mean. I think people are often far too precious about poetry or even about their own experience. I think it is best to experience experience then drop it and go on fresh. In the poem I am not expressing my thoughts or feelings; rather I am practicing discovering what it means to exercise language. Maybe this can be called self-expression. But I say it is not self-expression to make the point.

I don't see my poetry as unique or groundbreaking in any way. I think there are unique and groundbreaking poetries but mine is not one of them. If you look at contemporary poetry, you will easily see the many sources I am influenced by. About a month ago I gave a poetry reading in San Francisco and the Language poet Ron Silliman (who has done groundbreaking work) said to me something like, "I don't know of anyone who writes so persistently in the moment of writing." (Incidentally, I think Clark Coolidge does.) So I suppose I would claim that, if anything. So I do not have a sense of the uniqueness of this writing or of other contemporary writers whom others feel are doing work that is so very, very different from what went before (sometimes this is said with admiration, but more often with scorn). I realize that for other people it looks that way (it is often striking to experience other people's reactions), but I am really used to it. I am really not trying to do anything special or amazing. I am actually saying what seems important to say now. So I think previous poets of the past are just like me. For example, many people are surprised to hear that I feel a great kinship with Shakespeare (of the sonnets) and Yeats, that I feel to a great extent my poetry is an extension, for now, of the work they have done. I have read both of them over and over again, and the sound and movement of their work are, I feel, extended and translated in my own (of course, I do not compare myself to them in any way). When I read very good conventional contemporary poetry, however, I am often, though by no means always, quite dissatisfied; it doesn't mean much to me. Because I feel that not to go deep and to grapple with the means of expression themselves (because that is what you find when you go deep, how much the means of expression condition us, as I've said, in another way, above) is to miss what's really important now. It's obvious that who we are now is built on what's underneath us (the past). So how to do what has already been done is always a new thing to do, and I feel often that those conventional contemporary writers are repeating something that has already been made for its time. This is not an idea I have but an actual experience in reading. I can read Yeats new for now and I am sure that what I will find will shock Yeats. But if I try to write Yeats now in the Yeatsian manner, it will really be stupid. You need to read a lot more to see what I am talking about. You can read Pound, Olson, Zukofsky, Creeley, Whalen, Williams, Stein (especially, for me), Watten, Benson, Silliman, Hejinian, Coolidge, Palmer . . . there are a lot more. I feel I differ from the Language Poets quite a bit, though I acknowledge a great debt to them.

I think there is a great deal of technique in my poetry; in fact, I think it is highly technical. But I like to have a sense of free play within the technique. I like to set up structures and then follow them, but only up to a point. In this my model is Thelonious Monk. I would aspire to the kind of humorous goof and yet tremendous technical skill that he displays (though for me this is much more an aspiration that a demonstration). But the technique is unique in each poem; each poem tries to answer the question "How do you write a poem now?" I confess, however, that my technique is a little simpleminded, and in this I have always had as a model the Chinese and Japanese Zen calligraphers, whose work I looked at in books quite a lot in my formative years. They have a great deal of energy and an avid honesty but are a little crude, it seems to me. So their art ended up to some extent in a separate category from other calligraphers: they were valued for their "Zen spirit" more than for their expertise, and, I suppose, for better or worse, this is true of my poetry as well.

I don't know if my poems are art. I would hope they are useful. I would hope that a poet will gain courage and direction from them and that a non-poet (if there really are any of these) will feel some warm understanding and realistic company, and will occasionally be brought up short by something that suddenly seems quite true, though you can't tell why. There are people who have to think about what is art and what is not art but I don't feel like that is my job.

Prose is writing that explains, makes a point, persuades, and fulfills a purpose. Poetry does not do these things; it lays bare the human heart and helps us to raise the important questions. After reading prose you have the idea you know more than you did when you started; after reading poetry you are perplexed, you are vulnerable. So it is the intention and the effect that makes the difference, not whether or not the lines go all the way out to the end of the page. It's hard to say what of my poetry I like the best. I am usually quite engaged with the next poem and that is the one that matters.

# In the American West:
# Portrait Photos by Richard Avedon

*An exhibition of Avedon's photos came to the Museum of Modern Art in San Francisco in 1986 and made a big impression on me, prompting this piece. As far as I know, it was never published.*

1. The portraits are super real, super intense. Nothing should appear this exact, precise, focused. Gigantic. The eyes screwed into the skull, every hair sharp, the lighting even, penetrating. Each face, body, a perfect image of . . . what? . . . a person? Photographed against a white background so that the people are standing in the middle of nowhere, ripped out of context. Is anything or anyone ever out of context? Is there ever no background at all? These are images of presences. They look like people but you don't see anything past the surface of the image, into or through the surface. They look like pictures of trees, gnarled, busted, blasted in storms, interesting shapes. The captions indicate that they function: "rancher," "coal miner," "pawn shop operator," "drifter," and they have names, but they don't appear to have, to be, anything else.

2. It is impossible to imagine what these people are thinking. They appear not to be thinking. It is impossible to imagine what these people are feeling. They appear not to be feeling. I say people but they are not people; they are images. The actual people represented by the images must think, they must feel, they must love or hate. If I meet them, I like them or I don't

like them. They are human, I am human. But these are images. I think I am supposed to imagine that they are people.

3. Avedon trains his fashion photographer's skill in the direction of ordinary people. He makes them look larger than life. Photographs them as if they were more than they or we could ever be, but they are clearly not. They are ordinary. The tension is tremendous.

4. It's about hands, tough dirty unconscious beautiful useful durable, conscious as speech, about eyes, intense steely unafraid exposed expressionless opaque unconscious conscious, clothes, durable weather-beaten ridiculous dirty plain, hair that flows, speaks, moves around, is alive more alive than the faces possesses a health and expressiveness that the faces don't, seems independent of the rest of the body.

5. The young people look like they might as well be a hundred years old. The prisoners bear scars and tattoos of Jesus. The mental patients pour tremendous energy into their hands, as though they could keep the world away with their hands. Everyone's been through the mill, worn down. There's no range of emotion. No development.

6. Nothing, no one, is an image, is clear, is without context, straightforward, fixed, subject to exact expression by means of technique. But if you can do it, if you can do it well, if you can evoke the image that arouses admiration, disgust, pity, envy, horror, etc., that touches the storehouse of images and triggers it, opens it up, then you can produce art that can be desired, described, bought and sold, and you can become famous and make a lot of money because the image, the description, the commodity, the clear perception, sells well in a mass market.

7. But nothing is like that. I want art so realistic nobody can tell what it is. I want art that doesn't take a person out of herself but reminds her who she is. She may not notice. She may not be interested. She probably won't pay.

8. No one I've talked to agrees with my view of the Richard Avedon exhibit of portrait photographs entitled "In the American West." Piet Groat

[a Zen friend, husband of the dancer, artist, and calligrapher the late Jennie Hunter Groat] writes that Avedon "sees with a compassionate eye. He is able to communicate to these people who volunteered to sit for him, that he is telling the truth about their lives, if they will let him. He is not a man taking a picture; he is giving them their picture of their life." I don't deny this. I think it's unfortunate that I can't deny it.

9. In his notes on the exhibition, Richard Avedon states, "A portrait photographer depends upon another person to complete his picture. The subject imagined, which in a sense is me, must be discovered in someone else willing to take part in a fiction he cannot possibly know about. My concerns are not his. We have separate ambitions for the image. His need to plead his case probably goes as deep as my need to plead mine, but the control is with me."

10. These pictures are powerful. They change reality. When I leave the exhibit, faces I look at look like faces from the exhibit. But this only lasts a little while.

# The One-Stroke Paintings
## of Kazuaki Tanahashi

*Kaz Tanahashi, activist, calligrapher, translator, and Dogen scholar, has been a friend since we—with many others—worked together on an early translation from Dogen's* Shobogenzo, *published in 1985 under the title* Moon in a Dewdrop.

I would rather live than have a lot of experiences. I would prefer that each minute occasion be clear. I will take a trip to the corner store. It will be the only time I will take this trip. It will not happen again and has never happened before. I will walk carefully; I will choose. Here birth and death tip the balance of my time all the time. The sense of art as dangerous is secured here, yet art doesn't need to be so significant. Compared to anything.

One could build a Gothic cathedral, write a symphony, eat lunch, or play with children. Or one could take a brush loaded with black ink and paint a line across a white stretch of paper.

Trained as a painter and calligrapher, developed as a scholar of deeply abstruse Zen texts, Kazuaki Tanahashi has a decidedly perverse and child-like approach to art.

He spends a lot of time looking out the window of his studio. He spends a great deal of time playing with his baby son. He becomes very excited about his ideas for artworks and he talks about them a lot. But he only spends a few moments making art.

He takes a brush loaded with ink and makes a single stroke on a white canvas. Often he cuts the canvas into several pieces, titles each piece, and claims that each piece is an artwork. Some of the canvases are almost completely black while others are nearly white except for a splotch of ink here or there. He is really amused by this. When he tells you about it, there is a particular joyful silly expression that comes upon his face. Then for a moment he is in earnest, deadly serious. Then, at a completely arbitrary moment, he breaks into a disarmingly boyish aw shucks grin. He seems to enjoy the fact that really, in the end, there is nothing to it.

On October 9, 1987, I visited Kaz at his home in Berkeley. He was dressed completely in black Japanese clothes, the sleeves of his hippari tied back, his long straight black hair swinging as he moved stiffly in a pair of black rubber boots.

He had just finished making twenty artworks in four minutes. He was walking around the twenty canvases spread out on the floor dragging an industrial vacuum cleaner behind him. He was vacuuming off any bits of dust that may have chanced to blow onto the still wet ink.

The single stroke that he had made across the twenty canvases with two fifty-pound brushes was three or four feet wide at its widest point.

Flashbulbs were popping.

This was a four-minute event that had taken six months of preparation (the twenty paintings are to be shown at an exhibit entitled "Surrender" in November and December of 1987 at the Cathedral of St. John the Divine in New York). The brushes were constructed of coarse reed wrapped in felt, of cotton rope, the strands huge, the brushes' ludicrous standing handles angled in metal buckets that held the remains of the five gallons of ink used for the project.

Yet Kaz did not convey any sense of triumph, culmination, or relief. He vacuumed the thirty-five feet of canvas that bore the single curved stroke quite matter-of-factly, carefully.

The stroke was black, the room and canvas white.

Outside the weather was cool, grey, a bit windy. It was an average October day in Berkeley.

Writing in Chinese has, even in modern times, maintained its physical basis. There is a bodily movement—as minute as the finger—as large as the arms shoulders and hips—in each character written, a fierce concentration necessary to carry out the embedded cultural enactment compressed and then extruded in every new performance of each ideogram.

Generations of boys and girls learn to write as if to dance. Poets are prized for their hand and eye as part and parcel of their composition. Calligraphy is drama, emotion, guts, wisdom, glee.

Like a score played over again through the centuries, each character

Or, with a nod to Zen philosophy, Western abstract expressionism, conceptual art, a single stroke.

With a single stroke the concern for form is arbitrary. There is a physical movement, a breath, the results are accidental. There is no manipulation of the medium: there is nothing but medium. What isn't there (white space of canvas) creates the work at least as much as what is there.

A one-stroke painting, since technique is minimal, is completely the naked expression of the personality that makes it—no personality—ink and space.

Some of Kaz's one-stroke paintings are monstrous, bold, chaotic, powerful; some are delicate, humorous, ugly, messy, harmless, just plain silly.

These twenty works today look out of control, distressed by the physical difficulty of manipulating the outrageous brushes.

When the canvases are separated and hung, there will be much to consider, contemplate.

It is impressive, the torque of meaning and depth pressed into each ordinary average moment of time, released quite simply by brush and body and ink.

The vacuum cleaner makes a domestic sound.

# *Waltzing Matilda* by Alice Notley

*I first met Alice Notley at Iowa and have been following her career ever since. Her long works of the 1990s and later,* Descent of Alette *(1996),* Disobedience *(2001),* Reason and Other Women *(2010), and* Culture of One *(2011), are tour de force rushes of language-flow dream narrative. This is a review of an early work of hers published in the* Poetry Project Newsletter.

Of current vital interest to poets is the question "Who is writing the poem?" The answer ("the poet") is not so simple, and there is a giant analysis that goes in this space ( ) which involves linguistics, philosophy, politics, and psychology, as well as poetics, that says the very idea there is the "poet" whose self is the motive force of the poem is great pressure at the root of the corruption of language and society. In part this is a matter of ideology, in part a matter of taste.

Short history of the poet: First, poets function as religion singers and shamans, singing to plants and skies, with very little sense of the particulars of their personal situations (if there are any). These poems not written down, much less authorship acknowledged. Next come the storytellers, whose works recount the "history" that starts off the self-consciousness of a "culture" identified as such. These guys may be anonymous or have names ("Homer") but we don't know who they are. Next comes "civilization," where you get "art" and a set of conventions that are strict in defining what the poems should be; so the poets craft the poems that way, you understand more "this is a sonnet" than that it's "a poem by Michael Drayton." Next comes Wordsworth, who claims that "Poetry is the spontaneous overflow of powerful feelings," and with *The Prelude* we get the first major poem whose main character is the author, all his inner life. This gets solidified and we get the revolt of poets like Dr. Williams and later the Beats, who want the real feelings. By mid-twentieth-century USA, we get, on the one hand, Olson, who wants, moving away from the person of the poet, to compose a "field" with "perceptions instanter" noted, and on another hand, O'Hara, whose "personism" is "all art" and "does not have anything to do with personality or intimacy, far from it!" What is it then? Central point is there is this "you" to whom the poem is addressed, opening it up thereby to a terrific recess of feeling, aesthetic passion-winds which translate into rushes of eloquence. Unlike Olson, and let's say, the Language Poets, where you get a powerful philosophical and intellectual basis from which the poem is purged of "the poem" and "the poet" in the name of a rigorous, powerful, open, and unbiased language.

All this to get off my chest to say the works of Alice Notley are the great continuation of the O'Hara tradition and that *Waltzing Matilda* is possibly her best book and for sure the one in which this character, this voice "the poet," is set out the straightest. Previous books have been very good and always moving toward including more, this one (and the later work in *How Spring Comes*, Toothpaste Press, 1981) includes it all, stories, sonnets, lyrics, playlets, journal poems, a novel in a page and a half, even a long interview with George Schneeman. Very straight personal stuff sometimes, but who is the person?

> My pastures of plenty must always be free,
> that's because they're mine. I possess
> where I do it. Where is it? Don't know.
> What is it? Don't know. Who is it?
> Dust friend wind gone river multiple.

This book also contains the best (simplest) poem on the death of John Lennon. The interview with Schneeman is very good, little by little the participants working their way toward a thought-provoking conclusion that illuminated me and is about Alice Notley's work as much as it is about George Schneeman's (actually this interview reads more like a "work" than an interview); where George finally says he's not painting real people but idealized people knitting in heaven because "everything that everybody does at every minute is in some other level than what actually is. Nobody is just doing the things they're actually doing. Everybody knows that they're not where they are. That everything is not what it is. Because if everything were only what it appears to be, they would all kill each other. I mean, they wouldn't be able to survive a day." So, three choices: think you are the person (false); abolish the person (difficult); or set up the person as a kind of convention, knowing in the end you don't know who that is (Alice). Read this book and be identified with yourself.

# Total Absence and Total Presence
# in the Work of Barrett Watten

*A fellow student with me at Iowa, Barrett Watten is one of the architects of the Language Movement. His work and thinking had an enormous influence on me in the 1970s and 1980s, when we spent quite a bit of time together. In 1995, Aerial, a literary magazine edited by Rod Smith, did an issue (Number 8) on Watten, and I think this piece, though dated June 1991, was probably written for that issue—though it did not appear in it. Instead the issue featured a long poem of mine on Watten, unpublished anywhere else. The online notice for this issue of the mag headlines this quite apt quotation from Andrew Ross: "Barrett Watten has challenged and vanquished every single petrified idea about what it means to be a poet in modern times."*

Among the many rearrangements and displacements of reality through the course of the twentieth century, I want to cite the decline of the future as the one most fruitful for a look at post-1960s' poetry.

In the early decades of the century (socialism, modernism), it seemed clear (to the West) that the chief player on the stage of history was The Heroic Individual, and that the drama had an organized plot pointed in the direction of not "a" but "the" future in which there were many dramatic possibilities, both positive and negative.

Many illusions about culture were shattered in the 1960s, but the idea of the future was the greatest casualty. Not only that there was for the first time confusion about and lack of confidence in the possibilities for the future, but further, that the whole notion of a linear historical continuum was seen as a particularly culturally bound ideology that was greatly to be questioned. Much of the mix of drugs, Eastern religion, and sexual and intellectual foment of the period amounted to a full-on attack on the concepts of time that had underlain earlier cultural developments of the century. There was a tremendous emphasis on presentness or timelessness as an alternative to historicity, and the influence of Eastern thought, Native American, and other traditional viewpoints—in fact the entire coming into view of a multitude of cultural perspectives each with a different stance on reality and therefore existing in effect in a different time period and pointing toward an alternative future all at what appeared to be "the same time"—cast doubt on the whole structure of reality as it had been described, and therefore on the nature and function of the individual and of language itself.

The concept of the avant-garde in art is, of course, deeply rooted in the sharply etched version of the Judeo-Christian historical-materialist idea of time, so the 1960s represented an ultimate challenge to the whole prospect of the avant-garde. Recasting the avant-garde in the light of what I will call "Total Presence" has been the particular genius and struggle involved in the work of Barrett Watten.

When time is seen as a steady and circular process, the future is the same as the past and there is security from one point of view and stagnation from another. Where time quickens and moves forward, there is a strong sense of a future that is unknown and yet is certainly going to be quite different from the past, and so there is a sense of elation and at the same time a sense of anxiety. But where there is a multidimensionality of times, each includes and alters the others and there is neither past nor future simply conceived. We are left with what I am calling Total Presence, which includes, indeed is enwrapped entirely in, a sense of history, but a history that isn't going anywhere. In such a situation the bottom falls out of the usual notions of personhood, and one is in a state of free fall among the structures of thought. This is what happens in Watten's works. The effect of this is, curiously, both tremendously calm and entirely full of anxiety.

Watten's work often appears to me as a version of science: the endlessly repeated experiment pushed up against the edges of what is known, a stubborn headlong assault that goes on until something gets broken. Or perhaps a reference book, a dictionary that can go on for a long time in a single reasonable, almost diabolical tone, relentless, patient, howling.

⁊

Notions of time are like threads in the fabric of thought: you pick one up and follow it along and everything unravels. Where there is a future, morality can be easily understood: the good or bad will be rewarded or punished later on. But where there's no future, ethics needs to be uncovered, broken out of its confinement in encrusted thought: ethics is difficult work. Where there is a future, the ethical values can be conveyed in writing through the agency of form or technique. Where there is Total Presence, ethical values precisely need to be created or fused in the form itself, not through it. In other words, form becomes, creates, or uncovers ethics; it doesn't carry across a preexisting ethics. This is a painful process that I find throughout Watten's mature work, which, I am arguing, is essentially ethical in character. It is a constant confrontation with form but not form as an external value. Rather, form as the most intimate heart of reality, which appears in no other way to senses and mind than through form of some sort or another. Hurling the mind again and again into the openness of form is to press up against reality in a thoroughgoing way, even below the level of what can be thought or felt. It is, if I can say this, a formalism so engaged with the world it becomes a kind of love; even exactly love. It makes of poetry not an aspect of language or a particular use of language but the essence of language, the twilight of language (twilight because here we cannot precisely see language and yet we are not in the dark either).

⁊

Criticism has been an essential path in Watten's coming to this position. In a sense he has thought himself to this place rather than written himself into it. His language for this reason strikes me always as coming from some distance, as if the present were in a way an echo of something that lies on the other side of language.

⁊

In the introduction to his prose work *Total Syntax*, Watten states, "Each (talk included in the collection) was intended, by its own argument, to make its way out of a situation in the total present in such a way that there was no going back, building a space to work in out of what were only nebulous imaginings at one time." The use of thought to find breathing space, room to work in, a sense of direction, and a means of proceeding . . . to create a way out of a situation in a total present that is unacceptable, even unbearable . . . into a further situation in the same place. Criticism with a primary rather than a secondary or explanatory function.

&

Watten's discovery of the Russian Formalists in the late 1970s was a crucial moment in his career. Here he goes back to a key movement of the avant-garde to find out where to begin to go someplace else. He identifies the main tenet of Formalism as "the self-sufficiency of the sign." In connecting the sign with the non-sign (referent) as its complement, ordinary language "familiarizes" (habitualizes) reality. Poetic language, on the other hand, assumes the sign's self-sufficiency, freeing language from the yoke of external reality, and so "defamiliarizes" (freshens) the human experience of reality. The function of poetry then is redemptive, is central to the ongoing creativity of things against the force of entropy. The logical conclusion of this thinking was a total emphasis on consideration of technique as the only important factor in understanding literary work. In his talk on the Formalists, Watten accepts this emphasis as the most fecund possibility for the present. ("I want a discussion of writing that leads to what can be done" rather than describes or, worse, defends, what has been done.)

But the Formalists weakened themselves in this: that in thinking to free poetic language from the world, they left themselves open to the eventual possibility of the exile of their work from the world. Formalism was pointed entirely toward a future, the failure of which was Formalism's downfall. Rather than poetry redeeming the world, the world overwhelmed poetry in the most direct and violent manner possible. Watten argues that in the developed West of the present, without any future, without even any "direct perception of the cataclysmic event" as it actually occurs, reality is a daily and painful deception, "familiarization," habituation, dullness of reality to the Nth degree. Technique then has to be a means of throwing us fully into the situation as we find it, a means to face it and transform it, rather than to remove us from it. In this, Watten's intention in emphasizing technique is in many ways the opposite of what Formalism ended with. As he states in *Total Syntax*, "We have doom on the far side of the media undermining our brains. We do not believe our senses; the level of automatism we have to deal with is of an order the Formalists would not have believed. The necessity for technique is absolute in the face of this."

For Watten, Total Syntax equals Total Responsibility within the work itself since there are no absolute shapes or standards outside the space/time/cultural context in which the work stands. Things aren't going to be culminated in a projected future, and there is no authority from on high that is going to help them along. And (as a necessary corollary to these statements) there aren't any eternal standards upon which we can evaluate literary works. In his essay called "Total Syntax," Watten quotes Robert Smithson (whose work has been of crucial importance to Watten's thought) to the effect that the present is "entropic . . . connects directly with the farthest, pasts and futures . . . and rejects any claims for progress." That the sign is self-sufficient means that there cannot be any rules, any sort of syntax other than Total Syntax; that the confrontation that takes place within the work is a confrontation within the Total Present. This view would represent, paradoxically, an absolutization of art itself were it not for the fact that Watten's criticism at every point insists against any form of absolutism, whether it be absolutism of the self or of the text. And in this lies, I think, the importance of criticism for Watten's total project in language: it serves as a means to cancel out all traces; it does the negative work of protecting the poem (though there is no "poem" as such in Watten's view) from any sense of limited meaning. Criticism for Watten is a stick you drag along behind you as you walk down the trail to be sure you leave no tracks. In his book called *1–10* (1980), Walton writes:

> He sees now (determined when he arrives) history
> (disappointments) not through interpretation (remember
> one another when outside) but death (only child). (p. 24)
> 1–1

❧

*Opera—Works* (1975) contains early works, written entirely before the crucial move I speak of above. In most of the works in this book, sign is still clearly wedded to referent. There is "subject matter" in more or less the usual sense; the poet appears as a voice speaking in space and time through the medium of the poem. Early influences (Olson, Creeley, Zukofsky) are clearly in evidence. There's a good deal of dream material, use of chance procedures, self-querying, formal experimentation. *Decay* (1977), a chapbook, contains material that feels similar formally, but the voice is more abstracted. In "Chamber Music" (in *Decay*) we have the beginnings of what I'd call the characteristic Watten style: a classical, measured, almost static arrangement of materials that appears very calm in its design, very elegant and organized, and yet contains within and between the parts multiple vectors of force in several directions, a highly controlled and yet at the same time passionate intellectual groping, almost a fury. "Chamber Music" is a series of one-sentence paragraphs, about fifteen words each, which seem to go everywhere at once, each one someplace else, but nowhere in particular. The title piece, "Decay," is an eight-poem series, each poem with a very ordinary but curiously enigmatic one-word title ("Call," "Outside," "Insist," . . .), the last of which, "Window," reads:

> This is the window. Then they
> showed me, through the window
> a depth like the Black Sea
> covered in a terrible dark &
> to the side of the depth, I
> saw a great mountain reaching
> up to the heart of the sky. I
> cried, "I know my way, I'm not
> going back." As if I had said
> this, everyone knew exactly
> what I meant. This is the door.

This poem is probably the last time in Watten's work that the pronoun "I" appears in anything like a usage that even remotely refers to the persona of the author. Here "I" walks through the door, never to return, and from this point on in Watten's work, the issues raised in the work are always universal contemplations of total situations without location in time or space. The sense of distancing in the language is completely realized. There is an almost ascetic perfection in the overall forms and in the word by word line by line or sentence by sentence pieces, all of which are held together by a tremendous pressure. (*Decay* has an interesting cover, designed by Watten himself: a very washed out, almost, indistinguishable photo of a downtown cityscape. In the distance a blank square hovers in the air, like an entity in boldface from another order of reality.

⁓

*1–11–10* (1980) is Watten's first book with an all-over compositional strategy. It is not a collection of pieces; rather, the sense of design and tight organization that we find in the poem "Decay" are extended here to cohere an entire book. It is a highly complex mix of alternating sections of prose and poetry, making use of ultra-dense paragraphs, cut-up techniques (including extensive use of quotation marks and parentheses to break up and distance the flow of the sentences) that pack the sentences with multidirectional and often self-conflicting content. This book also introduces the measured verse form that will be further developed in the book-length poem *Progress*, signaling a complete retreat from any sense of "organic" form flowing from breath or voice or syntax, these sonnet-like strung-together stanzas make no emotional or aural leaps in any direction. They read almost as if the Watten sentence had been arbitrarily set forth in predetermined line lengths. Such stanzas work completely against any sense of verse as we normally conceive of it; yet their scoring on the page cannot be denied: it cancels out any reading of them as sentences. A curious, almost painful, tension is the result. The book begins with a poem, "Mode Z," that seems to stand as epilogue. Here's the concluding stanza of that poem:

> Prove to me now that you have finally undermined
> your heroes. In fits of distraction the walls cover
> themselves with portraits. Types are not men. Admit
> that your studies are over. Limit yourself to your
> memoirs. Identity is only natural. Now become
> the person in your life. Start writing autobiography.
> 1–1

The statement of this poem can be seen as a further step, a direct progression from the position articulated in the stanza from "Decay" quoted above. Something like, now that you've begun, now that you've broken free, go completely into this freedom: merge yourself completely with the technique of your work, let there be nothing of you remaining outside the work itself. This is autobiography to the limit, autobiography that falls off the edge of autobiography. And in fact, the rest of the book does this, canceling out at all points any tendency not only toward reference outside the work, but also toward non-reference. (I mean that while the works cannot be understood to relate to the world per se, they also cannot be understood not to; they are not flaunting their quality as "language only," they seem to be saying something quite clear and almost self-evident; but one is not sure what, although I am always convinced that the work is somehow an exact record of Watten's thought; not "spontaneously," but formally.) The cover of the book (also designed by Watten) graphically illustrates the point quite well: an abstract three-dimensional grid of solid and broken lines, over which are superimposed black-and-white photographs of a mechanical pencil, a toy choo-choo train, a pushpin, a cup hook, a bent nail.

My argument then is this: that issues of self in writing and of the status of the sign in its relation to referent come together in Watten's work in a theory and practice of writing as Total Presence, as Total Responsibility, as, in the psychological and spiritual senses, the only possibility for survival and redemption in the face of what we find in front of us. And I am arguing that this viewpoint is responsible for a technique and a literary form that is essentially static, distant, and in a curious way, without imperfection anywhere. So the value of Total Presence in Watten's work turns out to be the opposite of what you'd expect from previous "present moment" writing strategies characteristic of the Beats or the Surrealists. Rather than a deep subjectivity in which the writer turns himself over completely to the workings of the mind in the present moment, we have here a notion of Total Presence, which has to do with an identity within technique. There is no question of freedom or release here. Rather, it is a question of complete consciousness and control within the writing. And this consciousness and control that are present everywhere in Watten's work often feel to me difficult or joyless: and even this appears conscious. This viewpoint, I'd argue, is operative in the work through the publication of *Progress* in 1985. That work, whose title represents a supreme irony, is the culmination of this decade-long exploration of Total Presence as perfect static troubled presentation of form. A single poem fully 120 pages in length, without any variation in form or break up into various sections, this work completes the pattern: it is made up of five-line stanzas, five to a page, each stanza containing somewhere within it an ellipsis (". . .") as if the static endless perfection of the form itself opened out at every point into an endless silence, which, however, did not signal a release but rather the eternal ongoingness of the problem of an unacceptable Present without future solution or past explanation. Again, as with all Watten books, the cover graphic illustrates the point quite well. A superimposed drawing in white, over a pale blue background, of some kind of circular machine, the main feature of which appears to be a large screw in the middle that suggests in some way a device of relentless torture.

> Already present in increments,
> Eternal.
> One man in a cage
> Equal to a thousand birds
> Not to be free in nature. . . . (p. 71)

Now I want to propose that there is a significant development that occurs with *Conduit* (1988). And this development is quite logical: it involves a consideration of Total Absence as the necessary corollary to Total Presence, a consideration, in other words, of the shadow medium, the unknowable uncontrollable form that lies on the other side of the total control and formalism of the work on the page and, in fact, completely conditions it. And this absence takes the shape, paradoxically enough, of a person, the person of the reader, the unknown person whose unknowable mind receives the message in the work and decodes it in some unknowable way, thus making the work what it actually is. While the writing itself can be controlled, made perfect, made static by virtue of powerfully intended technique in a Total Presence of the merging of author into text, the reader (and thus the actual act of communication) can never be known, can never be objectified. It is fundamentally dialogic and so can never be completely known either by any party of the dialogue or within the work. In this sense, from the standpoint of any of the pieces involved, it represents an absence that must be confronted in the working out of the writing. With an acknowledgment of this Total Absence comes a freer sense of technique and form, a loosening of control, an admission of the possibility of some sense of direction and spaciousness in the work, and an effort to clear a space within the work for communication.

❦

The title *Conduit* derives from the conception of language as a conduit: the "message" is sent through the conduit from the author to the receiver who picks it up, thus receiving exactly what the author has sent. This, of course, is not what actually happens. One possibility is that language is a conduit and meaning is what is sent through; but, in fact, there is no meaning outside the conduit; it is the conduit that is the meaning; there is no other message; all seeming messages are misunderstandings. The second possibility is that the conduit represents the structure of the mind, is, somehow, eternally determined, and so even though the message cannot be separated from the conduit, we can get outside the conduit and understand IT as the message. But this view implies a place to stand outside; it implies a past in which the conduit was formed and a future toward which it is headed. Neither of these possibilities is true and both imply a violence, an imposition that must be made on someone either to receive the message intended or to recognize the shape of the conduit as an object. In fact, language is not an object and it contains no objects. The work then of communication is to clear up the fallacy that there are any objects (any pasts or futures or possibilities for control). The conduit is not a passage through which something flows; it is complete openness itself. It is the unknownness of the reader, the author, and language itself that makes this openness possible, and it is possible, it is in fact the necessary struggle that is undertaken in any act of communication, especially poetry. This is the task that is undertaken in *Conduit*.

The book, again, as with all Watten's books from *Decay* on, is highly designed and organized: even the table of contents is typographically arranged so as to underscore the formal point being made. It consists of seven pieces, four in prose, three in verse, that, taken together, suggest a kind of access code to language itself (a seven-digit phone number). The first piece, "The XYZ of Reading," is a seminal essay that signals a new approach, much as the Russian Formalist essay of a decade previously opened new ground:

The writer is faced with adjusting himself to what accurately is the medium, a missing person that is the space for projections, the ground for what wants to be perceived.

This new medium is the resistance between writer and reader, speaker and hearer. [ . . .]

The speaker hears no longer only himself; he must also hear what the absence of himself would mean to another [ . . .]

It is not any collective "death of the subject" that accounts for the subject's removal from the work. Rather, it is the necessity of the very conditions of communication, without which reading or hearing cannot take place [ . . . ]

Here there can be no objects of thought, but only an extension of the temporal that effaces any motives [ . . .]

The world is everything that is *not* the case.

9–1 (pp. 9–12)

❧

The three poems in *Conduit* follow more or less along the lines of Watten's previous writing, but the prose works seem considerably different, exhibiting a sense of movement and even playfulness that is absent in previous work. "Introduction to the letter T" opens with an extensive quotation from Balzac's *The Wild Ass's Skin* and goes on to discuss techniques of typesetting, including instructions for creating an alphabet on a computer, complete with diagrams. The process of "going into the machine" to create the letter "T" from the letter "X," however, takes on added dimension. Here are the captions to the diagrams that describe this transformation:

Things should be absolutely solid,
in order to ward off blows.

There should be no spare parts from
which shattering impacts might originate.

The sun should be large and hot.
Estimates of its size should be correct.

People should point their fingers at
things in order to learn their names.

The voice should divide itself and
multiply in all directions.

Talk should be perceptible behind
closed doors.

Things should correspond to open
doors. There should be more outside.
(pp. 35–38)

❧

"The Word" begins with a page of random numbers, and includes some
notes passed between Pat and Jim and Joey, an "index," some mathematical symbols, some quotations from previous Watten works strung together with the words AND, BUT, and IF in capitals between them, and
an "oracle," which is in the form of a dialogue between Groucho, George
Fenneman, and the audience. "On Barnaby Jones" is an extensive comparison between the form of that television cop show and one from a previous
generation, "*Dragnet.*"

But the sense of movement and direction in these pieces is that: a
"sense." It is as if the movement was proposed not as a possibility of going
anywhere, but rather as a counterforce to the assumed movement, of "the
message" through the conduit of language. It is a movement, meant to ar-
rest movement, to open doors within language, not necessarily to go anywhere. In fact, there isn't anywhere beyond this to get to. And these works,
very effectively, take us there.

# Ted Berrigan, American Poet, 1934–1983

*Ted Berrigan was on the poetry faculty at Iowa when I was a student there, and his effect on me and the Iowa writing community was enormous. He was a supporter of my early work—blurbed my first book—and invited me to give my first reading, at the Poetry Project at St. Mark's Church, where I read, astonishingly enough, with the novelist Larry McMurtry to a packed house (all there to hear Larry, with Ted in the audience). My wife, Kathie, and I and our twin sons always visited Ted and Alice and their two boys in their famously tiny St. Mark's Place apartment in New York. His death in 1983, at forty-nine, came not long after one of those visits, during which he said that he had recently been to the doctor who told him that he had "a perfect heart." The tone and feeling of Ted's poems was constantly in my head throughout the 1970s. I have no record of the publication of this piece.*

There is a Zen statement, "Don't put a head on top of your head." It means, "Be the person you are, don't calculate," or "If you calculate, go ahead and calculate wholeheartedly." If I put my friend, the poet Ted Berrigan, in front of me to see what I think, this is what I think.

I want to write about Ted because it is the time to do that, now he is dead, but he is not gone. Someone like him, or anyone, remains with us very specifically, and we are in contact with that person very directly I think in the act of writing or thinking, the way Phil Whalen, in a poem long ago, is in contact with his (deceased) mother, or Ted himself in contact with Frank O'Hara. This is true because you know that it is. That's that. And when in addition to that, the person has left a body of literary work amplified by and embodied in the life of the person, the death of the person is not the ordinary one, and it is, I think, the proper form of address in all due respect to refer to that person as "is," not "was." (Another Zen statement: "No one is born and no one dies.")

So I don't want to write an elegy or deeply felt remembrance because it's what do I do now that concerns me and I think shows most respect for Ted.

What characterizes Ted's work is its resourcefulness, its commonsense know-how. With each poem, there is the open-minded feeling of what is a poem, how is it made, what can it be made into, and look what I've done with it. It's an innocent resourcefulness. Self-conscious, yes, but wholeheartedly so—no murkiness, no conflict, no sense of holding back. So finally there are five or six ways of making poems. Poems that are simple and dumb to poems that are like puzzles, with complex levels of meaning.

*The Sonnets* is a masterpiece and changed writing for the next generation period.

Ted Berrigan poems are always expressing that it is a great joy and an honor to write, joining the company of writers, but it is no big deal. It is just where I am and who I am now and the words I find myself surrounded by now, New York City, 3:17 a.m., now being fine and without further need of justification.

This is very liberating and democratic and makes a lot of people mad.

Ted put everything on the line in his poems and for his poems. He was going to be a poet then he was a poet, poetry was in particular poetry and was absolutely poetry, nothing else mattered—love mattered but love was included in poetry or was another name for poetry, friendship mattered but friendship was included in poetry, and there was the code of the West, a serious moral imperative that meant when you went into a bar to use the toilet, you were honor-bound to order a beer, stand at the bar, and drink half of it, and you had to be generous and careful about the way you treated anyone although with everything else going on there might be a bit of slippage here and there but you kept the code firmly in mind, and it was also included in poetry.

Ted had the single-mindedness of all great poets and great men. The person he was, he completely was, and you always knew who that person was; he was that person in, for, and because of the work he produced. He lived and died for poetry. "I am in love with poetry," he said. He completed his job as poet and left.

From him you get permission and encouragement to be who you are and to have that person be a poet.

This you do do but there is no way to do it in the way Ted did it.

It must be that, in Yeats's image, there are two gyres, one within the other, spinning out history, two ages simultaneously existing, one being born, one dying. The thesis and antithesis existing at the same time.

There is poetry as poetry and there is poetry understood as occupying a place in the world.

There are people who matter as poets and there are people who matter and are poets living as persons and practicing the art and the craft of poetry.

Ted gives you permission and encouragement to be who you are and have that person be a poet and because of Ted you do do this but you can't do this in any way like the way Ted did this.

Ted makes it possible but must make it so that although he must matter very much for you as a poet, it's yourself living as the person you are that makes poetry matter for you.

What makes *The Sonnets* great is the sense of excitement and discovery that they communicate perfectly. Everything is in the moment of composition, which is understood to be intense and unconnected to any other place any other time but this one.

This method matters to me as Ted matters to me and I can do it but not in the way Ted has done it. I want to find a way to write it so it is contemplation and I don't know how to do it but more and more it is deeper and I keep getting better as I get older; little by little I keep learning how so that I am writing it best when I am ninety. I will have to, to do this, pay a great deal of attention to technique, to method, to mind, to other people as they are the way they are, to history, to scholarship as best I can. I have the feeling I've got to treasure and preserve the possibility of writing for myself also others so I have a sense of mission. Ted makes this possible. But I think I've said too much.

# Ernest Hemingway,
## *Selected Letters, 1917–1961*

*I have an abiding affection for Hemingway's writing and reviewed this book, edited by Carlos Baker (Scribner, 1981), for the St. Mark's Poetry Project Newsletter.*

I picked up this book thinking it would be impossible to finish; just a few letters here and there, I figured. But I had to go on and read every word. Why is it, this writer, so fascinating to me to so many other readers, even now when I think it must be he is very much out of fashion, his attitudes very worn out, even offensive.

Well, there is a great deal of literary gossip here. Hemingway loved gossip very much. Almost no theorizing (Sometimes he tells you what writing is or how he feels about it but it is always pretty simple: "A writer is a gypsy. He owes no allegiance to any government. If he is a good writer he will never like the government he lives under. His hand should be against it and its hand will always be against him," he wrote to Ivan Kashkin, the Soviet critic, in 1935), no tortured intellectualizing, no enumerating of personal problems (When Hemingway can't sleep—which is usually—he says so; when he's depressed, he says he's got the "Black Ass," jokes about it). Lots of stories, lots of detail about writing, lots of detail about the business, a terrific lot of joking, black humor, seriousness. In short, these letters are interesting. They are as moving and as interesting as Lew Welch's letters, maybe three hundred times more interesting, say, than the letters of Wallace Stevens, who was a very good writer, but not of letters. Maybe you can be a good writer and write dull letters (Joyce, too) but to write interesting letters you have to be a good natural writer (maybe you can't write good finished works) and also a pretty interesting person. I think these letters are as interesting as they come.

Progress of the letters gives a pretty good graph of the career of the great American author, any great American author. An early period of learning and experimentation when things are terrifically exciting and fertile, usually at this point the associations with fellow later-to-be-famous artists are formed, usually against a background of a very romantic time and place. At this point, the writer knows how good he or she is but it's all promise. Five years later success starts. Five years after that the associations are different (less interesting), it's a different place, the writer is conscious he or she's got an audience, the pronouncements get more developed, more profound. Period of trying to beat the form he or she is working in. Great fame. Writer takes him or herself very seriously. Writing becomes less interesting than the necessity of being public spokesperson. Old age, self-imitation, stupidity, tragic end. All this is mapped out in these letters. You can see what "they" did to old Hem and how miraculously well he seems to have stood up to it, all in all. People then as now always trying to get underneath the pose, what really makes Uncle Papa tick, what really is he about. But I have always been convinced and remain convinced he was pretty simply this large tough guy who loved to hunt and fish, really could box, really was irresistible to a lot of women, really did know horse racing, bullfighting, skiing, etc., did all he could to make life seem continuously interesting to himself, and he could write better than just about anyone. He said, very simply, in answer to his most baroque critics, "No, I think how we are is how the world has been and these psychoanalytic versions or interpretations are far from accurate."

There are a lot of little tidbits in these letters you'll like though they've mostly appeared elsewhere in other forms (in Baker's previously published biography of Hemingway). Like his punching out Stevens in Key West in the early 1930s, his boxing match with Morley Callaghan, rounds timed by Scott Fitzgerald, who let one round go far longer than it was supposed to, on purpose, because Hem was getting beat, skiing in Switzerland, nearly ending up with a frostbitten penis (which I assumed was trigger for main character's problem in *The Sun Also Rises* but later Hemingway said it was his having been shot during World War I then having an infected penis due to bits of leather embedded in his skin), the clever way he slithered out of Boni and Liveright contract by writing *Torrents of Spring*, which he knew they'd have to reject, thereby freeing him from obligation to them (they handled Anderson, too). Well, you can imagine in nearly a thousand pages how many interesting things. Some letters really particularly striking documents. Like early exuberant letters to fishing buddies, full of outrageous puns and nicknames and, like they say, bursting with enthusiasm for life; or the letter to his parents describing wounding in World War I where he talks with great seriousness about how great it is to die for your country at an early age; or the letter to Gerald and Sara Murphy on the death of their teenage son ("We all have to look forward to death by defeat, our bodies gone, our world destroyed; but it is the same dying we must do, while he has gotten it all over with, his world all intact, and the death only by accident"). Or this, from World War II (during and after which Papa's particular brand of bloodthirsty lunacy became pronounced):

> One time I killed a very snotty SS Kraut who, when I told him I would kill him unless he revealed what his escape route signs were said: You will not kill me. Because you are afraid to and because you are a race of mongrel degenerates. Besides, it is against the Geneva Convention.
>
> What a mistake you made, brother, I told him, and shot him three times in the belly fast and then, when he went down on his knees, shot him on the topside so his brains came out of his mouth or I guess it was his nose.
>
> The next SS I interrogated talked wonderfully. Clearly and with intelligent military exposition of their situation.

When Mr. Hemingway wanted to tell someone off, he could. To Cardinal Spellman: "You will never be Pope as long as I am alive." To the FDR Birthday Memorial Committee: "Today we are gathered together to honor a rich and spoiled paraplegic who changed our world," or the truly outstanding letter to Senator Joe McCarthy: "Senator, I would knock you on your ass the best day you ever lived. It might be healthy for you and it certainly would be instructive." Occurred to me there's a great similarity between careers of Hemingway and Kerouac, the latest American writer who's enjoyed impossible popularity and personal fame, every detail of his life having been written about till I am sick of it. Different generations, of course, the one expressing the toughness and realness of the strong brave

USA, the other the corruption superficiality and sad lost hopelessness of the same sad USA, but really they are quite similar: super human energy and magnetic personality, terrific enthusiasm for people and places, fantastic success (though Kerouac never made the really surprising sums Hemingway did) and then the crashing paranoid ending. You would almost believe that a person like this won't come around again for a long time.

Coming back to the beginning, why is Hemingway so fascinating for me. Well, the writing is great, of course, and the music of it especially. Something new, some dignified version of what goes on, maybe that's it, the dignity of the people in the works, which maybe becomes a false or forced dignity, but still, there it is. That appeals to me. But when I read Hemingway, I don't feel better, I feel worse. Why is that. I think a really complete writer always makes you feel better (Williams) not worse, makes you see the value of what you've got, your own time and place, actually see it, not induce a feeling of nostalgia, like Hemingway's works do. So there is something wrong with Hemingway's works, these letters, too, what's wrong is he leaves something out, doesn't face something, glosses over something he wasn't smart enough or tough enough to include. What is it?

# The Poetics of Lived Experience
# and the Concept of the Person

*This piece and the one that follows were written for* Poetics Journal, *1982–1998, edited by Barrett Watten and Lyn Hejinian. Their tone, which now seems a bit forced and doctrinaire to me, reflects my effort to sound more like a theoretician than I was or am.*

For many years I have been concerned with the relationship between writing and so-called lived experience, and I have also been concerned with the concept of the person. These are things we take generally for granted but I have been puzzling over them in many ways.

Let me begin with the concept of the person.

In fact, our lives are completely permeated not, as we think, with ourselves, but rather with exactly a concept that we call a person, or ourselves. This concept is embedded in our language, our forms of thought, our forms of art. In traditional societies, with traditional social and cultural forms that are repeated over and over again, the society's concept of the person is strengthened and affirmed by the careful adherence to these forms. In our own society, we have decided, through the process of colonizing the world, fighting four major wars in fifty years, building the bomb, and all but assuring a serious wounding of the planet as a necessary by-product of our ordinary daily life, that the concept of the person we hold cannot be strengthened and affirmed, that there is, in fact, a certain unworkability to it. I say we have decided this, but I mean that artists, thinkers, social misfits, monks, psychologically disturbed people, etc., have decided this.

Perhaps most of the population has not decided this. Because of this, we have two distinct areas of or approaches to art: popular art (which assumes or accepts the socially affirmed concept of the person) and, what shall we call it, avant-garde art, or how about just art—which does question the concept of the person.

As a poet and as a Zen practitioner, I am always interested in questioning my own concept of myself as a person. In fact, this questioning is my project.

The word "concept" is I think exactly the right word. You think you know who you are, that it's not a matter for puzzlement, but if you were actually to stop whatever else you are doing and take a look, you would soon see that it is not obvious who you are. That what you know as yourself is in fact a concept, an idea that may or may not be relevant to your actual concerns.

For instance, commit yourself to sitting at home in your room, with the phone unplugged, no radio or TV, and repeating out loud steadily your name for one full hour. I think if you did this, you would not be so sure after one hour who you were.

Or better yet, sit there for a full day and watch your breathing, sit up straight facing the wall, and don't move at all. Then you would certainly feel many questions about who exactly you are. This is what we do more or less often in Zen practice.

I am not talking about creating an artificial confusion. I am talking about a shift in the depth at which we relate to ourselves. At a deeper than usual level, it is quite easy to see that there is, in fact, a self concept that is created by our society, our family, our language, or at any rate seems to come from somewhere, and that we do live almost completely through the filter of this concept.

You begin to see this very definitely. The more it comes into focus, the more obvious becomes the fact that there are two problems: first, most likely the self concept is an unworkable one that is causing or soon will be causing grief, and second, the fact that we are usually completely unaware that there is a self concept at work and that it does, in fact, completely condition our lives is much worse than the self concept itself.

It's as if we were trying to eat lunch while wearing boxing gloves and didn't know we were wearing boxing gloves and our failure to be able to

into our mouths seemed inexplicable and caused us more and
. At least if we knew—aha! there is a problem here. I seem
g boxing gloves—we could relax and try to do some problem

What does this have to do with poetry?

Language is the primary medium of the unexamined conceptual self.
The deep background voice speaks to us in unexamined words. Poetry is
the bottom line or it is the base line of the language we all use. Poetry is
the intensification, the spark, out of which other language manifestations
come. Poets are not necessarily gifted or insightful individuals; they are
those who are interested in or compelled to, or given to work in the boiler
room of language. So in my view it follows quite naturally that poets would
be primarily concerned with a close examination of language and poetic
form whose purpose is to uncover or provide us with a deeper look at what
a person actually is. And this deeper look comes not by virtue, certainly, of
the person of the poet, but rather despite it. Poets, in fact, need to be able
to enfold that person into language itself. It is language bared, not poets,
which create poetry.

This is why any poetry that I am interested in is concerned with form,
but this formal concern is not a "mere" concern with form but rather is a
concern that is political, spiritual, economic, educational in its implications.

Without this formal concern, what you end up with, whatever your so-
called content is, is work whose embedded unexamined assumptions automatically reinforce your own, and therefore the society's, self concept.

But with this formal concern, poetry becomes a kind of lens that works
two ways—from the poet's intention through the medium of language experience, to the reader whose experience of the poem changes his or her
life experience, and back to the poet through the poem. In other words,
poetry is an exchange; poetry counts. It is more than the expression of inspired thoughts. It changes minds and lives and provides a new way of seeing and acting in the world.

To talk about how poetry must use and be used by "lived experience,"
the second element of our title, let me quote Viktor Shklovsky, from his
book *Third Factory*. He says:

> If the line [he means the lineage of literary works] simply continues
> without being crossbred with the non-aesthetic fact, nothing is ever
> created . . .

We theoreticians have to know the laws of the peripheral in art.

The peripheral is in fact the non-aesthetic set.

It is connected with art [and "art" here is synonymous with poetry] but the connection is not causal.

Shklovsky means that in order for art to continue as vital expression, it needs continually to be altered by life, to be crossbred, as he says, with life. But life and art are two different things—art can't be about life as subject matter; it can only be life by being sensitive to its own winds and waves, forms, as life itself goes according to its winds and waves. The relationship of lived experience to art is, therefore, a strong one, but it is not, as Shklovsky says, a causal one. Lived experience and art are rather interdependent, mutually effective and influencing, but they do not cause each other. I want to be clear on this point. I do not advocate, and I believe Shklovsky does not advocate, the aesthetic as the primary. One wants, as Shklovsky says elsewhere in *Third Factory*, a sense of "destiny" in art, a sense of morality. But this cannot be achieved by imagining that direct reference to life is ever actually possible in a work of art. In fact, when such a thing is imagined, exactly the opposite of what is intended is achieved: far from aiding the cause of lived experience, art becomes a substitute for it. Since all of life is enfolded directly into the artwork, as we imagine, life itself, the act of living it on its own terms, can safely be ignored. This strategy, it goes without saying, is unworkable. In order for lived experience to be interdependently related to art, everyday life must be deeply attended to on its own terms, and art must be deeply attended to on its own terms, with no sense of hierarchy intervening between the two. As Shklovsky puts it in *Third Factory*, "Break yourself over your knee."

# Modernism, Postmodernism, and Values

I'd cite 1886 as the beginning of the Modern Period because it was in that year that, according to William James, psychologists first discovered that there is an area of mind or experience outside the ordinary limits of consciousness, which yet affects human behavior in a deep and unknown fashion. In other words (although the term itself and the refinement of the concept came later), there is an unconscious dimension to experience.

Prior to this, the world, despite its shortcomings, made sense. God was in heaven, we were here, and all things were explainable. Society's laws were fixed by God and every individual within the society, the artist included, knew where he stood. What imperfections there were in the scheme of things could be repaired.

But by 1886 it was clear that invisible and unknown factors that did not necessarily obey the rules set down by God were more and more operative in the life of society and the individual, and once this fact was noticed, the effects of these unknown factors and their number increased exponentially.

I understand cultural periods previous to the Modern to be characterized by clear and severe distinctions (I am talking about Western culture: the phenomenon of the Modern is a Western one that exists in the Orient [sic] only by way of the West). The development of Judeo-Christian culture up until the Enlightenment was certainly this way, with its emphasis on divinely dictated morality and a highly differentiated social order based on this morality. And of course, out of this tremendous interest in and need for evermore refined distinctions, science evolved and the world was tamed.

All of which unfolded in radiant light and with God's approval.

The Modern period began when someone looked back over his shoulder and noticed a dark shape there that hadn't been taken into account. It was probably very frightening.

I understand the Modern period to be about the breakdown, the blurring, of distinctions. Good and bad. Aristocrat and commoner. God and human beings. In the case of the arts particularly, for in the Modern period the figure of the artist supplants that of the religious authority as the driver of culture. It is a time therefore of tremendous exuberance for the artist. The nature of the object depicted, of the subject who depicts, and of the medium of depiction all come into question at once and we have an explosion in the arts mirrored in a social explosion.

If historical occurrence is like a building and consists of forces and impulses running in many directions which mutually reinforce or inhibit each other, then over time these forces or impulses will weaken the structure which, however, remains to all outward appearances standing just as ever it did. Until the first extraordinary storm.

However, this was, despite all the pain it entailed, also a happy experience because the crash cleared the air. The artist stood in the midst of the rubble perhaps in despair at the senselessness of a godless world of ugliness and human greed, but at the same time completely free and powerful.

The artist was a hero. He could completely affirm all his impulses to power, hatred, etc., because he was chosen; his blind creative fury was the spirit of the age. He was the anointed one.

And if he believed in the possibility of science and the new social order that science might create, he could look forward to a utopia in which he participated as chief spiritual guide and architect. (I use the masculine pronoun here quite pointedly.) However, it didn't happen like that, or if it did, the fact is disguised, or it takes a shape that appears quite otherwise when surveyed with the human imagination.

Now the artist stands with sword in one hand, prayer book in the other, looking at himself in the mirror (in costume) across the flaming seas, at the top of the mountain, etc.

But there is something seriously out of whack about this image.

The heroic stance of the artist, the willful personality of the artist, the artistic genius, creates more problems than it solves. It begins also to appear lurid, embarrassing, even comical.

Hence postmodernism, a term originally coined to describe architectural work whose whimsical punning on historical forms and human-scale building represented a complete turnaround from the heroic modernist perspective of glass and steel.

Postmodernism, an impulse created out of a combination of technical virtuosity, cynicism, business acumen, humor, and the logic of a situation that demands always that there be a further step following from the last. Parody. Borrowing. (Quotation.) No more frame around the picture nor cover on the book. So much self-consciousness, so much calculation, so much irony that every statement cancels itself out just as or before it is made. Art as anti-art. Art completely liberated from art. Art as life, or. . . . And perhaps a confusion of purpose under the weight of wit and skill.

So I find it useful to return to questions of purpose or intent. Apart from theorizing, what do I find in art that is necessary for myself and others, and why do I think that the appreciation of and creation of art is a worthwhile use of my time in a world full of marvelous amusements, horrendous need?

If I ask myself this, perhaps I have no answer, no ideology, but only the intense feeling of certainty, very clearly, that artwork is a necessity, that whether or not it is a necessity for anyone else, it is so for me. That's all.

And further, why do I think I feel that?

Because I want whatever it is that is, or is real, to speak to me, or I want to speak to it, for us to meet, so that life leaps forward and over itself. I don't want it, me, to, as Phil Whalen has put it, just lie there on the page, or on the plate.

I want to, in another expression of this, revise reality—make it grander, truer, deeper, more wonderful than it actually is.

Or yet another, to lift myself up out of whatever psychophysical habit it is my destiny to inhabit so I can see the world as what it is and truly be in it.

"Revise": reenvision, produce a vision, a value, and a plan implied in it, a way to proceed.

You can't do it with your bare hands because there is no way to get at the world with mind outside medium. There is always some form there: a chair.

So historically we find ourselves in what I think is an excellent situation, because the last century (it is just a hundred years since 1886) has produced some marvelous tools, both physical and artistic, and the dialectics of our situation have left us really flat, with all sides of the equation canceled out to a very peaceful zero, all the way around.

It seems quite beside the point, from where I am sitting, to argue for this or that point of theory; the arguments have been made and won and lost. We have through their use learned our skills, and no one need now be shocked or shaken, bumped or bruised. The artist takes her seat on the bus on the way to work and wipes the nose of the child sitting on the lap of the woman next to her. What we are dealing with is simply survival, and the simple human need for a language in which to convey a vision upon which survival depends.

I find it quite comforting to deal with distinctions as though there were none, and to face the unknown as though there were no fear.

Conceivably, the next job for the artist (after craftsman, magician, visionary, and successful entrepreneur) is historian. Or teacher. Or even physician.

# II

# Are You Writing?

# Are You Writing?

*In 2003, I published my first attempt at popular Buddhist prose,* Taking Our Places: The Buddhist Path to Truly Growing Up *(HarperSanFrancisco). Previous to this I had had no interest in this sort of writing, and had no style for doing it. But people liked that book, and benefitted from it, as they told me, so I began publishing more of this material, eventually becoming a regular contributor to the popular Buddhist magazines. The good editors at HarperSanFrancisco and later Penguin Putnam and the magazines helped me to figure out how to write for the Buddhist audience, and many of the pieces in this collection, this one included, were solicited by those magazines. A version of this piece appeared in* Shambhala Sun *in the Spring 2007 issue.*

Though they say writing is a bad habit for a Zen priest, I can't help it. I seem to be writing all the time. I write poems of several varieties in several voices, journal entries, Dharma talks, speeches, essays, books, blurbs, reviews, notes, lists, stories, e-mails, blogs. In doing all this, I have no special purpose I can discern or explain. I don't get paid much for it, and if I had a reputation or fame and notoriety (and I don't much) this would be a problem for me, because fame or reputation as a writer would be exactly infamy and disrepute for a Zen priest, which is one of the probably several reasons they say writing is a bad habit for a Zen priest. Though I hope my writing does somebody some good, I am not at all sure of this. It may even do some harm. Sometimes—very rarely—people do report to me that my writing has mattered to them. I appreciate that, but find it doubtful. Mostly it seems they have misapprehended what I was writing, making up their own text—which is fine, but they probably didn't really need my text in order to do that. Most likely, my writing is a waste of time—in the most profound sense (insofar as wasting time is always profound). I have always found this possibility to be as marvelous as it is disturbing. What a fabulous thing to spend one's life, as the essential gesture of one's life, on something that is completely useless. Something really pure about this. Whatever of purpose and effect one does, one could always do more or better. But doing something useless can't be surpassed. To perform a useless task is to perform an unsurpassable task.

What am I doing when I write? I am not documenting my life for my friends or posterity, nor am I telling anybody something they don't already know or need to hear from me. Why go on? I am compelled to, delighted to. There seems to be something crucial about working with language, something that wakes me up or brings a quality of density or significance to my life, even though I can't say what that significance is more than that it is a feeling or a texture. Besides, writing is a deep pleasure. And besides that, I have always written, seem to be a writer by temperament and impulse, and what writers do is write; they just can't help themselves.

Maybe I should get over this. Maybe there's an adhesive patch I can put on that will block the neural pathways that lead me down to the arteries of language. But if there were, I wouldn't put it on. Whether writing is good or bad, I affirm it like an athlete affirms her sport, a mother her child, or a believer his religion. I have noticed over the years in my conversations with writers that, for a writer, writing is a sort of absolute bottom line. "Are you writing?" If the answer is yes, then no matter what else is going on, your life—and all of life—is basically okay. You are who you are supposed to be and your existence makes sense. If the answer is no, then you are not doing well, your relationships and basic well-being are in jeopardy, and the rest of the world is dark and problematic.

Where does this need to splash around in language come from? Is it a disease? I'm not sure, but if so, I don't think (William Burroughs notwithstanding) we will identify the virus. I suppose the need to write comes from the intimate connection between human consciousness and language-making. Language-making isn't incidental or ornamental to human consciousness; it's not that we become human and then, being fully human, we decide it's time to say something. No, language is in some way the centerpiece, the defining piece, of being human. Yes, okay, other creatures also have language forms. Dolphins talk somehow; maybe mice do, too. But not the way we do, not with the same sort of desperate need to express—even if there's nothing to express. If no language, then no person. And if no language, then no concept of life, no concept of death, so no sorrow, grief, fear, joy—at least in the human sense. So no relationships. No fiction of a future. No tools, no imagination, no anxiety. We are what we tell ourselves we are in language.

Meditation practice brings the mind to a profound quiet that comes very close to the bottom of consciousness, and right there is the wellspring where language bubbles up. So does meditation get us beyond language? Is that what we're trying to do when we sit—to get beyond language to the pure place, the true place, the place beyond all that jabber? Is it true, as the old Zen teachers seem to be saying, that language is our whole human problem, the basic mistake we make, the mechanism of our suffering? Is this why it's such a big no-no for a Zen priest to write?

Yes. Language is the big problem because being human is a big problem. Language ruins us and makes us suffer. Language is certainly my big problem. All my dissatisfactions would instantly disappear if I couldn't identify them or talk about them. But so would I. Without language I'd have no experience, no life in the world. To say that language is the problem is to say that life is the problem: it's true, but what are you going to do about it?

Well, you live. And if you are a writer, you write. But here's the strange part: you write for the writing, you write alone and in silence, and you don't know if it does anyone any good—yet somehow you need a reader. This shouldn't be the case, but it is. Until there is a reader, some reader, any reader, the writing is incomplete. This is not true, for instance, with meditation practice or, say, with working out. You can run or bike or sit watching the breath without anyone ever witnessing it. It makes no difference whether someone witnesses or not. Because nothing comes of your running or sitting; there's nothing to share. But when you write you produce something that can be shared and somehow must be. You can't write without being read. This doesn't have to do with ambition or desire; it is built into the nature of writing. A word has built into it someone to listen and try to understand. That's what the word is, and to savor it, to fondle it, to hear and taste it, is to make the connection with whoever or whatever (maybe it's not even another person, but it's somehow someone or something) is on the other end of that word.

I have been thinking about this for a thousand years. In the 1980s, I sponsored a symposium in New York called "Meditation and Poetry," in which I brought together a number of serious poets who meditated. My idea was to try to discover what these two activities have in common. I remember Jackson MacLow, the great avant-garde poet, saying something like, "I am chary (I particularly remember his use of this word) about mentioning these two in the same breath. They exist in different worlds. Writing is effective and public; meditation is private."

But, one could argue, MacLow's writing was utterly private. He worked with chance operations and cut-up words for much of his career, so that there was no intention for conventional communication in his work. Even later, when he didn't use these methods, he was never interested in "saying something" in the usual sense. Many people found his works impenetrable. He was never trying to say or describe or explain anything, certainly not how he himself felt about life or the world. Still, he published copiously and was active in the poetry and arts community for half a century, all the way up until his death. Why?

A decade or more later I was involved in a similar symposium at Stanford. On the panel with me were the poets Leslie Scalapino and Michael McClure, both of whom practice meditation. We were asked by someone in the audience, "Whom do you write for?" And we all answered, in different ways, "No one." I remember that one of the professors in attendance (who, as it happened, was the Zen scholar Carl Bielefeld) took serious issue with this. Writing must always be social, he argued. What we meant was not that we were uninterested in readership—we all publish a fair amount—but that in the act of writing we did not consider who the reader is or what he or she is going to make of what we are writing. We write to someone, but that person is essentially nobody, without a name or social circumstances— we write for God. The beyond. The empty nature of all phenomena. Buddha nature. The Mystery. Zero. The empty nada. Nothing. We speak, and however little or much our words communicate, they touch something Out There. And somehow within the mind and within the words, that Out There is already implied. Words simply, by their very nature, imply and include a listener. A word, even spoken in one's aloneness, is always spoken to a someone. That's already there in the word as a word.

Years ago I went to the Wailing Wall in Jerusalem and did what all tourists there do: wrote some words on a scrap of paper that I tucked into a crevice in the wall. When I closed my eyes and touched my head to the warm stone, it came to me: "All language is prayer." This must be so. Who is it we are speaking to when we speak to anyone? To that person, and also past him or her to Out There. If there is language, it means there is the possibility of being heard, being met, being loved. And reaching out to be heard, met, or loved is a sacred act. Language is sacred, and all sacred observances always involve language, dedication, invocation, prayer, petition, commemoration, praise, lamentation—all language acts. We might call them special uses of language, but I think not. They are simply uses that sharpen and make more pointed the procedures that are always in effect whenever language comes into play—which is all the time, in every encounter, thought, perception, and deed.

And so, dear reader, know that at this moment of your reading this text, you are also touching the Mystery, the Nobody, at the center of your language-charged silence. I, the supposed author, about whom you may have formed some impression by now entirely of your own making, am not now talking to you. At the moment of your reading, amazingly enough, although I seem to be present, I am elsewhere, doing something else. I am unaware of who you are, and I don't know that you are reading these words in this exact moment, when you have this text in your hands, holding words I have written in a present for you that is past for me, while I am in this moment (not this moment, that one) mowing the lawn or eating lunch or out walking—or writing something else. Or no longer exist at all. And yet, at this moment, the moment when I am composing these words and you have not yet read them—a moment in the future for you but piercingly immediate to me now—I am as close to myself, and to you, as it is humanly possible to be.

# On Buddhist Writing

*Another magazine piece written for* Shambhala Sun.

I began to write as a boy out of a need to respond to the world by making something of my own. The world was asking me to do this by virtue of its being so present, so heavily present. Words were the only things lying around available for my use. Besides, I heard stories and knew the Bible so naturally I wanted to produce writing like that. This was not as easy as it looked. I went to the University of Iowa Writers' Workshop but this seemed not to help. For years before and after that, I wrote constantly but none of it ever came off. In despair (but also because it made perfect sense to me as I understood it at the time, and because it seemed essentially cheerful, as I was not), I began Zen practice. Things were then still worse. My experiences in intensive meditation, more immediate and real to me than the biographical events of my life, simply couldn't be explained in words or dramatized in scenes or stanzas. I felt forced to find a way to work with words beyond their explanatory, descriptive, or dramatic possibilities. I saw that I needed to get myself and my literary notions out of the way in order to allow the words themselves to come forward. Little by little, through reading, experimenting, and paying attention to the efforts of my close literary friends, and finally trusting what came out of all that, I developed a sense of how to practice with words, and writing became quite easy.

Mostly now writing is a joy for me. It comes freely, and I never think or worry, though I think I must practice some inchoate form of rumination. I do often revise, but even this has a feeling of play, a form of doodling. Writing is like playing a musical instrument: you have to practice for a long time, always, especially at the beginning (decades), but once you develop your chops, it's easy to keep them up, and once the music starts, it carries you along.

Of course, not everything I write is worth publishing; in fact, most of it is unpublished and unpublishable. But this does not make it a waste of time. All writing is worthwhile and can be read with profit by someone, who can find in it a secret message that might be, in any given moment, crucial. It is amazing that human beings, living always with such complexity, can say anything at all. Any writing evidences human saying so is worth reading, however clumsy it may seem according to canons of style.

Trying to write about Buddhism is more difficult. I have always tried to avoid it. Instead, I prefer to write about immediate experience, which when you are writing is writing, a particular kind of experience. People tell me that my writing has always sounded like it is about Buddhism, but I never really intended that. If I am supposed to be writing about Buddhism, I remind myself that writing about Buddhism is a dubious and probably impossible undertaking but that someone can be perhaps encouraged by my attempt. Then I can write something.

I give a lot of Dharma talks and often write them. This is again something different. Because I know I'll be offering the words I'm writing to people in person, and I can see their faces, and I know who they are, there is a friendly atmosphere already generated for the time of writing, and that friendliness bleeds into what's written, and inspires it. In a way, then, the talk is from the beginning a collaboration with my listeners. Because of this, the words don't have to work so hard, because my being there with people, our mutual presence, will generate most of the meaning. The words can be almost incidental. It's good if the words can be skillful, true, or beautiful, but even then this is as much a matter of the way the words are spoken at the time as the way they are written, in the time of writing. And people are usually meditating while I speak, and have been meditating for a while before I speak, which makes a big difference.

I think the most difficult thing of all is sitting down to write a publishable popular book about Buddhism. To write such a book is to write about Buddhism as a set of notions whose purpose is to help people radically change their lives. The notions themselves are not so important, and can even be counterproductive if they are taken too seriously. To write about Buddhism in this way, you have to take those notions seriously enough and at the same time let the reader know that they are not so serious. This is a bit of a trick. In writing a book about Buddhism, too, you face an audience you will never meet, with its presumed expectation that your words will make sense, be inspiring and wise. This makes the task even more daunting.

When I wrote *Taking Our Places: The Buddhist Path to Truly Growing Up*, I had a hard time adjusting to these new problems, finding the proper tone and voice. Before that, I always thought I was simply writing. But now there seemed to be so much more that needed to be going on. I wrote that book because someone asked me to do it, and it seemed a good way to avoid going to meetings—I had already been to too many meetings at the Zen Center—and a book contract, which would bring large amounts of money to the Center, where I was abbot, seemed a perfectly understandable excuse. But I found it impossible and eventually, in frustration with the publishers and the writing itself, tore up the contract. Later another publisher asked me to write about Buddhism (it was a time—unlike the present—when publishers were actively looking for such material) and I resurrected the project, and this time, despite the unpleasantness, managed to persist. Later I got used to who I was writing for when writing a more or less popular Buddhist book, and the process became easier in subsequent books and articles, though I continue to find this kind of writing completely different from what I am doing in poetry—in which there is, in a sense, no audience, only the words and the silence.

Given all this, though, why would anyone write a Buddhist book, and why would anyone read one? Like all writers, Buddhist writers write out of personal necessity, and for fame and fortune. Some Buddhist teachers, who are not really writers, write because they find it challenging, and they enjoy challenges. I suppose, too, that people who write Buddhist books feel, as I do, that there is a benefit in trying to express Buddhist teachings in a more general and broad way, to more people than you would ever be able to meet and get to know. Readers of Buddhist books want to hear a voice reminding them that deep sanity is possible in a troubled world. This is the main thing. It also does happen from time to time that the reader of a Buddhist book finds something—an example, a phrase, an idea—that causes his or her world to shift. These moments do occur in reading now and then, in Buddhist reading, or any kind of reading.

The poetry is, as I say, another matter. It's more a matter of necessity. Unless I engage in it, I feel out of sorts, and am not so easy to live with. When I do engage in it, it relieves something in me. I find the process of being a person very perplexing and problematic. How did it happen in the first place, how is it maintained, and where is it going? Nowhere good, it seems. But when I am able to write, writing acts as a counterprocess and then the person process becomes motive and fodder for whatever it is I am supposed to be trying to discover in the poem—which is, however, never clear. I find that all my poems (these days I resist the idea of "poem"; writing poems feels more like simply writing, a primary form of writing, rather than "poem" as a special instance of writing) are unsuccessful. There are successful poems more or less, but I have never written one of them though I have read many. But I consider the failure of my poems to be a good thing—it provides energy for the next writing, which is always, despite everything, a hopeful proposition. It's the unwritten writing that's the great writing. How could the written writing ever measure up? So I keep going. Writing's a form of investigation, a form of contemplative experimentation. I don't necessarily know what I am writing and certainly do not approve of the various forms my writing has taken or the opinions that seem to be expressed in it. When I meet another writer who understands all this (and there are some, not many, but some), I find it a great relief.

# Do You Want to Make Something Out of It?
# Zen Meditation and the Artistic Impulse

*This essay, probably written in the early 1990s, was my first attempt to back up with sources and antecedents some of the ideas I had been working out on my own for some years. It was my manifesto on "art and spiritual practice," and many people took heart from it. Somehow the essay appeared in many places, most of which are now lost in the haze of memory and not findable on the Internet. The late Gil Ott, publisher of* Singing Horse Press, *knew of it, and it was his idea to reprint it along with the collection of diary poems (one a day for a calendar year) that Singing Horse issued in 2000 under the title "Success." Versions of it appeared in* GIA Reader *(Volume 12, Number 3, Fall 2001) and in the online magazine* Big Bridge.

Allen Ginsberg begins his essay "Meditation and Poetics" (in *Beneath a Single Moon, Buddhism and Contemporary American Poetry*, edited by Kent Johnson and Craig Paulenich, Shambhala Publications, 2001) with this paragraph:

> It's an old tradition in the West among great poets that poetry is rarely thought of as "just poetry." Real poetry practitioners are practitioners of mind awareness, or practitioners of reality, expressing their fascination with the phenomenal universe and trying to penetrate to the heart of it. Poetics isn't mere picturesque dilettantism or egotistical expressionism for craven motives grasping for sensation and flattery. Classical poetry is a "process" or experiment—a probe into the nature of reality and the nature of the mind. (p. 94)

And the poet Philip Whalen makes the same point in a poem when he says something like, "I don't want to be another pretty poety-boo; I want to be a world."

For me this sense of making poetry or art as a heroic and grandiose undertaking whose cost and goal are everything sounds about right—providing you don't get too excited about it, seeing it as anything more or less than any human being is doing, or would do, if he or she reflected for a few minutes about what is a worthwhile and reasonable way to spend a human life. So: (1) art isn't just another job, it's an endless exploration, and as with any exploration there are proliferating avenues of pursuit and no final successes, and (2) art is a necessity for humans, and we all need to find a way to participate in it.

The reason we need art so desperately is that the world and we ourselves persist in being made. There is something exhausting and troublesome in the madeness of the world and in the madeness of ourselves. What is made has always the quality of limitation or unsatisfactoriness. Madeness captures us into a vicious cycle of desiring more madeness or better madeness, and the madeness we get only makes us want to make improvements or additions. Art making is an anti-making. It is an anti-making because it is a making of what is useless—this is what makes art art, that it is useless, that it doesn't do anything, that it is something inherently unmade and this is the source of its liveliness. Any piece of art stares us in the face with the fact of its being what it is uselessly; it is a record of a person's commitment to the confrontation with the made, a confrontation one is bound to come away from second best, and yet one does it, and reaches a peak of exaltation in the doing of it, and the artwork facing the viewer or hearer is a phenomenal testament to that useless confrontation, which, by virtue of its supreme failure, calls our life into question. If you really look at a piece of art or hear a piece of music or poetry or see a dance, you walk away wondering about your life. This is what these objects are supposed to do; this is why artists make such sacrifices in the doing of what they do, because this doing is the undoing at least temporarily of what has done them in in their lives and would do them in to the point of death or madness if it weren't undone in the process of making art.

One of the qualities of artwork that has always impressed me is its unstable nature. The artwork is its physical presence—its words or notes or paint—and yet it isn't that. If you are hit in the face by a plank, you will definitely be hit by it and will feel the effects of it no matter whether you believe in planks or not, no matter whether you are in the mood for the sensation of pain or not. But if you make an effort to experience an artwork, you may not experience anything at all—it may strike you as a meaningless hunk of this or that, hardly worth a second look. Or it may strike you as profoundly moving one day, and completely beside the point the next day. Imagine an artwork sent from one gallery to another for a major show. Of all the people who will come into contact with that work—movers, drivers, curators, technicians who hang the work, security guards, the perhaps thousands of people who will file by to see it—of all these only a few, a very few, will actually experience it as an artwork, and even those few might come back to the gallery the next day and not at all be able to fathom why the day before the work moved them so, or even if they could say why it moved them, and explain it, that would only be a memory. The actual experiencing of the painting has occupied only a few minutes in the many hours of human contact with the work. In other words, real experience of art is extremely rare, and it is fleeting, unstable.

The poet Paul Valery said in his essay "Poetry and Abstract Thought" that poetry is "completely irregular, inconstant, involuntary, and fragile, and that we lose it, as we find it, by accident" (from *The Art of Poetry*, translated by Denise Folliot, Vintage Books, 1961, p. 60). It is a fantastic thing that people place such enormous value on something like this, something so evanescent that we are really hard pressed to say whether it actually exists or not. I suppose, to some extent, we value art out of long habit, or perhaps because it has become a good business: in art's aspect of non-art, it can become just as much a commodity as anything else people will pay good money for, probably even more so, because some sorts of art are even more subject to sudden economic inflation than an Internet or gene-splicing stock. Yet, at bottom, there remains the mystery of the uselessness of art, of the shifting and unmade quality of it, and of the tremendous need that we have for the unmade and the undone, no matter how unstable or accidental our experience of it may be. The experience of it is precious and life-changing always.

I want to go a little further in considering what the actual experience of this unmadeness might be. In ordinary waking life we do make clear and hard distinctions between separate things. This distinction-making is what perception and thought are all about, and all day long we have perception and thought, piling one thing on top of the other, until there is a great weight of them. We define ourselves in the same way among or within our perceptions and thoughts, and get buried in the process. Life is very practical and very weighty, and there is a great deal of conflict that comes from the bumping into each other of the various perceptions and thoughts that cannot occupy the same space at the same time. So there are decisions and considerations and there is desire for organization, yet there is less organization always than one would like, because as soon as the world is organized, along comes something else, and there is disorganization again, then the need to make something else to counteract what has just been made, and the weight of it wants to pull the house down. The problem of being human is always more or less the same problem, but it is tempting to imagine that in our current historical period all of what I have been saying is more true than it appeared to be in the past. There seems to be, simply, more going on, more piling up, more that cries for organization and will not be organized.

The work of art, by contrast, is entirely organized and therefore peaceful. Formally it may not be organized at all, but our experience in appreciating it, if we are fortunate enough to be in the situation of having such an accident befall us all of a sudden, is that of organization, radical organization. Artistic form is the expression of this sort of organization that is essentially an unpiling of the piling up of distinctions that make up our lives. The work of art unpiles everything and undoes us in the process; it raises a million questions that amount to one question: who are we and what are we doing here? This question is the essential question that undoes us every time because we never can answer it. So it keeps us fresh and it allows our life to fully enter itself.

What I mean by organization is a feeling of connection or inclusion or completion beyond thought. In the light of the experience of the work of art, the world makes sense because it is no longer made of weighty and disparate parts; it is a world of nuance and shimmer: what we call beauty, though this word has become fairly useless because it has become confused with pretty. Beauty is not necessarily pretty; it is, rather, this accidental sensation, before we think about it and therefore make something of it, of connection, unmadeness, uselessness, perfection, freedom.

Paul Valery states:

> I recognize it *[he speaks here of the poetic experience, but I think his remarks can be extended to any sort of art]* in myself by this: that all possible objects of the ordinary world, external or internal, beings, events, feelings, and actions, while keeping their usual appearance, are suddenly placed in an indefinable but wonderfully fitting relationship with the modes of our general sensibility. That is to say that these well-known things and beings—or rather the ideas that represent them—somehow change in value. They attract one another, they are connected in ways quite different from the ordinary; they become (if you will permit the expression) musicalized, resonant, harmonically related. . . . (p. 59)

What Valery is describing here is a trancelike state that is more real to us than the real world we live in every day. It is a state that is oddly brought on by a formal arrangement of ordinary stuff in such a way as to discreate the ordinary stuff, take it apart, which is so startling, when we actually notice it, that we become literally entranced. The Jesuit poet Gerard Manley Hopkins once hypnotized a duck with a straight white chalkline, then lifted his hand. The duck kept staring at the chalkline and did not move. Hopkins wrote in a notebook entry, dated April 27, 1871: "They explain that the bird keeping the abiding offscape of the hand grasping her neck fancies she is still held down and cannot lift her head as long as she looks at the chalkline which she associates with the power that holds her. This duck lifted her head at once when I put it down on the table without chalk. But this seems inadequate. It is most likely the fascinating instress of the straight white stroke."

"Instress" is the term Hopkins coined to refer to the potentially torqued nature of pure unmediated holistic perception, which he considered to be clear evidence of the presence of God. The duck in this case was mesmerized, Hopkins says, not by becoming habituated to the hand on her neck, but by virtue of her utter fascination with the chalk line as such. For us, art is that chalk line; it points to the instress, to use Hopkins's term, of every experience in the perceptual world, the only world we can ever live in—inner and outer.

The experience of art is an experience of connection beyond thought. The curiosity of it is that the experience, as a human experience, can't take place anywhere else but in thought or perception. This is exactly why it is so hard to pin down what an artwork actually is, and it is its unpindownable nature, always the case, but lately more appreciated and examined than heretofore, that probably accounts for much of what took place in the history of art in the twentieth century. This has been the job of this time: to point out directly and baldly that doubt and accident lie at the heart of what art has always been. And in doing this one comes close to the boundary between art and life and immerses the boundary itself in doubt and accident. The words "art" and "life" become quite indistinct and imprecise. One could substitute for both the words "reality" or "being." That the job of all art or living is to appreciate and authenticate what is—our life simply as it appears. Viktor Shklovsky, the Russian literary theorist, wrote, "To make a stone stony: that is the purpose of art."

Why don't we experience a stone as stony? Why do we persistently forget to come alive to the world as it is in front of our faces? Why do we have to go to all the trouble of making art so that we can return to where we are and have been all along? I think it is because of the way thought works in us. To be present in the midst of our being what we are is a pure sensation that we can never exactly apprehend. It is fleeting and ungraspable. Thought is always coming a second afterward, telling us something, singing a song of the past. Thought includes the aroma of our being alive, but it also includes so much that is made, so much of doing and piling up, that it tempts us necessarily away from ourselves. To find within our thought and perception (for perception is already thought) a settled free and unmade place takes effort; this is the effort of art. Valery again:

> There is no other definition of the present except sensation itself,
> which includes, perhaps, the impulse to action that could modify that
> sensation. On the other hand, whatever is properly thought, image,
> sentiment, is always in some way a production of absent things. Memory
> is the substance of all thought . . . thought is, in short, the activity that
> causes what does not exist to come alive in us. . . . Between voice and
> thought, between thought and voice, between presence and absence,
> oscillates the poetic pendulum. . . . (p. 73)

This reminds me very much of the saying of the Heart Sutra, "Form is emptiness, emptiness is form."

All of what I have been saying is a Zen perspective on art, although I have a strong resistance to the idea of a Zen perspective on anything for reasons that are probably obvious from what I have said already. So take the words "Zen perspective," please, with a grain of salt, and understand them as shorthand for a way of looking at the world that is essentially unmade and undefined. We can't get away with that, of course. We will always have to be someplace and called something so we will have to use terms somehow in the hope that we will remain willing to have them deconstructed right before our eyes, and to find their deconstruction amenable. In the practice of Zen meditation, we are not trying to do anything other than to undo everything and simply be present as directly as possible with all phenomena that arise. This necessarily involves a moment by moment letting go of definition and perception and thought. I do not mean that we would attempt to become stupid, blank-minded, and unthinking. Rather, that we would let the world come and go as it naturally does, without trying to stop it at some arbitrary point of our own conscious or unconscious choosing. Which, of course, is what we do try to do by making a world up, piling it up, as I have said, and becoming its victim. In Zen meditation we happily enter a radically simple, even an absurd, situation—just sitting still and breathing—so that we have the possibility of seeing how this troublesome world is made. Although we may not be able to do anything with this meditation practice, it does serve as a kind of training, helping us, by familiarity, to become directly used to the actual situation that prevails more or less within being. Meditation practice is a return, over and over again every moment, to that particularly odd situation, which we can see as time goes on exists in the middle of any situation, no matter how simple or complex.

The sense of artmaking that I am advancing here is, after all, following Ginsberg and Valery, an inherently religious one. I do not want to conflate art and religion, of course. I recognize that they are not the same thing, and yet I am arguing that what we call the aesthetic impulse is, at bottom, identical to what we call the religious impulse. Certainly the cultural history of Zen, particularly in Japan, would attest to the close relationship between the two activities.

Insofar as both art and religious practice always manifest in the world as we know it as particular things, both have serious built-in problems. Religion solidifies into doctrinaire narrow-mindedness or institutional power-brokering, or usually both, and art solidifies into money, if it is successful, and despair if it is not, a defeat in either case. I am not the first to point out that art in our radically mercantile society is more or less doomed to become commodified, and that it is generally made for the wealthy, and becomes for them in various ways a kind of sanitized and enriched currency. Even artists who do not make economically valuable artwork must create economically attractive explanations to attract funders to pay for the generally high costs of the art habit. Even poets, who require only about ten dollars' worth of materials to create their works, must earn a living somehow, either by doing something else, which means they will eventually have little time or energy for poetry, or working as professors. In either case, anyone these days who writes poetry must brand and promote their work as culturally relevant in order to remain in the game. (The poet Nathaniel Tarn affectionately refers to this as "pobiz.") Despite this, I do not think the situation is hopeless, and that is why I have taken the time to think about this topic. I believe that if the artist can be clear about the nature of the project that he or she is finally concerned with, and actively work at being clear about it—for clarity is never a given, it needs constant revision—just as if the religious practitioner, which is any of us, can be clear about the project he or she is engaged in, it is possible to proceed with liveliness and integrity, despite the difficulties. Life well and seriously lived has never been without these difficulties; it is part of the fun and simply a given in the situation.

A final quote from Valery:

> The mind is terribly variable, deceptive and self-deceiving, fertile in insoluble problems and illusory solutions. How could a remarkable work emerge from this chaos if this chaos that contains everything did not also contain some serious chance to know one's self and to choose within one's self whatever is worth taking from each moment and using carefully? (p. 77)

And a poem of Zen Master Dogen:

To what shall
I liken the world?
Moonlight, reflected
In dewdrops
Shaken from a crane's bill

# Bewilderment

To the Sufis, words precede existence,
perhaps because a cry brings people running.

—Fanny Howe

*This epigraph is from Fanny Howe's essay "Bewilderment" (which appears in her astonishing collection of essays on writing and life,* The Wedding Dress: Meditations on Word and Life, *University of California Press, 2003). She originally delivered it as a talk in San Francisco, which I attended on September 25, 1998, for the Poetics & Readings Series, sponsored by Small Press Traffic. I remember the room was packed, the audience enthralled and excited, and the talk fascinating, though completely incomprehensible to me at the time. And yet the basic thrust of it—that bewilderment was not a problem to be avoided but instead a state to be sought, cultivated, and cherished—made perfect and immediate sense to me, and struck me as an essential religious and literary insight. I am sure that I wrote my own essay with the same title soon after I attended that talk. Rereading Fanny's essay now, I appreciate its complexity and brilliance. It circles round and round its central theme—which is itself circular and murky. There is no forward motion—neither in Fanny's essay, nor writing in general, nor in life, or time. Just gyres turning in fits and starts, full of disjunction and reversal:*

At certain points wandering around lost produces the (perhaps false) impression that events approach you from ahead, that time is moving backward onto you, and that the whole scenario is operating in reverse from the way it is ordinarily perceived. . . .

Each movement forward is actually a catching of what is coming at you, as if someone you are facing has thrown a ball and stands watching you catch it.

Watching and catching combine as a forward action that has come from ahead.

All intention then is reversed into attention. (p. 17)

*Fanny is a poet, novelist, essayist, activist, and Catholic mystic, spiritual daughter of Simone Weil and Edith Stein (about both of whom she writes), and all her writing reflects this commitment and exploration. As a gnostic, she is both inside and outside the Church, both faithful and unfaithful in her faith, and her religion is powerfully resistant to all boundaries, cranky and fiercely compassionate. My few and yet for me potent and intimate conversations with Fanny over the years—conversations in which the apparently vast differences between our respective traditions and experiences have meant nothing at all—have been a treasure and relief.*

*A version of this piece appeared in* Dharma Life, *Issue 23, Summer 2004, at http://www.dharmalife.com/issue23/puzzled.html.*

Whenever anyone asks me how I came to be a Zen priest and abbot, I always say "accidentally." This is true. While I admire religious people, people who seem to have a religious destiny and interest—and I know many people like this—I am afraid that I am just not such a person. Mainly I am and have been all my life bewildered. I mean this in the literal sense: "bewildered," meaning not knowing what is going on, being lost, astray, wandering about, ruminating, meandering, uncertain, distracted: being aware of the many situations that obtain in any given situation, the many perspectives contained in any one perspective, the unlimited possible alternative explanations for, definitions of, and ways of looking at anything, understanding anything, the basic paradox, tragedy, and perplexity inherent in being human and living in a world humans make with their fractured, limited (and at the same time inconceivably precise and complex) sense organs and minds.

The dictionary tells me that the "be-" of "bewilder" means "be," as in "to be"; but it also means "completely and utterly." "Wilder" means to be lost in a place where there are so many conceivable paths you can't tell where to go. It means to be in the wilderness where there aren't any paths—only empty spaces or full spaces without any clearings so that everything is surrounding you, embracing you, which means everything is felt at once and all possibilities are equally compelling. So to be bewildered is to sense the many paths that must be possible and also to realize that there are no paths at all, that the whole world is open and wild. Wherever you go, wherever you are, whatever happens is a path that leads somewhere—and also a question: a path that leads to another path.

This is how I have always felt. The world is truly bewildering, truly incomprehensible, completely resistant to meaning, sense, interpretation, and this is what makes it so impressive. You can never explain. Of course, you can and probably do explain many things, but these explanations, imaginative though they may be, do not really tell you anything about anything. The real world—and anyone's life—is too strange, too bewildering, to be explained.

I started my Zen practice not as a spiritual person but as a poet. Although I did not become a poet on purpose, neither was it an accident. I was forced into it by circumstances. I was born at the very end of World War II, when the soldiers were returning home from the battlefield with a great hope that things could now be normal and that life would certainly be better now than it had been during and before the war. People in general are admirably able to imagine hopefulness, no matter how hopeless things might seem. This is something to remember and to count on in hopeless times. But although everyone in those days was trying to imagine hopefulness, in fact, people were traumatized by what had happened to them in the war. (And in my case, growing up in a Jewish family, the trauma also included the unspeakably impossible-to-digest fact of the Holocaust, which directly affected my extended family, as it did all American Jewish families.) As a child I felt this universal trauma as a kind of coating on top of things, like dust that was constantly swirling around in the air and would inevitably settle on whatever you brought into the room. I could feel it but no one ever talked about it or even seemed to know that it was there. But children always know what's there, even if they can't say what it is. Instead they feel it mythically, and they are bewildered by it. Which is, I think, a normal feature of childhood that accounts for many of the anomalies that stud adult life like so many suppurating boils that no one seems to notice.

We all grow up knowing somehow that there's a gap between how the world actually is—how we feel it to be—and how the adults in our world see things and explain them to us. It is one of the great travesties and mistakes of human culture that we always think of children as childish. Actually we to ought seek their advice, and try our best to consider their point of view as being of the essence for human understanding. Of course, it would make no sense to ask children for practical advice about how to run the government—this is our unfortunate task as adults. But when running the government causes us to forget the profundity of the child's point of view, we are truly sunk. Jesus must have meant something like this, I think, when he said, "You should be as little children."

Because of being bewildered in a traumatized world, I was constantly forced to doubt the world as it was given to me to understand and to try to understand it on my own. This was the only form of self-defense I could think of. I began writing as a way to understand what I otherwise could not understand because thinking could never get me there. I could see how limited thinking was. I kept thinking the same things over and over again. Although poetry has never helped me understand anything, it has helped me to keep on trying to understand by giving me a method larger than my own mind and personality. But poetry also makes it clear that the gap between how things are and how we live is immense. So poetry can make your life a lot worse.

This was what happened to me. Here is a recent poem of mine that may have something to do with this:

These pages are years, days, nights
Words pasted on like flashes of black light
Points of space that swallow apples and dates
Until all that's occurred—places, moments, events—
Folds into the general whole
As a sea humps waves that fall and spray against rocks
Then rock out again, swaying—
How the heart can be a rock
How it can be blue, a curtain or a sky
How it can be a royal crown upon a noble skull
Sliding out from the general scheme of things

I walked along the shore and saw
Two dead cormorants, an eyeless pelican, flies walking in the sockets
Sky with banks of golden pearl gray cloud
A smeared rainbow flaring indistinct against the horizon—
Objects are neither solid nor discreet
Subjects repeat themselves as waves
With variations, spray, trajectory, rhyme—
Birth comes this time of year

To those who wait it, doubled

Poetry was making life really impossible so I could see that what was required was to close the gap by finding a way to turn all of life into poetry. This was the only hope. I was feeling this when I first encountered Zen books, which seemed to provide me with what I was looking for. This is how I understood Zen then—as a way to live so that all of life could be poetry, so that the gap between the way things actually are and the way people live and think could be somehow closed and you could live life whole and true, and it could be beautiful and purposeful, even if things were difficult, and even if you could never really know the purpose.

So my motivation to practice Zen wasn't really spiritual. I suppose you could say it was aesthetic and practical. I wanted to find a sustainable way to live. When I found out about zazen practice, it immediately struck me as desperately important. I don't know why—possibly because I could sense that in order to do what I wanted to do, I needed to approach things from an entirely different angle. I didn't like statues and bowing and robes and so on—it all seemed objectionable to me, an iconoclast by temperament and upbringing. But I really liked zazen: the idea of zazen but also actually doing zazen. It was never boring. I could never figure it out or get tired of it because it was so simple it was almost nothing at all, which made it by definition and experientially inexhaustible.

I started doing zazen every day and I have continued. It just so happened that keeping on doing zazen intensively required me to bow to statues and, eventually, to wear robes and take ordinations. Of course, I had a lot of resistance to all that but the resistance was small compared to my certainty that it was absolutely necessary to live in such a way that I could keep on trying and failing to understand my life. The resistance was only me and my little preferences and conditioning, whereas zazen and the necessity to keep on with it was something much wider than that. So I persisted. This may sound nobler than it actually is. The fact is, I was terrified not to practice zazen, not to live out this desperate and impossible quest for the truth. I imagined I wouldn't be able to bear life in any other way. I could not imagine any other possibility. So I was willing to do whatever it took to go on.

Of course, we all have theories—to be human is to theorize—and all our theories are autobiographical. My theory is that to be human is to need to live a life that is whole and meaningful and beautiful, a life devoted to the pursuit of the real—although I am, of course, doubtful about all the terms of that sentence—"whole," "real," "meaningful," and "beautiful" are all suspect words and may not mean anything, though they do convey a flavor close to what I might mean. It seems to me, starting with my own experience, that all human beings want and need to make this kind of effort, and that this is why there is always art and religion of some kind in all human cultures. From childhood we have dreams and images and longings that ripen into a vision of life that we need to understand for ourselves, uniquely and viscerally.

This is why there is such a thing as spiritual path. To me, spiritual path isn't separate or apart from ordinary life, it's not an unusual life, an alternative to emotional life and material life. Spiritual path is simply a way to stay true to what arises in the course of a human lifetime, whatever that may be. For this we need some methods and rules and techniques and teachings. These things are practical, the food and clothing of the soul. There are many kinds of good food and many kinds of appropriate and useful clothing—there can also be foods that are bad for you and clothing that is uncomfortable and wrong for the weather. We need to find what works. But in any case, the teachings and techniques and beliefs of a spiritual path aren't themselves a spiritual path. Spiritual reality, spiritual truth, is always bewildering, never entirely knowable. We can know some things. For a little while anyway we can feel we know something that is true. Mostly we can be surprised by a feeling of wonder—or a feeling of gratitude or gentle perplexity. But we can never really possess the truth. That's a kind of craziness, to think we know the truth. My favorite line in the Zen ordination ceremony is: "The path is vast and wide. Not even a Buddha can define it."

I say that everyone without exception wants and needs to live with spiritual integrity, but I know that there is not much evidence for this. Now and in the past the vast majority of people are not concerned with spiritual integrity. Even if they say they are, they probably actually aren't. They are concerned with economic well-being, with their families, with social status, power, and so on. Or maybe they are just concerned with physical and material survival. It is now and has always been a minority of people who have devoted themselves to a thoroughgoing exploration of reality.

Nevertheless I believe that all human beings have that need in them, and that everyone has some native sense of its importance. Anyone is stopped short on entering a silent meditation hall or a cathedral. Taking a minute to just sit still there, anyone feels something larger and wider than—or at the very least strangely different from—the literality of mundane life. Sometimes the same thing happens when you read a poem or see a great picture. Everyone knows about this because everyone knows, whether she thinks about it or not, that she has come here from nowhere, and that when she is done here, she is going to return to nowhere. The minority of people who are devoted to a thoroughgoing exploration of reality do it on behalf of all the others. In the end, this is the only way it can be done.

# Beyond Language

*The popular notion that Zen is "beyond language" is something I have thought about for a long time—thinking that is reflected in many of the essays in this volume. The idea raises many questions such as: What is language? How does it function in consciousness? What would being beyond language look like? Could language be beyond language? A version of this piece appeared in* Tricycle, *Volume 20, Number 4, Summer 2011.*

A seemingly inescapable fact of my life is that I write poems. Why would I feel the need to do this? I don't think of poetry as self-expression or making something beautiful with words. So these ideas furnish me with no motivation. And I don't get paid. But I seem to be convinced that there's a point to poetry: to clarify language through a process of ongoing exploration, so that I can more and more find out how to live within language as joy and liberation, rather than as bondage, which it can be and is when I am constricting myself and the world in language, without knowing I am doing this. Think about political discourse and how hopelessly entrapped within itself it is, and we are when we are talking and talking within a narrow, conflictual framework. This happens in our inner lives. We are our own CNN and Fox News. It's terrible.

So I am interested in and fascinated with language and its grip on us; language is a vital social and personal force that cries out for clarification—or exorcism. I realize that not many people see language this way. But whether or not you do, language is important to you because language describes and creates the world you live in; language describes and creates you. If the world is difficult and life is difficult, it is not so much that there is something wrong with you or the world (though there may be something wrong with you and the world—but what does this mean outside language?), it is rather that there is something wrong with the way you employ your various descriptions of self and world.

We usually think there is something and then there is talking about something and that the something is substantial and real and the talking about it is secondary. But in fact, there's no way to separate something from talking about something. Even perception is in part (the greatest part) a process of talking about something. As in phenomenology from Husserl to Heidegger; as in Wallace Stevens's "Description Without Place":

> Thus the theory of description matters most.
> It is the theory of the word for those
> For whom the word is the making of the world,
> The buzzing world and lisping firmament

Language is humanness; human consciousness is language-consciousness. We are so close to language (it is us; we are it), we can't understand it. We are in language as a fish is in water: for the fish there's no such thing as water; water is just the way things are; it's the medium for being. Language is that for us. I have been wondering about language and I cannot understand it and I cannot get used to it. I have been trying to understand language and yet I am no closer to understanding it now, after all these years of exploration, than I have ever been. Still, I am always writing about this effort to become familiar with language. It seems to be my chief topic: can we get friendly with language; can we know what we are? In "The Meridian," the poet Paul Celan writes, "Whenever we speak with things in this way [in poetry] we dwell on the question of their where-from and where-to, an open question without resolution" (*Collected Prose*, translated by Rosemary Waldrop, Sheep Meadow Press, 1986, p. 50).

So language is, on the one hand, a prison: we're locked inside it, created by, defined by, it, and can see only as far as we can say. On the other hand, language frees us: it unlocks our imagination, allowing us to reach out to the world, and to fly beyond it. This is what poets try to do. Of course, they always fail. The point is not to succeed but to make the attempt; in this there is already some freedom and some delight.

In Zen practice you are always trying to stand within language as an amazement, to open up the hand of thought and gawk at language, let language gawk at you. This means coming to understand and dwell within language in many ways. A word means something and not something else. But also a word is gone even as we speak or write it and so it isn't anything. When we speak or write something, we think we are understanding or communicating, but actually that is not so. When we are speaking or writing, we are speaking about nothing. Primarily what we are doing when we are speaking or writing is articulating humanness. Speaking or writing is just being ourselves, expressing that. When we get tangled up in something we think we are speaking about, we suffer. All language is music. Music doesn't meaning anything, but this doesn't diminish its importance. We need music. Air and water don't mean anything either. And yet the paradox of language is that meaning is part of the medium; words have meanings assigned to them, but meaning doesn't mean anything, it's just part of the procedure.

This is a simple point but mostly we don't appreciate it. We grip objects we have created with language, objects that don't exist as we imagine that they do, and we suffer for it. If we could experience language as it really is for us, and truly abide within that experience, no need to change it—probably we can't change it—we could be free from the suffering language creates. This doesn't mean that we'd be free from pain or sorrow. Only that we'd be free from the special sort of anguish that human beings feel when they are lonely and estranged from themselves, others, and the living world.

This thought lies at the heart of Buddhism, and has from the beginning. The first three members of the eightfold path—right view, right intention, right speech—all hinge on language. These make right conduct (fourth) possible, and when there is right conduct there can be correct effort and mindfulness (six, seven), which lead to correct concentration (eight), reinforcing right view—and liberation is possible. So from the first, Buddhist thought recognized language as pivotal to human conditioning—that views, intentions, and uttered words need to be examined and revolutionized. In later Buddhist thought this insight was strengthened and made more explicit with the teachings on emptiness, which understood the nature of human experience to be "mere designation," language, empty of any fixed definable reality.

As a spiritual teacher operating in the real world with real students, the historical Buddha was sophisticated and quite practical in these matters.

He knew that getting caught up in language was a trap. He saw that nothing was more fundamental than right view—out of right view everything good unfolds—but he also saw that right view isn't some specific propositional truth. People sometimes ask me what is the Buddhist view of this or that. But there is no Buddhist view of this or that. The Buddhist view is a non-view, but not a non-view that is the opposite of a view, a wishy-washy noncommitalism. Non-view includes various views that arise in response to conditions. Non-view is an attitude, a spirit of openness, kindness, and flexibility with regard to language. Non-view is a way to stand within language, to make use of language so as to connect, without being caught by and separated from the world and others by language.

Buddha spent his life talking to people. Like Socrates, he was one of the greatest masters of talking to people in recorded history. One gets the sense in the sutras that the Buddha talked not because he was particularly loquacious, or because he was given to elaborate explanations, but in order to help people see through the smokescreen of their own language and views. Once someone asked him for his secret in answering questions as effectively as he did. He said that he had four ways of answering questions: one way was categorically—simply to say yes or no without ambiguity. The second way was to examine the question analytically, clarifying definitions of terms, trying to determine what was actually being asked, usually by deconstructing the question. Most of the time when the Buddha employed this method, there was no need to answer the question: under analysis the question proved meaningless. The third way was by posing a counterquestion, whose purpose was to bring the questioner back to his or her own mind, redirecting attention away from the entanglement of the language of the question to something real that stood behind it. The fourth way was simply by putting the question aside, because some questions are so hopelessly entangled that to take them up on any terms at all would be to get stuck in them like flypaper—which doesn't help. Trying to answer these questions is like trying to get through a wall by beating your head against it—it is ineffective and you get a sore head. To put the question aside is to walk around the wall without beating your head bloody. This way you do get to the other side, which is after all the important thing. So sometimes the Buddha's response to a question was silence.

In his discussion of right speech, the Buddha similarly evidenced the subtle and nuanced understanding that words do not have fixed meanings and ought never to be taken at face value. The meanings of words depend on context: who is speaking and listening, the tone of voice employed, the underlying attitude, the situation in which the words are spoken. The very fact that the Buddha did not recommend that his words be written down, that he allowed others to explain the teachings in their own words, and did not designate a special sacred language for religious discourse, but insisted that ordinary common language be used, shows that he understood language to be a process, essentially a dialogue, a dynamic experience, rather than a tool of exact description or explanation. Far from being a neutral conduit for the conveying of preexisting meanings, the Buddha saw that language is an ever-shifting vehicle for the self, and that the way to clarify the self, and the world, is to hold language in an accurate and sensitive way.

Of all the teachings of Buddhism they inherited from India, the Zen masters of ancient China emphasized most this point about language:

> A monk asked Zhaozhou, "What is the Great Perfection of Wisdom?"
> Zhaozhou replied, "The Great Perfection of Wisdom."

—From *The Recorded Sayings of Zen Master Joshu*, translated by James Green (Shambhala, 1998), p. 89

> Another monk asked him, "What is meditation?"
> Zhaozhou replied, "Non-meditation."
> Monk: "How can meditation be non-meditation?"
> Zhaozhou: "It's alive." (p. 42)
> Another monk: "What is one word?"
> Zhaozhou: "Two words." (p. 90)
> A monk asked Feng Hsueh, "How can I go beyond speech and silence?"
> In response, Feng Hsueh quoted lines from a famous poem.

—From *The Gateless Barrier*, translated by Robert Aiken (North Point Press, 1990), p. 155

What makes us miserable, what causes us to be in conflict with one another? It's our insistence on our particular view of things. Our view of what we deserve or want, our view of right and wrong, our view of self, of other, of life, of death. But views are just views. They're not ultimate truth. There's no way to eliminate views nor would we want to. As long as we are alive and aware there are always views. Views are colorful and interesting and life-enhancing—as long as we know they are views. These Zen masters are just pointing out to us that views are views. They are asking us to know a view as a view, and not to mistake it for something else. If you know a view as a view, you can be free of that view, beyond views through views. If you know a thought as a thought, you can be free of that thought, free of thought through thought. Views are language, thoughts are language. To train ourselves in language, to open language up, is a practice that cuts to the heart of Buddhist liberation. It is why the Buddha never engaged in metaphysical debate and kept silence in the face of language-trapping questions.

Going beyond language through language is something we can actually practice and develop through meditation, study, awareness in our daily life acts, and through a practice of writing. In meditation we can learn to pay attention not only to sensation, but also to emotion and thinking. Learning to let thinking come and go, we can eventually understand a thought as a thought and a word as a word, and with this understanding we can find a measure of freedom from thoughts and words. With study, we can begin to appreciate Buddhist thought not as a new set of correct concepts, but as mental yoga, counterweight to the concepts we already, unconsciously, hold, and that hold us locked into a small atomized selves. When in daily living we learn to return again and again to where we are, in body, emotion, and mind, we are learning to hold our language and views lightly, to see that they are ever-evolving currents of being, that are ours and everyone else's. Playing close attention to the way we talk to ourselves, we won't fool ourselves too much. Another old Zen master used to call out to himself and answer himself. He'd say, "Don't be fooled by anything." And he'd answer, "I won't be!"

# Phrases and Spaces

*Here is another piece for a Buddhist audience on language. This one focuses on the traditional Zen practice of koan study, meditation on phrases. A version of it was published in* Shambhala Sun *(March 2008).*

The technique of working with phrases is the special genius of Zen practice. This technique consists of living with, penetrating, being penetrated by, phrases, until they become large and strange, revealing themselves to us. That is to say, through them we are revealed to ourselves.

By "phrases," I mean literally phrases—clusters of meaningful words, identifiable, explainable, conceptual. But "phrases" also means the silence, the expansive, ineffable space that you will find in the middle of and surrounding all words and concepts if you meditate on them long and deeply enough.

In Zen meditation this is accomplished by practicing zazen—meditation—with phrases, breathing them, inquiring of them, casting off usual notions of linguistic comprehension. Practicing, as Zen Master Dogen puts it, "thinking not-thinking." That is, allowing thought to arise and disappear, without grasping, without entanglement, without driving thought through fear, desire, smallness, stupid unrecognized circular habits, as we usually do. So that instead of going out toward the phrases, as if they weren't alive, interpreting or explaining them, gaining mastery over them, you allow the phrases to come forward toward you, until you feel them on their terms, free of the usual aggressive activity of the conceptual mind. Feeling them in the gut; letting them work on you.

In Zen there are various specific traditions and methodologies for working with phrases. In contemporary Western Zen, there are several koan traditions, all influenced by Rinzai Zen. Some of these traditions are very well organized, with koan curricula and prescribed ways of responding to koans in a fairly regimented format; others, though based on this kind of system, are more free-form and various, with a curriculum of stories used according to need, and with more flexibility in responding. In the Soto Zen that I practice, working with phrases is practiced in a fuzzy and disorganized way. There is no curriculum and no particular format. This has suited me, because I find I resist things that are too well organized; real life is fuzzy, and spiritual approaches that seem organized (they never really are organized; they just seem to be) and therefore suggest progress and reasonable development strike me as less honest than disorganized approaches that admit progress is a problematic concept to begin with. Though I have always been fascinated with religious systems, organized or not, I have a hard time taking them literally. But I realize that for many people, maybe most, organized approaches are good. They provide a map and a way of checking yourself.

I have said that the Zen practice of phrases involves actual phrases—word clusters—but also the silence that's always inside and all around words. Like the vast spaces inside atoms, without which what we call the "solid" world could not exist, silence makes words possible. In Soto Zen there's a way of practicing with phrases without any words. This is Zen mindfulness, which is not mindfulness of something, but mindfulness of silence, spaciousness, or emptiness or—another way to say it—of presence, of being itself. This is practiced using the breath or whatever is in front of you—a person, a task, a physical object—as the phrase. Life becomes the phrase, not in the abstract but as it appears uniquely, wherever and whenever you are. You pay close attention to it, avoid pegging it down to an explanation or an evaluation, and you wait with intense inquiry. The hope is that everything will illuminate you. Everything will open you up. Everything will surprise you. Although in real practice this doesn't always happen; it is a direction, an aspiration. In any case, the main point is to keep up a continuity of practice.

It doesn't make much difference whether you are practicing with what's in front of you or whether you are using a literal phrase like "Who is this?" or "What is love?" that may have arisen from the issues of your life; or whether you are using a classical Zen koan phrase like Zhaozhou's "Mu" or "cypress tree in the courtyard." The more you meditate with the phrase and maintain your meditating with it through your activity (because, like phrases, which are more than phrases, meditation is more than literal sitting meditation), the more your practice can be continuous and the more will be revealed.

In the mid-1980s I was living in a Zen Center led by Bernie Glassman. We practiced phrases in the Greyston Bakery, which was at that time the main project of the Center. The bakery was a crazy place; we had more business than we could handle, and it was always a special time for breakneck effort: Halloween cookies, Christmas cakes, Thanksgiving pies, Valentine's Day heart-shaped tarts. It was always something. We were working very hard from morning till night. Bernie was tireless and expected everyone else to be tireless, too. And we were not professional bakers; in fact, we didn't know how to bake; we were learning as we went along. So it was exhausting work, going very quickly all the time, trying to fill rush orders, to get things right, and of course, making many mistakes and having constantly to do things over again. In the middle of all this, Bernie would open up shop for *dokusan* (in his tradition it is called *daisan*), the traditional Zen interview in which the teacher examines the student's understanding of his or her koan phrase. He'd sit in his manager's office at his desk while you—in your baker's whites, covered with flour—sat in the outer room on a chair taking a few moments to quickly come back into touch with your phrase, which was right there at your fingertips, easily brought back into full consciousness. When Bernie rang the bell, you'd go in and respond and he would respond back and then he'd ring the bell and you'd go back downstairs to the assembly line as the next person came in. Such things are possible.

One of my favorite phrases is "Who is sick?," which comes from the koan collection *The Book of Serenity: One Hundred Zen Dialogues*, translated Thomas Cleary, Shambhala Publications, 1998:

> Guishan asked Daowu, "Where are you coming from?"
> Daowu said, "I've come from tending the sick."
> Shan said, "How many people were sick?"
> Wu said, "There were the sick and the not sick."
> "Isn't the one not sick you?" Guishan said.

Daowu said, "Being sick and not being sick have nothing to do with the True Person. Speak quickly! Speak quickly!"

Guishan said, "Even if I could say anything, it wouldn't relate." Later Tiantong commented on this, saying, "Say something anyway!" (p. 352)

It seems as though Daowu had the practice of visiting the sick, a marvelous spiritual practice. I do this practice, but not nearly as much as I would like. Walt Whitman spent the greater part of the Civil War visiting the sick.

It is also possible that Daowu was not visiting the sick. "Where are you coming from?" is a Zen question meant to evoke a response perhaps different from the mundane facts. When Daowu said he had come from tending the sick, he could have meant anything or everything by it. This is an answer we could give on any occasion: What are you doing? I am tending the sick. What else are we ever doing? This is the first noble truth of Buddhism: sentient beings are by their nature sick. To be alive is to have a terminal illness. The whole world is a hospital ward.

But then Daowu says, "There are the sick and the not sick." Who are the sick? The ones who think they can escape the pain and loss, who think they aren't sick. Who are the not sick? The ones who know we all are sick together, and have sympathy. They know the world is a hospital ward and we are always tending the sick, ourselves included. When we know this intimately, we are not sick. Ultimately as Daowu says, the True Person is beyond sick and not sick. The True Person simply "is," and in this "is" is living and dying, sickness and health. In the face of this, Daowu asks Guishan to speak, and he does. Guishan was a great Zen master. He understood Daowu perfectly. Saying something won't explain anything, he says in so many words. Which is surely true. It's like asking someone, "Explain your life to me, I want to understand it." It's not possible to explain even a moment of life. But as Tiantong chimes in, "That may be true, but still you have to say something." That's right. Not saying anything is not an option. We tell our stories. We try to help.

# Blizzard of Depictions

*I seldom attend academic conferences but this talk was written for and de-livered at a conference called "Speaking for the Buddha? Buddhism and the Media," held at the University of California, Berkeley, February 8–9, 2005. Most of my fellow panelists felt that Buddhism was being unfairly or superficially depicted in the media. My thought was that there is no possible hope that Buddhism—or anything else that engages essential subjectivity, like, for instance, poetry—could be depicted in the media in any way at all— that you'd inevitably end up with some sort of caricature.*

A week or so ago there was a huge blizzard in the Northeast. I was watch-ing reports about it on television. You'd see, in the tiny box of the tele-vision, pictures of snow-covered streets and buildings, with snowflakes whirling all around. There would be a reporter standing in the foreground all bundled up in a winter parka, his or her face barely visible, clutching a cold microphone. The reporter would be saying something like, "There is really a lot of snow out here!" I watched these reports in Vancouver, British Columbia, where the weather was mild, with a light drizzle.

Wittgenstein famously said, "Whereof one cannot speak, thereof one must be silent." But he didn't mean by this that what you can't speak about is irrelevant, illusory, or nonexistent. In fact, Wittgenstein felt that the un-speakable was the most salient reality. He also said, "The mystical is not how the world is, but that it is."

The world depicted in the media is not the actual world that I, or pos-sibly anyone else, live in. The world I live in is more or less difficult to talk about or to depict in any broadcastable way. It's a quiet world, an unspeakable world, an intimate world. I am not saying that I don't watch television or go to the movies or read books or pay attention to the current buzz in Washington London or Baghdad. I'm only saying that I pay attention to these things knowing that they are different from the world I live in. (Of course, the intimate world I am talking about also exists in Washington, London, and Baghdad—only you don't see it on television). I pay attention to the media because I care about all worlds, not just the ones I happen to inhabit. I also know that "Norman Fischer" exists in several worlds, including the media world. I try to be clear about the difference between the various worlds so as to avoid getting them mixed up.

I realize that the title of this conference is "Speaking for the Buddha? Buddhism and the Media," but to me it is doubtful that anyone who can appear as a spokesperson in the media, including "Norman Fischer" or the "Dalai Lama," would actually be speaking for Buddhism. Because I don't think that Buddhism—at least as I understand it—is that sort of thing. I appreciate that in the title of this conference as it appears on the website there is a question mark after the phrase "Speaking for the Buddha." I am also doubtful about the language of the conference description that reads, "The notion of what it means to be Buddhist in America is determined not only, or even primarily, by learned monastics, but also by publishers, film producers, marketers, and entertainers." As far as I am concerned, what it means to be a Buddhist is not determined by any of these.

I wanted to get that thought off my chest so that I could go on. In this panel our specific topic is authority and transmission in Western Buddhism. This is something I know about and I am happy to address it. As a Zen priest and teacher, I have been given the authority to transmit the Dharma to worthy disciples, and I have done this several times. One of the things we do in the lengthy process of Dharma transmission is to study together. We study, among other things, texts of Dogen that talk about the ineffable intimacy between teacher and disciple, and between person and world, and about the fact that Zen transmission is essentially undefinable and undepictable, even in the realm of thought. I am not trying to be mysterious here, and Dharma transmission isn't anything mysterious. It's just a fact of ordinary life. In our tradition there's no test you can give to ascertain whether someone who has received Dharma transmission actually has received it. All you can do is examine the documents of transmission and hear the testimony of the people involved that the process of transmission actually took place. In the tradition, authority in the Dharma is conferred not as a reward for skill or brilliance but mostly out of a sense of faith and confidence, on both sides, in this ineffable yet quite ordinary intimacy.

Some years ago when I was involved in the formation of an organization called The North American Soto Zen Buddhist Association, a professional organization for Western Soto Zen priests, we considered how we would choose our members. In other words, how would we ascertain who was and was not a qualified Soto Zen Buddhist priest. In fact, our solution to this problem was quite simple: since we all understood that there cannot be any objective, in other words, media-worthy, way to suss out a Zen teacher, all we had to do was to trust that anyone who had been through the recognized Soto Zen Dharma Transmission ceremony in a recognized lineage was, in fact, a Soto Zen priest. Within the small world of Soto Zen Buddhism in the West, which has very little media exposure, this has worked quite well.

A few months ago someone came to me asking, in so many words, for certification as a Zen teacher. This fellow was not only a bright Zen student with lots of talent and understanding—he was also already a Zen teacher with a thriving Zen group, and several members of his group had previously come to talk to me, telling me of his compassion, wisdom, brilliance, and so on. But I had to tell him that I couldn't give him Dharma transmission without getting to know him well, practicing side by side with him, and going through the long process that all Soto Zen Buddhist priests go through. Although the fellow really was in some ways a good Zen teacher, I could easily see the difference (although it would be hard for me to describe it, other than with a dubious phrase like "a particular feeling for life") between how he was practicing and what he understood, and how Soto Zen Buddhist priests practice and understand.

Even though I couldn't help him out by endorsing his teaching, I had no problem with his going on teaching if that suited him and his group. Why not? If someone has something worthwhile to teach, and if there are people around who want to learn it, and keep on showing up, who's to say that the person can't do this? And if he wants to call what he does Buddhism, or even Soto Zen Buddhism, who's to say that this is a misnomer? "But," you might object, "uncertified Buddhist teachers could be charlatans, and could do serious harm to their unsuspecting and possibly charisma-addicted students." That's true. But certified religious traditions, including Soto Zen Buddhism, are full of instances of serious harm done by certified charismatic or uncharismatic religious leaders. Real religious practice is dangerous stuff; it is hard to tell the difference between the fake and the genuine, and both the fake and the genuine have the potential I am sure to be helpful or harmful to our lives. Students just have to trust themselves and hope for the best, I suppose. This is the postmodern Wild West, after all!

The media will always be depicting something about Buddhism, and people will follow those depictions, which will always (when it comes to the Buddhism I am interested in) be incorrect. Despite the great influence of the various media on all of us, I have a lot of faith that the Buddhism I am interested in, the unspeakable, intimate Buddhism, will persist and will be carried on through the various traditions quietly amidst the snow flurries. I have no evidence for this. I just believe it.

Any religious tradition is and has to be an open system if it is going to survive. A religious tradition is constantly being revised, influenced by its surroundings, and usually this revision is not conscious or deliberate. If, as I believe, the various Western Buddhist traditions we have inherited from Asia will go on quietly, outside the media glare, they will not go on unchanged. Each practitioner affects a change in a tradition, as does the weather, the landscape, and yes, the chatter of newspaper, radio, television, internet, movies, and so on. Change is inevitable, necessary, and positive in the long run, I think, so I am not worried. To be honest with you, I feel that the postmodern media-crazed world is a bit off balance and deranged. Nevertheless somehow out of this blizzard, what's worthwhile and true will emerge; at least it is cheering to hope so.

# Saved from Freezing:
# Spiritual Practice, Art Practice

*An earlier version of this piece appeared in February 2005 issue of* Tri-cycle, *a Buddhist magazine, Volume 14, Number 3. In it I am trying to explain again, to myself I suppose, what my various concerns—writing, Zen practice, and Zen teaching—might have to do with one another. The idea of "imagination" appears prominently in this piece—as it does later in this collection—a concept, a faculty, an experience, I am constantly trying to understand.*

Almost every day I listen to or read or watch the news, some days all three of these, because I want to stay tuned to what is seemingly going on in the world outside my house. These days this is an unpleasant experience. The longer I watch or listen, the more worried I get. Things do not seem to be going well. The news about what is going on out there seems to rhyme with an idea of myself in here subject to these difficult conditions—and the world and that self seem mutually to freeze one another into place eventually with the sense of what seems to be the case. There's something desperate about all this.

It occurs to me that world and the self as we usually understand them are exactly frozen: rigid, cold, painful to the touch. Icily conceptual. My personal problems, my conditioning, my attitudes, my self-definitions, what I hear from those around me, and the general conception of what the world is and where it is going—all of which is infused with an unspoken and general sense of dread—all this fuses me to concepts, positions, and anxieties chilling in their effects. Palaces of ice that hold a world and a self in place, stunned, fixed, frozen. But when I switch the news off to write or read a poem or otherwise access the art experience, I thaw out. The world disappears—or at least the sense that it is impossible and intractable does. I relax. My burden is lifted. I am engaged in a way that's active, not frustrating. This is more than mere distraction, taking my mind off my, or the world's, problems. Engagement with art produces a state that is the opposite of distraction. Art saves me from freezing.

Religious practice can have this effect, too. It can provide me with a larger view of my life, a hopeful, flexible, warming view. Possibly. But anyone who's done religious practice for a while knows that it doesn't always work this way. In fact, spiritual practice can provide its own arctic blast sometimes, icing up the soul into more grotesque shapes than the ones you were in before you began, perhaps in your desperation, to do it. Why? Because people naturally tend toward ice: we crave ideology, organized explanations for things, truths we can forever depend on. So though it turns out to be quite painful in the end, we crave the very frozenness we seek to melt. We bind ourselves even as we long to be free. Religion always ends up being a big problem because we are problematic.

Art practice—which necessarily includes engaging art as viewer, reader, listener, etc.—makes a big difference. Art, if you actually encounter it as art, acts as antifreeze—it melts the viewpoint, opens the mind and emotion, deranges the fixed normalcy of apprehension—at least avant-garde art does, and for me, any art that really challenges is always avant-garde (which is to say, is involved with the terms and tools of its own making).

Art engages the imagination, a faculty whose function in consciousness is rather vague and fuzzy. Imagination evokes a more mysterious reality than we can directly sense or rationally confirm. Imagination sees into and through the apparent world to a world more luminous and significant. Without imagination, we plod on in our two-dimensional ice palace, merely surviving the day without rhythm, quickness, or vitality. Technically alive but not really living. Imagination isn't just entertaining: it is vital.

But this is tricky business because imagination is wild. It does not play by the usual rules. It cannot be controlled or manipulated. It appears when it feels like it and leaves without notice. From the point of view of the rationally, ideologically, organized world, imagination is dangerous, for it scorns the world as a mere backdrop for its colorful activity, and in this way casts doubt on everything the other faculties (reason, the senses, the emotions) hold dear. No wonder Plato wanted to exclude the poets from his Republic. And no wonder religion equally mistrusts and fears the imagination, which in addition to its conceptual transgressions, is also forever evoking energies—sexual and creative—religion would just as soon forget about, they are so messy, so hard to control or predict, so impolite and antisocial.

Imagination feeds off desire, transmuting and magnifying reality through desire's underground energies. Imagination confronts desire's discomfort, intensity, and impossibility, deepening and problematizing the world, opening up abysses where there was solid ground. Fantasy is the opposite: it avoids any drastic confrontation with desire's problematics, fleeing instead into a crude and far safer wish fulfillment. Fantasy is teddy bears, lollipops, superheroes, or maybe whips and chains; it is also voices in one's head urging acts of outrage and mayhem—and it is the confused world of separation and fear we routinely live in, a threatening yet seductive realm that promises us the happiness we seek if only our fantasies could be fulfilled. Fantasy and reality are opposing forces. Fantasy is an attempt to escape a reality that it correctly senses can't actually hold. Imagination seeks to enter a truer reality, shaping and evoking it at its most poignant levels.

So although religion seems inherently to be, and has been, at odds with imagination, the truth is religion requires imagination and is, in fact, possibly imagination's chief production. Of course this is true! Where else does the whole edifice of religion come from, with all its rituals, practices, mythologies, and intensity—if not from the imagination? How else would we go beyond the thin ice of things to the passionate flow of the moving waters below—the actual experience of being alive—which religion exists to encourage us to do—if not with the imagination as ally and guide. The senses, the reason, even the moral and emotional faculties are not enough.

Small children have an easygoing and natural sense of imagination. For them there's no serious difference between the world of matter and normal causality and the fluid world of dreams. To the child, these worlds (which seem so diametrically opposed to the rest of us) crisscross and mix all the time. Children have to be carefully taught to freeze the world, to get it to hold still, so they can figure out how to be fixed persons in it in an organized way in the insane world they will have to live in eventually.

Religion, as many believe, is childish. It should be. It should help us recapture the innocent accuracy of vision lost in the process of growing up. It ought to foster senses of play, magic, and humor. Probably it's too much to ask that these qualities be encouraged within the normative forms of any religious tradition, which, after all, have their doctrines, organizations, and real estate to tend to. That's simply practical. And this is why working with the imagination through art—challenging, questing, and questioning forms of art—is so important for religious practitioners. And the reverse holds as well: religious practice is good for artists. As a Zen priest, I have been saved from freezing by my practice as a poet; as a poet, I have been driven deeper in consideration of my art by my practice of Zen. Zen has probably saved me from myself; poetry has probably saved me from Zen.

Art requires discipline. The materials you are working with (even conceptual artists can't avoid materials) discipline you. At first, perhaps, you approach art with a passionate personal need to express your inexpressible feeling. But you soon find that the medium—whether words or paint, movement or sound—is extremely resistant to your self-expression. Things don't fall into place. You can't say what you thought you wanted to, and the very effort to try to do so obscures whatever you thought was the original message. You end up grappling with the materials, which reshape you to suit them. It turns out that making art is not so much self-expression as a dialogue between what we think we want to express and the materials that seem to have their own demands. Engaging in this dialogue moves you to a degree of attentiveness and concentration beyond the private and the personal. It also moves you to encounter art's own traditions, constructed on terms much different from those of religious traditions.

Art practice provides a path into the rich and unique content of your own life. It appears that I don't need art to know what I think and feel. But without art, what I think and feel becomes quickly circular, self-centered, and limited. Engagement with art gives me a way to start with what I think and feel (or almost think and feel) and then to plunge deeply enough into it that it becomes not only what I think and feel but what anyone thinks and feels and, even beyond this, what isn't thought or felt at all. When I write or read poems I am met, through my own thought and feeling, by what's outside my thought and feeling. In this sense, art practice promotes a profound empathy, a widening of my sphere of awareness.

Art practice is an antidote to religious doctrine and dogma—or dogma and doctrine in general. It's a way to discover truth, but not the sort of truth that's handed out already vetted. The sort of truth we have found ourselves, for the first time. This is a much more difficult, intimidating, frustrating, nearly impossible, and essentially joyful proposition.

Those of us engaged in religious practice should never forget how painful and destructive religious practice becomes when our enthusiasm for the truth of whatever tradition we are pursuing becomes exclusive and obsessive. Not only does narrowness of view cut us off from others who practice and believe differently than we do, it also cuts us off from ourselves, as we slash away at our own thoughts and feelings in an effort to fit them to the shape of the doctrines we hold dear. Art practice can move the inner life of the religious practitioner out from under the dictates of tradition and challenge it with a demand for freshness. This has been my experience. My lifelong involvement with poetry has kept me sane within a fairly narrow and rigorous life of religious practice.

We need art as a form of recreation, re-creation of ourselves and our world, a freshening of what goes on day by day in our ordinary living. Viktor Shklovsky, the Russian formalist critic, arguing for attention to formal detail in art, said, "To make a stone stony—this is why there is art." In defamiliarizing the familiar, art makes it new. Artists know this, but not only artists. We all know that in engaging the world outside our own personal interests and habits, and with some rigor of discipline and attention to detail, we feel something of the divine, of the whole. If we approach our daily tasks with this heightened sense, taking care of our homes, our relationships, our communities, even ourselves, with attentiveness and love, we can live as artists, grappling with the materials of our life. In fact, this is exactly the intervention that conceptual art proposes, beginning with Duchamp, and it is no accident that Zen in particular, with its emphasis on the paradoxical and uncanny nature of time in the present moment, was so influential with the early conceptualists in New York.

Being human is a big job. So much to do! Taking care of body, mind, soul, taking care of each other, repairing the world, earning a living—it's endless. There's no use worrying about finishing the job, no use even fretting about how well we are doing it. But to brightly begin and to continue: that's the great thing.

# Attention en Route: Buddhism and American Avant-Garde Poetry, a Personal View

*A version of this piece appeared in a special section, "Poetry and Spirit," in* Facture, *a literary magazine, Issue 2 (n.d.), edited by Lindsay Hill and Paul Naylor. Naylor, in particular, who inherited Singing Horse Press from Gil Ott when he died in 2004, has been interested in the intersection of spiritual practice and the avant-garde for some time, as has Hank Lazer, an essay of whose on this topic also appears in this issue of* Facture. *Naylor solicited this essay, and it would not have been written without his encouragement.*

The avant-garde poetry scene in San Francisco in the early 1970s: all assumptions about poetry and the world were open to question, and the main idea was that everything needed to be thrown out in order to begin over. That was the spirit, and there was much contact; everyone seemed to have no job or a job that allowed plenty of time to go to readings, hang out, publish mags, argue, write much. No one had a family, wanted a career; being a poet was the opposite of that: stay away from serious worldly commitment, which was corrupt and irrelevant, especially the academy (this notion later on reversed itself when the analysis focused politically, and noted that there was no such thing as "great poetry" in the sky, it was all socially determined, had to do with who was in control of the discussion, the academy was in control, so, in order to wrest control, one had to join). San Francisco was the place to be, and there was consciousness that we were "West Coast writers," and as such, even more at the edge, the frontier, looking away from Europe, in the other direction. Close associates of that period included Barrett Watten, Carla Harryman, Bob Perelman, Ron Silliman, Lyn Hejinian, Kit Robinson, Steve Benson, Leslie Scalapino, Rae Armantrout, Bob Grenier, Tom Mandel, Jerry Estrin, and probably many others I am forgetting to mention, and there was also frequent contact with New York avant-garde writers. At first the New York School writers and the Beat writers were allies, being anti-academic, but later on, there was a conscious effort to distinguish the new poetry from what the New York School people (who were older and already half a generation established) were doing. Both the Beats and the New York School writers featured to one degree or another the person, the image, of the poet as a central organizing principle. O'Hara had invented personism, and the Beats were all great romantics. We young poets were digesting everything—beginning with Williams, Pound, Stein, Zukofsky, we went on to Creeley, Olson, Whalen, Snyder, Kerouac, and later on reading Clark Coolidge, who became a key source, and then the Russian Formalists, who prompted us into theory, and then the discovery of linguistics, Wittgenstein, and the great postmodern theorists. The Beats and New York School people rejected the whole notion of thinking about poetry, but we started writing critical essays, at first whacked-out essays that were not intended to make cogent arguments or be susceptible to conventional understanding, and then later dense polemical stuff, delineating a perspective, even a definitive school. There were important magazines and important issues of magazines. Leaders of the school began to emerge. Things were taking shape, and had to do, as it developed, with language as language: seeing that language was not, as writing had up till then assumed, a more or less neutral conduit for thought and personality (of course, there had always been style and form but that was just the way you made language do what you wanted it to do), but that it was instead a heavy and opaque, conflicted and politically determined indigestible shaper of thought, controller and confuser of thought. Language was something in its own right, not in service of something else. It was not transparent. It conditioned everything, was what all writing in the end was reducible to, and so was the only fit subject of poetry, and we began to become acutely interested in how language worked to make what it made. It did not take much further thought to see that the whole sense of the person, the poet, the author, couldn't be the one we had inherited from the past; that the author, the poet, as unified person could not be assumed, that the whole notion of coherent intelligent literary self was highly suspect. Thus the Language School was created and it was extremely testy and insistent on its austere precepts, which made a whole lot of other poets, older and contemporary, mad. But this is, I suppose, what it takes to get something going.

I say "we" here but I was off to the side of all of this, and so am a bit sketchy about it. I did go to the readings and the parties and hang out as much as I could, absorbing all of this as it got filtered through the very intelligent and exciting work of my friends, because poetry was where I mainly lived, but I also lived in the midst of a different set of circumstances: for one thing, I was married and had two children (some of the others also had children, but not until ten years later, except for Bob Perelman and Francie Shaw, whose children are close in age to ours, and Lyn Hejinian, whose children are about ten years older); for another I was a committed Zen Buddhist practitioner. I had begun daily practice in 1970, and by 1976 had gone to live in a monastery and in 1980 was ordained as a priest. During this period I continued writing and publishing and staying connected, but was necessarily elsewhere, often physically and otherwise. Oddly I had the feeling that, although off to the side, I was still, by virtue of my Buddhist practice, very much in the middle of things, though in my own way. Because of my absence and spiritual practice, I could not take part any longer in the debates and discussions, could not read the reading lists, yet I seemed to be going along the same track even though on another train. This is because Buddhist thought and the postmodern theory that was beginning to become the key source for the poetry that was being written were quite consonant. I could pick it up in the discussions I did participate in on breaks in the monastic schedule, when I came to visit friends, and attend as many events as I could.

Nearly all the writers I have mentioned had been at one time or another interested in or had practiced Buddhism. Buddhism was a corner of the avant-garde of the 1960s and 1970s certainly, a wedge that the Beats and others used to pry themselves loose from the American culture they found so objectionable and destructive. If you were coming of age at that time, and if you were thinking about things, and especially if you were on the West Coast, you were probably going to encounter Buddhism. But by the late 1970s, Buddhism seemed too exotic and romantic, insufficiently intelligible, too "spiritual" and maybe anti-language. Most of what the poets were thinking about by then sourced from Europe, so it became, in the way that attitudes and currents of thought become desirable or not desirable in the cultural foment, not a positive thing to be involved with Buddhism and most of the writers dropped their active interest. (It reemerged much later, in the 1990s, for these writers as well as for many others, as things got tougher, people got older, and some actual solid practice for making life kinder and more bearable became necessary.) I seem to have a great capacity for thickheadedness and for a certain degree of cheerful oblivion to what is going on around me, so I didn't particularly notice this. I was aware of it to some extent, of course, but it didn't really have much of an effect on me. I was studying Buddhist thought deeply (along with my Zen practice life, I was getting a master's degree in Buddhist studies), finding it useful for my writing as well as for my living, and not minding particularly what anyone else thought. And my friends were all always quite tolerant, even, I would say, interested in my viewpoint. Although many of them would, at the time, have expressed no interest in Buddhism, they remained interested in me, and our exchanges and friendships during the 1970s and 1980s went on as fully as they ever had.

In fact, there is no doubt that my reading of Buddhism over those years was always deeply influenced by my work as a poet in that particular time and place, with those particular associations, and certainly the reverse is true. In the history of Buddhism in the Far East there has always been a close connection between poetry and the teachings, and one could argue that in China, Zen (the school of Buddhism I practice) was the result of the encounter between Buddhism and the Chinese poetic tradition, and that the poetic tradition in China was in turn radically altered by its encounter with Buddhism. So I was in good company. In China and Japan there are traditions of poet monks and monk poets. The former were poets who took on Buddhism, either as literary device or sincere religion, or both; the latter were Buddhist priests who wrote poetry as a way of expressing their insight and faith. I suppose I am neither of these exactly, though I have always felt that for a Buddhist priest I am a pretty good poet, and for a poet I am a fair priest. In other words, I seem to be between jobs almost all the time. But that suits me and I probably could not do it any other way. Poetry for me has always had that deeply private and inward sense to it, almost anterior to communication, speaking through the text to a "you" that doesn't exist, even as an ideal reader, the same "you" that melts into individual consciousness when you sit on your meditation cushion, the "you" that you dissolve into when you leave this world through death's supposed doorway.

All of this then leads me to trying to think through some of the ways in which what I've absorbed of Buddhist thought and what I've found in avant-garde poetry relate to each other. This will necessarily be an impression-istic stab at it, because I do not as a rule think about things very systemat-ically (for years the idea of not thinking about things at all was one of my main thoughts and methods of working; this is no longer the case but there are shadows of it still in my style of thinking) and am highly conscious of the tenuous nature of both poetry and Buddhist practice.

Most central is the notion I've already mentioned: the deconstruction of the person, deconstruction of the voice or sense of "I" that propels the poem. Mid-twentieth-century academic poetry offered a "poet" who speaks the words of the poem; so did Beat poetry, Black Mountain poetry, New York School poetry, etc. There may have been, in some of the new poetries, a problematizing of the figure of the poet (in Ashbery's all-over fractured wit or Creeley's taut and tortured forms), and yet it was still there. Someone is talking in the poem, and that person, "the Poet," is heroic-tragic-omni-scient. But the actual fact is that the "poet" is not a coherent person but a style of organization of poetic form: it is arbitrary and contrived. In fact, poems are organizations of words, and these can be made to fit varying circumstances. The idea that the subject is a fiction and ought to be avoided in favor of what is more clear and accurate, the denuding of language itself, is, as I have said, a key insight of postmodern thought in general, and of the late twentieth century in avant-garde poetry in particular.

The essential fictiveness of the person, the subject, and the effort to take a closer look at the materials that make up such a subject, is also key in Buddhist practice and thought. The Buddhist notion of "no self" means that psychologically the sense of self is a construct, a designation placed upon a flow of experience. The Buddhist practitioner trains him or herself to recognize the mechanism that produces the notion of self, and seeing the disadvantageous nature of that notion, to undo it, and instead see expe-rience as arising and passing away on its own. Self is seen as a conditioned convention, and there is an effort to see more deeply how the mind works, so that one's view is not occluded by the sense of "me." This kind of thing is a major focus of meditation practice.

At this point in my work as a poet and reader, it is difficult for me to sit still for poems that are self-consciously inhabited by "poets" who feel think see hear and say various things. The whole thing strikes me as quite false, a contrivance that is too easy to see through. By contrast, poems that move along according to their linguistic necessities seem much more lively and true. In writing and in reading this way, I am apt to discover something along the edges of my experience, something that would be unsayable except in the form of a poem. In such poems there is the sense of feeling one's way along in the dark, of skirting the boundary of the sayable, of pressing on language so that it begins to speak what would not be speakable if the limited idea of "me" and my ordinary emotion, physical experience, and so on, formed the parameters of what could be said. If "I" write the poem, if the poem is only big enough to encompass the territory that an "I" could inhabit, then it is quite limited indeed. Without that limitation the scope is immense. Every new poem is a question of the reinvention of poetry. For a long time I had an argument with a doctrinaire application of what I have just said: it becomes limiting to have a strict principle against any sense of persona in a poem. It always seemed to me as if the occasional appearance of a constructed persona were an option that could be exercised if the poem called for it. So I have used this and have had various voices and characters appear in my poems. I find the occasional sound of someone's voice to be a welcome relief, even if it is fake.

Another aspect of avant-garde poetry (as I have already said) is its sense that language as such is to be dealt with as the major material. Not image, or meaning, or emotion, or some idea of beauty or shape, but simply the quality of language itself as exploration, uncovering. Avant-garde poetry has been criticized for this in that linguistic exploration or experimentation seems to many readers bloodless and pointless, abstract and reader-unfriendly. But in the light of Buddhist practice, I can see a great virtue in it: in fact, when you look at your mind, when you look at the constituents of "me" and of confusion and suffering in living, you do see very clearly language standing right in the middle of what the problem is. In Zen practice you are always trying to stand within language in a fresh way, to open up the hand of thought and let language be flexible. This means it is necessary to understand language in many ways. On the one hand, each word means something and not something else. But also each word is gone even as we speak/read/write it and so it isn't anything. When we speak/read/write about something, we might think we are understanding it or controlling it, but actually that is not so. It is not that we are speaking/reading/writing about anything—rather we are being human, we are expressing ourselves. It's when we get tangled up in the something we think we are speaking/reading/writing about that we suffer. It is, then, a very good idea to take a close look at language, and to have a practice of loosening up the grip we have on language (and language has on us—language that is controlled by whom? The state? The marketplace?). Avant-garde poetry can be such a practice; it has been for me, and I think for most of the poets I know, poetry is more a practice than an art, not a means of self-expression, but rather a way to freshening up vision and an avenue for living.

Two other factors in avant-garde poetry that are corollaries to what I have been saying are (1) a resistance to any notion of closure, and (2) silence, the extralinguistic, as the always-present limit of the poem.

When "I" writes a poem conveying emotion/thought from "me" to a reader using the transparent conduit of language, a whole series of aesthetic considerations come into play. There are aesthetic canons, and my success in the poem depends on how well I manipulate these canons. So poems have literary punch lines; they run artfully toward conclusions and afford the reader the satisfaction of a job completed and well done. But leave aside the "I" and begin to explore language as practice or as process, and you are already militating against any sense of closure in a given poem or in a series of poems (no accident that in the postmodern period so many poets write in series, endless series). There is the sense that no poem ends, that there is only the one infinite poem, and that the ending of any poem is just a temporarily convenient resting point. (I do not know if poets of the past used a technique that I have many times used and that is so common in avant-garde work: you get a notebook, begin to write on the first page, and the poem ends on the last page; the size of the line is determined by the width of the notebook.) Witness here also the many experiments with erasure and revision, and the high consciousness of the tenuousness of language, its endless possibility to remake or disturb or confuse itself. (I have seen poems with words in type crossed out, but still legible, and replacement words printed above. There are also many cases of the same poem being reworked and rewritten as a series. All of this, of course, is heightened by the technology of "word processing.") Closure gives an entirely false sense of security and solidity. It also closes off possibility. The classical argument against closure is found in Lyn Hejinian's essay "The Rejection of Closure" (1983). It argues for "open" (without closure) versus "closed" texts, and hinges on the essential point that the world, experience, life, personhood, is essentially vastly complex and completely without boundary or fixed definition, an endlessly open story, so why would we want literary works that give us a false notion of our actual human experience—thus increasing our confusion.

Buddhist thought everywhere implies this same insight. In Buddhist psychology there are six, not five senses: the thinking mind is considered a sense; and each sense is associated with a "consciousness." This means that mental and intellectual experience is an ever-fluctuating continuum just as are the other senses; and that although it is different from the others, it is not their boss and chief explainer; which is to say that mental and intellectual experience is not a discriminating apparatus capable of accurately looking over sensual experience in order to define it or fix it in time. It is just another form of flux. Also Buddhist thought speaks not of life and death (death as the conclusion of or the opposite of life), but of life-and-death as a single endless continuum. Death is not the end of a story but a transition in the continuum of transition after transition. (I do not mean here only ideas of so-called "reincarnation" but the notion that every moment we die to the past and go forward, and that there is no final moment in this process.)

Without closure there is no separate place before or after the poem that could be called silence (just as Mahayana Buddhism starts with the proposition that nirvana and samsara are not a dichotomy, enlightenment and confusion are not different states). Both Buddhism and avant-garde poetry want to say that the silence or darkness that lies on the other side of language is not, in fact, elsewhere than in the words. At its best, avant-garde poetry is a practice of metaphysics, and most avant-garde writers that I am aware of do have this almost religious/philosophical sense of the practice they are doing as a kind of confrontation with reality, a practice of questioning and investigating the impossibility of language and conscious life. Impossibility is, of course, only a problem if you are expecting something else; as long as you are not, you can delight in it, and find it profoundly satisfying, perhaps the most satisfying of all possibilities. The difficulty of avant-garde poetry comes from this, I think: that it always needs to push on the place where language disappears into itself, that that poking is the theme, in the end, of all poetry that matters (otherwise it would be prose, explaining, showing, or attempting to mimic something).

This raises the question of the reader. Someone might complain: What's wrong with these poets? They do not seem to want to be understood, do not seem to be interested in communication. Who can understand/appreciate this rootless barrage of words? Well, there is certainly a point here, and I would argue that in a sense the reader is not important (just as, in Buddhist meditation, there is no audience and nothing produced, I would argue that with the avant-garde poem there is also no audience and nothing produced; there is only the process itself, into which the reader is invited to peer, and thus participate). Of course, there are readers/hearers and there is the poem on the page or read out loud, but this is only something technical, a necessary step in the completion of the work. In other words, it is not that the poem is completed and then presented. It is that the completion of the poem is its presentation. I have myself wanted, out of some sense of friendliness for the reader, to make my poems to some extent amusing or easy to read (although their point is usually obscure), but in the end, despite this tendency, I really feel as if there is no audience in fact, and that an "understanding" of the poem either in myself or my listeners is only an impediment to what I am actually trying to do.

Lately I have been reading the poetry of Paul Celan. In an essay of his called "The Meridian," which was delivered as a speech on receiving a literary prize in Germany, he gives eloquent voice to what I am here trying to get at, so I will end this essay with some quotation from and discussion of that piece. (I am using Rosemary Waldrop's excellent translation of Paul Celan's *Collected Prose*, Sheep Meadow Press, 1986.) Celan is one who, with a great sense of seriousness, sincerity, and even desperation (he was a Holocaust survivor) felt compelled to write the kind of work I am talking about, not out of a need for aesthetic positioning, but for sheer survival.

In his essay, Celan speaks of the poem as intentionally promoting obscurity and distance within itself and from the reader for the purpose of promoting the possibility of "an encounter." The poem, therefore, he says, "speaks on behalf of the stranger—no I can no longer use this word here— on behalf of the other, who knows, perhaps of an altogether other. . . . Perhaps poetry is a turning of the breath. . . . Nobody can tell how long the pause for breath—hope and thought—will last."

"The poem today shows . . . a strong tendency toward silence . . . the poem holds its ground on its own margin. In order to endure, it constantly calls and pulls itself back from an 'already-no-more' into a 'still-here'" (pp. 48–49).

I have always been struck by the tenuous nature of poetry—as well as of life (it is probably less obvious in the case of life, which seems so much more substantial). For many years I was astonished and horrified by the fact that a poem that one day could seem life changing to me could seem entirely opaque boring and meaningless the next day. Somehow, it became clear to me, the actual poem, the poem itself, what was so important to me, wasn't the words; the poem wasn't the poem; it wasn't something other than the poem, and yet it wasn't the poem. The poem was also not my experience of it: it was its experience of itself, which required an author, and required a reader, and there was not really any difference between these two. And this was something almost impossible to catch hold of, define, or properly know. All kinds of analysis of language, form, and so on were beside the point. Life (as Buddhism is fond of teaching) is in the same way radically contingent, fleeting, ungraspable, relational. Like the experience of a poem, one is hard put to say whether it occurred or not, whether it is located there or here, whether it is present or already gone. One can never say where yesterday has gone: and today is already yesterday even before it arrives. Buddhism tells us that all things, time and human experience, are empty, not really here at all in the way we think they are, like mist, a bubble, a phantom, a mirage, a reflection, a dream. The poem's job is to suggest this for us—even more, to bring us to it, an experience which is perhaps always available, but seldom noticed. The poem therefore is, as Celan puts it, something "lonely, it is lonely and en route" (p. 49).

Working with language in this spirit, one finds a measure of freedom. Intently concerned with language and its relation to the human mind at the deepest and most intimate level, one comes to see language finally disappearing, its weight falling away entirely. In the end the whole process of poetry is seen to have been an exercise in attention, the calling forth of our human conscious awareness from struggle and confusion out into the spaciousness of freedom, by means of language itself, because there is no other way. Celan writes, "The attention which the poem pays to all it encounters, its more acute sense of detail, outline, structure, color, but also of the 'tremors and hints'—all of this is [achieved] . . . by a kind of concentration mindful of all our dates (i.e. the whole range of human joys, tragedies, perplexities). Attention [and here Celan quotes Malebranche quoted by Benjamin—the theorist of quotation—in an essay on Kafka!]—attention is the natural prayer of the soul" (p. 50).

## NO SANDART ANYMORE, NO SANDBOOK, NO MASTERS

Nothing in the dice. How
many mutes?
Seventeen.

Your question—your answer
Your chant, what does it know?

Deepinsnow,
Eepinnow,
I-i-o.

—From Paul Celan, *Breathturn*, translated by Pierre Joris (Sun and
    Moon, 1995), p. 107.

Room's dark but light comes through big square window
Vivaldi's playing, the dog's sleeping nearby
Life's arrayed around me lightly—things I see
Words I want to hear, birdcage, piano, book
Things cancel their contexts
I do not know about that
I only see what's in front of me where I am standing
When it gets dark I will be in the dark
When it gets cold in the cold, hot in the heat
That's as far as my thinking goes
And when it goes further
I stop
And remind myself
That there are many thoughts
But they are all unknown to themselves
Now (which is then) I am writing someone's thoughts
As physical words

Whose physicality can be deciphered later as meaning
Giving rise to someone's thoughts
Producing a false record of this moment
But there is no moment whose record is false
No moment whose record is of that moment
Each record is its own moment
As we know
Soon I will stand
Turn off the music
And be gone
This
Will remain

—Journal entry, dated July 15, 1999.

# On Questioning

*This text was delivered several times in retreats and talks venues. It was originally written for the annual Mindful Lawyers' Retreat, held in the Angela Center, Santa Rosa, California, in the spring of 2009. Endless questions, without answers, have been a constant theme of my thinking, the indeterminacy of everything an attitude that has always been natural to me. It may come from my Zen practice of questioning—the essay's main thrust—or perhaps it is entirely Talmudic. In any case, this is probably my most direct statement of it.*

Traditionally, the Zen stream in Buddhism is said to begin with Bodhidharma's triple dictum: a special teaching outside the scriptures ("beyond words and letters"); pointing directly to the human heart; without mediation. And the legendary Sixth Zen Ancestor, the paradigmatic Zen person, is an illiterate temple rice-pounder, whose intuitive understanding of Zen has nothing to do with training or education. From the start, then, Zen presents itself as the ineffable essence of Buddhism, the kernel or core sense of it, with everything extra stripped away. Direct, intuitive, experiential. Having nothing to do with faith, piety, or doctrine.

The style and tone of the literature of Zen throughout its long history bears this out. Zen stories are full of slang and roughness, and often seem to violate Buddhist canons of conduct and observance. It's not that the Zen tradition is particularly reformist or iconoclastic; in fact, throughout its history in China, Japan, and elsewhere, Zen has seen itself as the bulwark of all Buddhist schools, and has held fealty to tradition. And yet all the schools of Zen have understood the essence of Zen to be something deeper and wider than any particular school of Buddhism or even any particular religion, including Zen itself. You might say that Zen is the only one of the world's great religious traditions that explicitly makes going beyond itself the essence of what it is. Of course, that's only what Zen texts seem to say: people who've read them, especially in popular form, without commentary or qualification, are often quite surprised when they observe Zen life and find that it is just as conservative and literalistic as any tradition will be, after a time. But the exceptions to this throughout Zen history—the groups and individuals who have seemed to be quite free and open—are always valued and strongly validated. And in any case, taken at face value, Zen literature seems clearly to be pointing to a radical freedom from doctrine and preconception, which is why un-Zen or amateur Zen enthusiasts like Zen so much.

What is the essence of this radical freedom that Zen teaching seems to be proposing as the core of the religious quest?

It's questioning. The active, powerful, fundamental, relentless, deep, and uniquely human act of questioning. Questioning that's radically a feature of the human mind, and of language. If there's a word, a statement, its opposite can be imagined. Anything that is—as a human being can know it—is inherently subject to questioning. Questioning that leaves any possibility of or notion of answering far behind. Questioning that produces a doubt so deep and so developed it eventually becomes indistinguishable from faith. Questioning that starts with language and concept but quickly burns language and concept to the ground and enters silence. Questioning that brings humanness to its edge and pushes it off. So that the feeling of being, of existence itself, as manifesting in a particular time and place and person, becomes foregrounded.

Despite the fact that Zen is full of texts, stories, doctrine, and concepts, all this is understood to be for the purpose of erasure. Zen discourse is an anti-discourse. Inspired by Madhyamika philosophy, which asserts that all ideas, doctrines, and existents are empty of any fixed reality, and that emptiness itself is empty, and so no words or doctrines can ever stand up to scrutiny, Zen holds its various statements about reality very lightly. The punchline of so many Zen metaphysical jokes is just this: that which was asserted as true a moment ago is not true now, it's gone. Zen presents itself as nonideological, as fundamentally an experience, a feeling for life. But it can't be an experience either because experience always begs description and explanation: experience, understood as such, is ideology. Questioning questions experience and moves beyond it.

A child learns speech after she grasps the illusion of the persistence of objects. So she names. But soon after naming is in place, almost as soon as nouns give way to sentences, objects organized in their relations and activities, questioning begins. Where did Daddy go? Why is Mommy crying? Why can't I have more candy? When will we have to leave this place? And later, why must I speak nicely to her? Where did Grandma go when they put her in the ground? Why do I have to grow up?

The child's questioning begins with noticing that things in the world don't make sense, and that the explanations we are given are bogus and conventional. This is why children always ask questions that are impossible for adults to answer. So adults laugh or smile or scratch their heads, which is a way of avoiding the issue entirely. And, in fact, leaving childhood behind, growing up, turns out to be about putting aside these childish questions, which are, after all, expressions of wonderment, uncoverings of the boundaries of speech and thought. Growing up turns out to be about suspending questioning, burying it, so that we can get under way with the practical work of getting a living and cooperating with the existing arrangements of the world. Growing up is the submergence of questioning.

The questioning, of course, doesn't go away. It is still present with us, though below the surface. It manifests as anxiety in the middle of the night for no reason, or as a vague dissatisfaction with conditions as we find them, or as an out-of-scale feeling of anguish at instances of loss or defeat or disappointment. Somehow it is necessary for us to return to our questioning, but we don't know how. We don't even know that we need to do this.

On a psychological or discursive level, questioning seems disruptive and distracting. It causes us to hang back from activity, creates in us an inability to commit ourselves to anything because we can't seem to leave aside our concerns and doubts that seem to stand between us and full-blooded, full-bodied, fully engaged life. This kind of questioning flows from and goes only as deep as the personality: our history, our desires, our fears.

Zen drives questioning deeper than this. In Zen meditation we concentrate on the breath in the abdomen and on the posture as a way of resting alertly and radically in the present moment. We eventually let all thinking fall away, but not by striving to eliminate it. Rather we allow thinking without becoming personally active in it. We let thinking think thinking, and in this way it comes to rest. This powerful focus at a single point, with spaciousness, in the present moment with all its depth, hones down and develops questioning until it goes beyond language. Language beyond language, a kind of sub- or proto-language: silence. Until the questioning is reduced to an intensity that burns up inquisitiveness and desperation, living is questioning and nothing but questioning. Everything else dissolves. Everything else seems partial or exaggerated.

This questioning is basic to the Zen method of taking Zen beyond itself. No belief or doctrine stands up to it. Only what is confirmed and sustained by what happens, and trusting this absolutely, even though moment after moment it disappears like smoke. And going deeper and deeper with questioning until there's no possibility of an answer one could repeat, define, know, or depend on. Instead the dawning of a feeling of absolute certainty. And the constant letting go of that certainty in the willingness to stand in the middle of uncertainty, because uncertainty is the only thing that has the rock-solid feel of truth. Uncertainty is readiness. It is only a problem and a weakness when there lies underneath it the desire for a secure outcome. But in reality no outcome suffices; no outcome can rise to the level of this thoroughgoing questioning. No outcome can match the panoramic glory and color of the imagination. Uncertainly is pregnant with constant possibility. It's an endless adventure. Time is eternal because questioning drives time out of time. Questioning simply goes on.

I realize that what I am saying here is drastic. Maybe it makes questioning sound heroic—and maybe questioning is heroic in relation to the usual placid acceptance of social reality. But questioning is, at the same time, very ordinary, and Zen practice is nothing if not practical and grounded. One of the cardinal aspects of Zen questioning is that its profundity and thoroughness are identical with the actual shape of ordinary everyday affairs. With everyday practice in the temple or out of the temple, one gradually integrates questioning into all ordinary tasks. Questioning purifies and enlivens everyday life, functioning like a scouring pad or a torch, scrubbing or burning away the patina of desire, confusion, and mindless habit that generally covers ordinary activities, so that they can't appear as they are; their luminosity is necessarily diminished. With questioning, when we walk we really walk; when we eat we really eat. Nothing false and misleading beyond the moment can withstand the fire of questioning.

With a spirit of questioning in our lives or as our lives, there's no possibility of a thoughtless acquiescence to personal, social, or political injustice. One accepts convention as convention, and one is forced to look deeper at the implications of actions or institutions and follow through on what one sees. So, despite the checkered history of Zen Buddhism as an institution, I am convinced that the Zen spirit is one of radical kindness and righteousness. Throughout Zen's history in all cultures there have been examples of this spirit and there will continue to be.

# An Everyday Zen Letter,
# Mid-June 2012, Muir Beach

*A few times a year I send a letter to supporters of my Zen community, the Everyday Zen Foundation. This is one of those letters.*

Dear Ones,

It's summer at Muir Beach. Bright warm days (not the usual fog and blustery wind). I have been reading and ruminating. Two thoughts keep returning to mind.

First, the strangeness of life. I can't seem to get used to it. How days pass by, time moving on, but to where and from where? I am often working on my calendar, planning events for a supposed future that the calendar defines. But where is that future? When is it? It seems to be right here, as I contemplate being somewhere else at a later time. I can imagine it all in my mind. And then the time comes and where am I then? Here, where I have always been. Now, in the time I'm always occupying (or is now occupying me?). And soon that here and now is past, and where is the past? Did anything actually happen? The truth is I have no real evidence of the past or future except in my presence now. And in my presence now no clear sense of who the person is that's experiencing (if that is the correct word, I think not, but I do not have a better one) these things, thinking these thoughts. Time is time; something seems to be occurring; someone seems to know this and say so.

The second thought I keep coming back to has to do with religion. I like to spend time reading religious thinkers of ages gone by. I have been reading Dogen closely for more than forty years. And other Buddhist and Zen texts. And Jewish and Christian texts as well. Just today I have been reading Augustine's *Confessions* (again) and the inspired poems of G. M.

Hopkins (again, again). And I wonder: what were these people thinking? Augustine wrote in the fourth/fifth centuries, and when you remove the "thees" and "thous" of the archaic translation, he seems quite contemporary in his self-consciousness and verbal dazzle. He prattles on and on with tremendous urgency, talking to God as if God were present, pleading, explaining, speculating, wondering, but always full of faith that the Whom he is addressing is listening with transcendent loving interest. Hopkins writes of the Christ he is meeting everywhere, in hawks and marshes, in clouds and seascapes, as though this Person were the most palpable, actual thing in the world. But is there any way that we or I can feel what Augustine or Hopkins (or Dogen, Nagarjuna, Zhaozhou, etc.) was intimately meaning when they were saying what they were saying? I think not. No way being a person then could feel like being a person now. A whole universe of conceptual and historical frameworks has shifted since then, and to read their words as if we understood what they meant, to dismiss or validate them, to project our contemporary prejudice onto them—would be hopelessly myopic. And yet something in their speaking speaks directly to me. Religion is so odd in this way. How many learned books have been written about Augustine or Hopkins? How many interpretations and reinterpretations? And Augustine and Hopkins are themselves already reacting personally to primary religious teachings as they felt them in their time. Commentators decide what this or that religious teaching supposedly means, and what this or that religious thinker of this or that historical period is supposedly saying, but the truth is they don't know. No one does. Any more than any of us knows what is really going on in any average day of our lives! I have always found it comforting and very helpful to contemplate religious texts. Although I never know what they mean, I find something that helps me to live. My ruminations are illuminated.

Meanwhile, days slip by and the world goes on in its stunning confusion. In past letters I have expressed my dismay over the state of the world (and my latest poetry book, *Conflict*, is all about this). But for some reason lately, and especially today (maybe it's the sunshine) I feel quite hopeful. More than hopeful: I feel certain that despite everything, it's okay. We have, of course, much to do, internally and externally (if there's any difference between these two). No end to that, ever. And yet I feel confident. The world's rightness is here already.

Yours, Norman

hinking

# Poetry and Faith

*This essay appeared in the Autumn 2013 issue of* Religion & Literature, *in a Special Forum entitled "Twenty-first-century Poetry and Hospitality." Its editor, Romona Huk, solicited it from me.*

Going around my house and the landscape outside and the city and the world I inhabit, I am aware of how much I see and hear and taste and touch and feel and how much I do not see and hear and taste and touch and feel, that there is so much going on in my daily experience I am aware of and so much going on that I am not and can't be aware of but that yet affects me, moves me, and makes my life what it is. So that anything at any time might floor me with its known and unknown dimensions, I might stagger back at a sunrise, a tree, a bush, a cup, a floor, a window, or a person speaking to me facing me with her face that has lived through these many days and years and all that has happened in them. I think I know what it is that is going on in my life in this world, I operate normally as anyone does, I would never think to deny the person that I am here among others (and I do appreciate others, it would be so lonely without them), but also I marvel at the darkness and vastness of what I don't see or hear or feel or know in any way, that seems to be the basis of it all. I know I don't know. The passage of time, therefore, shakes me up all the time.

I have always been impressed with the Torah's strong prohibition against visual images of the Divine. The people in their hour of greatest loneliness, uncertainty, and need fashion a golden calf, as anyone would, for consolation, and God, in consequence, causes the tablets, the most precious of all human things, the keys to living and knowing how to live, to be smashed.

That's how severe the prohibition is. Don't look: you can't look. You can't see My face (Moses is permitted only to see the trailing glory). That's forbidden because it's impossible. Yet you want to look and you will look, and you will see, and you will inevitably be fooled by what you see because what you see is not real, and because you will act on what you see, things will not go well. Hence the Torah's story is not a happy one.

You can't see but you can hear. God speaks. God doesn't fashion the world with his hand. God speaks the world into being. In English the text reads, interpretively, "God said, 'Let there be light,' and there was light." The Hebrew literally says, repeating the same words, "God said, 'There is light,' and there is light." This makes it unclear whether God was making a predictive pronouncement—saying words that would invite or invoke light, as the common English interpretation indicates—or whether God's saying and the immediate luminous being of the light are one and the same action.

Being as hearing. Not seeing: hearing. Seeing: active, reaching out to touch and hold a world. Hearing: receptive, remaining present to receive a world.

Seeing is a moment later, a construct. You see in the light (after the light's spoken/as being); you hear in the darkness (the moment prior to the light as spoken being). Seeing is outside. Hearing is inside. So seeing is idolatry. Seeing is making something out of being, something you can hold and manipulate. That can manipulate you. Seeing is the physical world, the world of space, its image in your mind.

But hearing is in the moment of being, of time. Hearing is inside. Hearing is presence. Hearing, you're not outside being, holding it or longing to hold it. You are in it. You are it. You are present, presence, reality in which manipulation and desire and being overcome by the world don't apply because in such wholeness of identity there could only be belonging and love (though these words, with their sentimental overtones, are not quite right: we are talking about something larger than what these words usually connote)—which is what the whole of the Torah, in very realistic and drastic narrative tropes, is struggling to express. It's a struggle for sure. *Israel*: literally, *who struggles with God*.

The text ends with no resolution, Moses about to die, speaking, speaking, speaking, pages of text, retelling all that has already been told as the people are about to enter the Land of Promise (Promise: itself a speaking, a word given and committed to) that they have not yet entered as the fifth of the Five Books ends.

The basic Jewish prayer, to be said many times each day, is Shema: Listen, or Hear. *Shema Israel Adonai Elohenu, Adonai Echad*: Listen, you who struggle with God; listen and you will hear that there is only, there is nothing but, Adonai, our God.

This tells me three things that are central to my living and writing:

First, to privilege listening/hearing, over seeing. Time over space. Or within physical space, the space around and between objects, in which the objects appear, rather than the objects themselves. Seeing (seeing objects as such) will never bring me whole; it will only give me a world out there against which I'll have to stand.

Second, if I will listen deeply enough, I will be granted the feeling of union with the world I live in, with others, with myself, and this union will by its nature be unknown to me—essentially unknown (God is unknowable; I can't know nor depict nor explain nor express God, but I can touch and be touched by God through my listening).

Third, this feeling of union is personal ("our" God) and familial; it's not metaphysical, abstract, distanced. It's close to me, as close (and as problematic) as my friends and family—as the sense of myself as a person among persons. So there's love, there's feeling involved in this. I am met and held in it. My exile can be ended.

When I practice zazen (Zen meditation), as I have been doing all my adult life, I am practicing this listening. I am sitting still without trying to do anything, not trying to control thinking, or direct attention in any way (yes I do begin by paying attention to body and breath but not as a meditation object or a task to be performed: simply as a way of undoing my usual preoccupation with being myself in a world). Instead I am listening. Literally listening. My whole body becomes an ear listening to the world inside and out: I literally am listening to, am hearing, the sound of the ocean, the wind, and whatever feeling of being or thought of being arises inside or out. Ideas for poems or daily tasks do not occur to me, or if they do, I forget about them. Listening is always radically in the present, which is to say, timelessly in time. There is no later in which I must remember to do something that occurs to me now.

Then, later, if I go to my desk or my chair with my notebook and pen, I listen for the words that will appear on the page at that time. Call this improvisation, but I don't feel like that about it. I am not improvising, I am listening. Words come through. It's more like dictation, though I don't hear words spoken to me (as Jack Spicer apparently did), or written out visually (as Hannah Weiner did), they just seem to come, I don't know from where. They seem not to follow any intention or shaping on my part. I am not thinking them; they come on their own. If, as might occur, it seems that the words are "mine," that is, refer to events in my life (usually quite sketchily, without narrative) or thoughts and themes I seem habitually to be given to, that is only because my listening can't but include references to the particularity of my being myself in the world I live in. Of course it would be that way. Those who wrote down on scrolls the words that appear as Torah were the same. They were listening just as fiercely—certainly much more fiercely because their situation was so much more dire—hearing the words that came to their hands in their time and place, which would appear as they did, not as mine do. "Our" God is always of the time and place in which "we" find ourselves. All writing that is real, that aspires to reality, that will sit still for and humble itself for reality, would do that— would appear in its own guises, its own vocabularies.

Vocabularies are not invented. And even if they were (I could write invented words, though I don't do that), the characters in which the invented words appear (the Roman alphabet) are not invented. That is, my listening comes not only in the form of (as if squeezed through the tube of) my own circumstances but also through the agency of the alphabet I have historically inherited, and the particular language within that alphabet I have grown up speaking and have continued to speak all my adult life. (Though it has been a persistent thought of mine—growing more urgent with the passage of years—that English is my second language, that Hebrew, the language of my ancestors, is my actual language, but I have never known that language well enough to speak and read it with fluency, so that I am in a perpetual state of discomfort, speaking someone else's language, not knowing or having ever known my own: this might be so for everyone who speaks any language.) This means that whenever I speak or write anything, I am always joined with all those who have spoken and written in this language, my mouth is literally full of the words others' mouths have been full of: I am literally in my listening and speaking/writing out of my listening conjoined with others, speaking the lives, the words, the thoughts/ feelings of others. When I write poetry, I am especially aware of this, and it is what makes the poetry so powerfully satisfying (though also unsatisfying at another level, since I cannot ever write the poem that is wanting to be written, the poem the listening is drawing me to: that poem will never be written, so that every poem longs for and implies the next, and there is no end to this).

When you listen, you hear sounds, of course. But you also hear silence. Silence is exactly not a sound, so you can't hear it in the same way you hear a sound. But all sound arises from silence and only deep listening will make this clear. When you listen fully and completely, you will hear sound and you will hear the silence from which the sound appears and that is the heart of the sound, the truest aspect of the sound, its basis and meat. Sound, we could say, is being. Silence (unbeing?) makes sound possible—it's the hiddenness within the sound that makes it sound. It's the truth of the sound. (What in the world would that word, "truth," possibly mean, otherwise?) When I am writing poems (which could also be prose/unpoems, but there is always some form, form is endlessly various), it's the truth of the sound that I am following and that will take shape in the unique form and sound of the poem.

The world is awash with stuff, stuff you can see and must get hold of in order to continue to live another day. It's relentless—the speed with which we need to pay attention to this stuff is ever-increasing, we are literally getting sick with it all, sick of it all, the world is becoming daily more problematic, and the increases in speed and articulation of stuff are causing our institutions, our economies, and our psychologies to be in a vertiginous state of teetering. Everything teetering.

Listening is the opposite of this—it is in the middle of it all, is the basis of it all—yet the activity of listening on purpose (in silence, which could be prayer or contemplation; in writing it is poetry, which is listening to and reflecting the silence) is the opposite of the activity of rushing around dealing with all the stuff. There is no escaping that rushing, of course, until the body is outlasted by time, but there are better and worse ways of going about it. It is hard these days to sit still and pay attention to the poem—the poem one writes or the poem one reads (increasingly there is less and less difference between reading and writing). And yet the poem, though perhaps now quite rare, is more essential than it has ever been. Because of the rushing.

When I refer to "poem," I mean not possibly what most educated readers would mean by that word—a short elegant elliptical narrative that expresses an aspect of the writer's subjective experience. Such poems can be satisfying and are often quite well written, but this is not what I am talking about. I am talking about the sort of encounter with listening/speaking in which the subjectivity or life story of the writer is not centrally important, in which the trying to express one's self or one's viewpoint is not the method or the goal, nor is competence or elegance in writing: rather, the point is—the poem's energy is—an encounter with the real that is so vague and chartless that one is hard pressed to define it or "teach" a way to write or read it, though all poets who practice this encounter know exactly what I am talking about.

In this sense, the poem I mean is essentially a "hospitable text." Hospitable not because it is easily accessible or understandable—because texts like that would of necessity be a display for the other, a display the reader is meant to behold with envy admiration or recognition—of the poem's—and my own, as poet—otherness (disguised as "identification"). But hospitable because the poem's surface would resist the smallness of my interpretative mania, so that if I would allow myself a moment of not knowing, of simply listening, the poem would draw me in, encourage my largeness by stripping me of the smallness of my preconceptions—it would be the place where I might find my deepest sense of belonging—belonging to the Oneness the Onlyness that's at the root of the silence/listening/speaking that is the poetic process; belonging to the endless others who have spoken/hollered/ wailed/yapped in the language I am now so deeply and so fully engaged with—and the belonging to other poets dead, and, especially, living, who are engaged in this same process and with whom in the darkness of the poem I am now engaged with as deeply as speaking people can be engaged with one another. The hospitable text makes the world hospitable because it offers as nothing else can an occasion for friendship and hope. Though, as I have said, the poem I mean isn't "personal" in any of the usual senses of that word; it is, in fact, more and more fully personal than anything else I can experience. I am never closer to myself, to others, and to the proposition of being a person, than I am when I am in the unknown midst of my listening to and in the poem.

POETRY AND FAITH

Let all the things we touch—
As if roasted by the time we last touched them—
Be increased by our presence & allow please

That the music of our breathing collapse easily
Into the three or four pieces we had in mind from the outset.
Heart isn't hand but head isn't heart either.
All things count the limit of themselves fairly
Particularly. Enemies of that
Limit in our system order prayer.
So leaving we enter there.

•

Two trees on a street
Coffee in an old can
Destitute distributions on cant &
Eyes' blades make destruction
Reaching for later

Always limiting what's perceived—
Our knowing self lingers like fingers
Over preferred objects

All thinking is of something never everything
And nothing's never apart from that,
Its sad inaccuracies

Without ever looking
We set down empiricisms
Cold abstractions
On warmly set tables
Of our affectations

•

In a minute all edges
Fall into substancelessness
All curves ride the borders
Of their reminiscence

On hold what's dearest to us
Lingers in a fever-touch

Writing, we totter in the breach

Longing for the message
But getting just the copied instance

So hold onto what's presented
Nothing's less
Toward our anchor's testing
In ache of spades

●


Woe to the charcoals in our brews
Diving or living I saw no way
The whole of it came not at once
But murder by degrees is far worse

So writing opens up the pen a crack
To ease the sphere's distance a speck
And hurt us less I suppose than perishing

It doesn't sound so terrible
To diminish a little every day
Otherwise swim backwards
And go anyway

●


Weighing in further than ever yet
Not gathering what's clept

Wooing wonders, wearing worlds,
Sentencing borders, measuring worths
Not called for nor burdened to
The voice. I'll holler likely

Anyhow, and wake up the death

●


Wooden extractions
Painful rumblings of the gut
Heartfelt renderings
Into the pits or ruts

Inchoate meanderings
Along the rails of rhyme
Fitful patterings
Foolish attempts to slide

•

Cornering mischances I wonder
What makes the elephant tardy
Why does the chameleon change its shape
How come the dragon sucks up fire
Who's arranged that the rhino knit like that
Why's the willow green in summer

Where's the hare when you need him most
Why's a circle the shape of sunshine
Who organized the color of the flood
On what ground is the snake stamped
Over whose wall does owl clang night

Where's the Nile's source
Under what shall we file our darkest dreams
How measure the shape of wholes
Calibrate the distances of despairs

Why not throw off eyesight or
Angle in further toward the steam
How differentiate cube from contortion
Deliberate over chairs
Order relations among amphibians
Or confabulations among recalcitrant stars

Integrate integers organize organs
Deplete reproductions repeat ancient signs

There are quite a few details to attend to
Before we write the final lines, acuities
We're suspended to, diarists still to unwind

Like lustrous burning eyeballs
Borne lazy in our minds

Fit the eager portions
Into the rinds

•

Hoping for some revulsion in the shuddering rhythms of times
I rear back & hurl my conversations into roils of ricochetting rhyme
Letting my mustaches fall silent I reckon stations where
    communication's perfect
Where whatever one means by what one is registers perfectly in tarnish
In spoilage nasty's clever productions across rampant designs
So hold forth in faith that's perfectly jarless, teeming, and bright
All-over regression
To flight

•

In synch
The old women knit fragments
In pitch
Perfect
To latter
Their old felt broken
Their hairnets patched
They refigure their birthing
And wander liquid
Among the dunes
In sweetest wonder
Left only to themselves
The sun shines down
Branches cross

•

He dips who caresses
What's occurred in his hands
As airs blend & fire
To spirit the earth

Organized ascensions link laughter
To greater lengths

Hairs twirl in the dragnets
Of our Souls

Bother me not, weird World
Lather me all over
With Wishes and Pearls
Evening comes, morning of another Swirl

Anti-matter in black holes sucks mind
Down avenues of depleted pride
As souls blend in poetry's endless remorse
And words lock their silences
In peals of Dread

# Introduction to *Beyond Thinking: A Guide to Zen Meditation by Zen Master Dogen*

*Kaz Tanahashi, calligrapher and activist artist, is also a Dogen scholar with whom I have been working on translating Dogen off and on since the early 1980s. When he published this collection of Dogen works on zazen, he invited me to write the introduction reprinted below, and originally published in* Beyond Thinking: A Guide to Zen Meditation by Zen Master Dogen, *edited by Kazuaki Tanahashi (Shambhlala Publications, 2004).*

The year 2000 marked the eight-hundredth anniversary of Dogen's birth, a good time to appreciate the crucial contribution this great teacher has made not only to Japanese Soto Zen Buddhism, or even to Zen Buddhism in general, but to religious practice the world over. The latter half of the twentieth century has been perhaps the strongest time for Dogen's work: in Japan and in the West he has been studied as never before, and his thought has been influential, not only for a Soto Zen school that is now thoroughly international, but also in a wider philosophical discussion, in which he is often compared with Heidegger, Whitehead, Wittgenstein, and others. Dogen's thought has proven useful and germane to many postmodern discussions in fields like metaphysics, epistemology, language theory, and the like. When I began practicing Zen in 1970, and encountered Dogen's writing for the first time, he was very little known and understood in the West. While much of his writing has yet to be brought into European languages, several English translations of his master work *Shobogenzo* (from which many of the pieces in this volume come), as well as other materials, are now available, and Western Zen practice centers based on his work have been established. With all this, I think we can say that serious study of Dogen in the West is well under way.

It seems natural then at this moment to take stock of where we stand with Dogen, both in Japan, and in the West. Who is Dogen, what is his teaching, why is he important? For those of us who have been practicing Soto Zen for many years, studying and trying to put into practice Dogen's ideas, a new spirit is emerging. There is a greater willingness to view Dogen critically, to see the problems as well as the tremendous and sublime depths, and to recognize that the religion he founded has had its ups and downs. In Japan, the Soto establishment has in recent years made a strong effort to reach out to the wider world. It has forthrightly apologized for past mistakes (supporting Japanese militarism before and during World War II, and going along with the Japanese anti-Chinese racist policies of that period), and more than this, has engaged in its own internal debate about how and why these mistakes were made. In many ways the Japanese Soto church has made sincere efforts to accept non-Japanese practitioners not simply as colonial subjects of their religion, but as robust and authentic practitioners in their own right, who may have something to contribute to a wider-ranging study of the master. All of this was unimaginable twenty-five years ago.

Western Zen practitioners are beginning to grow also, retaining a good deal of the initial wonder and adoration of Dogen, but tempering them with a critical eye. It is true that Dogen's writings are lofty, difficult, and profound, great treasures of world religious thought. And yet, we are now beginning to admit that Dogen's thought is also at times cranky, narrow-minded, elitist, fundamentalist, even violent at times in its expression. We are beginning to admit that no human being, Dogen included, is perfect, unchanging, or always right, and that no person or institution remains unaffected by the social and political conditions that form the context for what happens.

While Dogen was a religious reformer and innovator, he was also, deeply, a traditionalist. A traditionalist religious view is more often than not narrow-minded, authoritarian, and rule-bound, more likely to cut off real and vibrant life than to foster it. We need only study the record of any religious establishment to confirm this—from jihad to the Crusades, religion's effect on the human world has often been disastrous. And even when religion has fostered relatively peaceful times, it has often left scars of guilt and inner anguish on its most loyal adherents. Because of this, the last few hundred years have been understandably hard on traditionalist religion. The modern secular psychological and scientific viewpoint, which has taken religion as something old-fashioned and counterproductive to real human values, has been a source of liberation for many people. But now that the developed world is, to a large extent, free of the old religion, and at the same time clearer about the limitations of the human species, the secular perspective is wearing thin. We are finding a new way to practice religion—not superficially, not rigidly, but flexibly and widely, lovingly not crabbily, with a gentle idealism that is not, as idealism all too often is, toxic.

One of the necessities of this new kind of religion is actual practice—daily practice. It is admirable and important to have the right ideas about our lives—to believe that goodness is possible and can be cultivated; to view compassion as the most important of human achievements; to want to be mindful not mindless, and so on. But these attitudes, wonderful as they are, aren't enough to carry us forward in the present world. We also need some concrete form of spiritual practice we can be committed to—an everyday practice, which can be a strong basis for those beliefs and intentions, and can help us to work with our daily conduct. By spiritual practice I mean activities that we actually do—that we take the time to do; activities that are, in a rational sense, useless, done merely for their own sake with no other goal or object, and done with devotion and dedication to something larger than ourselves, and as much as possible without self-interest. Here is where Dogen's writings, particularly those included in this volume, which bear specifically on his understanding of meditation practice, can be immensely useful.

Soto Zen practice, Dogen's practice, centers on zazen, sitting meditation. But zazen is not, as one might imagine, a concentration technique to still the mind and produce religious insight. Dogen's zazen is much simpler and far more profound than this. Even, as the reader will soon see, close to ineffable. I have always marveled at Dogen's sense of zazen practice. It is, on the one hand, extremely lofty and difficult, maybe even impossible to do, the most advanced and demanding of all possible spiritual practices; and at the same time, it is a practice so easy and so accessible that anyone, no matter what his or her beliefs, skills, or level of commitment may be, can do—almost can't avoid doing. As Dogen says, zazen is a form of meditation so basic it can't even be called meditation. It is simply the practice of being what we are—of allowing, permitting, opening ourselves to ourselves. In doing that, we enter directly the depth of our living—a depth that goes beyond our individual life and touches all life.

Dogen's zazen defies description or explanation. Though Soto Zen teachers sometimes offer practical suggestions about how to sit, they make it clear in their fuller discussions that zazen is no mere technique. Many have noted the paradoxical language (whose originator, as you will see, is Dogen himself) with which zazen is typically described. This is not to mystify the student—it's because there is no other way to speak of zazen accurately. The zazen that Dogen is advocating is neither devotional nor experiential; it's not a form of concentration or relaxation—though it may or may not include any or all of these things. It is simply sitting in the midst of what utterly is, with full participation.

Dogen speaks to this in the very first sentence of the very first text he wrote explaining zazen, "Recommending Zazen to All People." If it is true that enlightenment is everywhere complete already, within us and outside us (as I suppose a theist would assert about God) then why would we need to do anything to bring it about? In fact, Dogen tells us, we do not. We practice zazen not to produce enlightenment, but to express and manifest the enlightenment that is already there. As he says in "Rules for Zazen," (p. 7), zazen "is not conscious endeavor; it is not introspection." Still, there is a simple way to go about it. In this text Dogen goes on to explain exactly how to practice zazen—down to what temperature to maintain in the room, what to sit on, what to wear, and exactly how to arrange the body in the correct posture. The text is about a page long. It tells you all you need to know. Zazen practice is not difficult. Anyone can do it, and instruction takes only a few moments. Yet even many lifetimes are not long enough to mature it.

Zazen is a physical practice. We don't usually think of spiritual practice as physical, and yet, life, soul, spirit, mind don't exist in the sky—they exist in association with a body. In Dogen's way of practice, body and mind (or spirit, soul) are one thing, and so to sit—to actually and literally sit down— paying close attention to the body as process, unifying consciousness and breathing with that process until you can enter it wholeheartedly—is to return naturally to what you most truly are. You have been this all along, whether you sit or not. But when you sit in zazen, you return to it, and embrace it completely.

I suppose that the most widely quoted and misunderstood aspect of

Dogen's zazen is the line that comes toward the end of this text: "think not thinking. How do you think not thinking? Non-thinking. This is the art of zazen." (Note that this term *hishiryo*, coined by Dogen, can be rendered as "not thinking" or "nonthinking" or "beyond thinking." In this book the latter two renderings have been used, sometimes together. As is often the case in translating Dogen, whose use of terminology is often purposely multifaceted, one English word for one term is not sufficient to give the full flavor of the meaning.) I spent many years pondering this line, and practicing with it. It has turned out to be not so difficult to understand and to practice as I had thought. To think not thinking doesn't mean to stop thinking, or to try to stop thinking. In saying "think not thinking," Dogen is talking about an alternative way to think—a way that is not enmeshed in desire and confusion, but is rather fluid and free. Usually our thought is either dull and dim, or it is agitated. In both cases thought is being pushed by anxiety or desire. When we do zazen, we let go of all this, letting thinking simply rise and fall, by returning to awareness of breathing and posture. Thinking may be going on, but there's no more pushing—it's just thinking going on, not "I am thinking." This kind of thinking is what Dogen means by non-thinking, thinking beyond thinking. It is no problem. Sometimes in zazen there may not be any thinking—or very little of it. This is fine also.

In the final line of this short text, in a deceptively simple sentence, Dogen expresses the secret essence of his notion of zazen, and of all spiritual practice: "Zazen is the dharma gate of enjoyment and ease; it is undivided practice-enlightenment."

A great deal is said in these few words.

I think the real fruits of spiritual practice do not became apparent right away. If you do almost any kind of serious practice even for a day or a weekend, you will see some powerful effects in your life. It is not at all unrealistic to think that someone can have a life-transforming experience in a short retreat or even in a morning at church. I have seen this happen many times. But the real fruits of spiritual practice grow over longer periods of time. As you go back day after day to your cushion, through times when you like it and times when you don't like it, times when it is very difficult to keep it up, times when your soul aches so badly you can't imagine sitting there for even a single moment more but you do it, and times when your mind is raging or your mind is so peaceful you can't believe there could ever be a troubled moment ever again—when you experience all of this year after year on your cushion, you begin to find a deep appreciation and satisfaction in your practice. And in your life. You feel as if your cushion is your home, your true spot, and that when you sit there, you are always all right. If you are a Buddhist, maybe you will say, "When I sit on my cushion, I am sitting in the palm of Buddha's hand, and I feel this no matter what shape my mind is in"; and if you are a Christian, you might say, "When I sit on my cushion, I can feel Jesus's love flooding my heart." But whatever you say, I think there will be that deep sense of satisfaction in your time of doing zazen, and not only then. You will feel that satisfaction in your life because you will know that you have come into contact with what is most basic and fundamental in the human heart: with love, letting go, and silence, and the taste of these will pervade your life. Even when the day comes when you lose everything to death, all your possessions, your friends, your body, your mind, even then you will have some serenity knowing that the big mind, the larger reality, will always be present, and will carry whatever you are to become exactly to where it needs to go.

By "undivided practice-enlightenment," Dogen means that our life is always whole. We have always been enlightened beings—this has always been the nature of our minds, the brightness of our cognizing consciousness. To really know this is to accept a deep responsibility, a joyful responsibility, for our living. For Dogen, "practice-enlightenment" is one continuous event. It's not that we practice now in order to become enlightened later. Rather, because we have always been enlightenment, we must practice—and our practice is the expression of that endless and beginningless enlightenment.

Enlightenment sounds very lofty but it is something quite ordinary. The enlightened person is simply the person who isn't selfish—who sees things as they really are, loves them, and acts out of that love. With zazen practice we see a world that is lovely, and that calls out to us to participate in it. We are glad to do it. We can't not do it.

As you study the texts that comprise this book and continue with your meditation practice, I think you will find difficulty in explaining or understanding what you are reading or experiencing. Dogen's expression of zazen practice, of human life, takes us to the very edge of what we can say or know. For Dogen there is no linear path connecting ordinary life to enlightened life, no scale of depth in living or understanding from superficial to profound. Each moment of practice is already the last as well as the first, and even a beginner is already finished. As he says in "On the Endeavor of the Way," (p. 16) "the zazen of even one person at one moment imperceptibly accords with all things and fully resonates through all time . . . each moment of zazen is equally wholeness of practice, equally wholeness of realization." In other words, in our daily zazen practice we entrust ourselves to the wholeness of our experience, and to all of experience, moment by moment. We are not so much trying to calm down or improve as to give ourselves to the holiness that has always been at the center of our lives.

Although this is something we literally touch with our own bodies, as Dogen insists throughout his writing, it is also not something we can know, in the usual sense. We sense it, feel it, are it, as is everything else we come into contact with throughout the course of our lives; and yet as soon as we think we know it as an object or an experience, and begin to define or take credit for it, we lose track of it. In the same text Dogen says, "earth, grass, trees, walls, tiles, and pebbles . . . all engage in buddha activity," and inspired by them and in concert with them, we express the depths of what's true, "unfolding widely inside the endless, unremitting, unthinkable, unnamable buddhadharma throughout the phenomenal world."

This is lofty indeed, and lest we get too excited about it, and want to rush out with our good news to the world, Dogen reminds us that "it does not appear within perception, because it is unconstructedness in stillness; it is immediate realization." Unconstructed. Immediate. This is how we begin to make efforts in our lives, then, inspired by our practice of zazen. Letting go of our assumptions and preconceptions and coming forth in our lives from a stronger place. Not that we can ever eliminate our assumptions and preconceptions, but rather that, seeing them come and go in daily practice, we know them for what they are, and can once and for all break their spell over our minds and hearts.

Passages such as these bring us face to face with one of the most often-mentioned aspects of Dogen's writing: its difficulty. We are speaking here not only of problems having to do with translation or cultural distance, but with the sheer and inescapable fact that Dogen's writing, in places, is almost perversely opaque, to the point where one wonders whether he actually intends communication at all. For Dogen the central fact of our existence, and the source of its profundity as well as the problems inherent in it, is that we are at once severely limited and, at the same time, limitless, and that these conditions depend on each other. In other words, as existent creatures we are bound by time and space, and yet also we have a foot in eternity—which is not a limitless span of time and space, but the true, imperceptible shape of each moment of our lives. Since this is Dogen's point over and over again, how can he not find himself immersed in linguistic spirals and verbal somersaults?

Underlying almost all Dogen has to say about meditation practice is this sensibility in regard to the paradoxical nature of time and space. As he says quite directly in "Deep Ocean Samadhi," (p. 71), "Past moments and future moments are not sequential. Past elements and future elements are not aligned. This is the meaning of deep ocean samadhi." ("Samadhi" is meditative concentration.) We experience ourselves conventionally, in the world of our own perception and emotion, as sequential, as within the realm of time and space. But the actual reality of time and space also must include non-time and non-space, which are always present with us. To do zazen is to open ourselves to this reality. For us, dying is the limit of time and space. Dying is present with us always, in the midst of every passing moment, although we usually do not think of it. Dogen thinks of it, and in doing so, how can he not come up against the limits of language, which is time and space bound. So, in a text like "King of Samadhis," (p. 50), he cannot avoid expressions like, "Know that the world of sitting practice is far different from other worlds. . . . Study the world at the very moment of sitting. Is it vertical or horizontal? At the very moment of sitting, what is sitting? Is it an acrobat's graceful somersault or the rapid darting of a fish? Is it thinking or non-thinking? Is it doing or non-doing? Is it sitting within sitting? It is sitting within body-mind? Is it sitting letting go of sitting within sitting, or letting go of sitting within body-mind? Investigate this in every possible way. Sit in the body's meditation posture. Sit in the mind's meditation posture. Sit in the meditation posture of letting go of body-mind."

These are not rhetorical questions; they are open questions, crucial questions. It is passages like this that have made me appreciate my practice and my life, hold myself always as open as I can to new possibilities of meaning and experience, and incidentally, never tire of going back again and again to reading Dogen.

It is a very curious thing that this wonderful wide-open practice that Dogen so eloquently advocates became in his life and in the centuries afterward identified with a rigid and formalistic style of severe monasticism (the third section of this volume, "Zazen in Community," contains important texts that reflect this). Many readers of Dogen, baffled by this, choose to ignore or dismiss this as historical baggage, but to do so is to miss an important point.

The monastic life is strong. It involves dedication and total participation. There are no breaks, no hiding places, no profane moments. The monastic life honors a rule whose essence is simple: always think of others and always act with others in mind, for we have no life without others. Dogen sees monastic life as the template life of the awakened person—he sees it as the life of the historical Buddha himself. In living the monastic life, we re-enact ritually the Buddha's own life—our lives become his. The elaborately detailed rules and guidelines, the formalized bows and words, the minutely described marking out of sacred space through ceremony, the solemn rules and gestures of seniority—all these serve to make this ritual life concrete through all our daily acts. Although most of us will not live in this way even for short periods of time, we can recognize the point that such a life illuminates—that we are all Buddha in essence, and seen in that light, every moment of our lives is a timeless crucial moment. And so we are challenged to live, making all our acts, large and small, buddha acts, because each and every one of our acts carries the moral, metaphysical, and symbolic weight of absolute truth.

In other words, Dogen sees that through monastic ritual profound meditation practice can pervade our whole lives. This explains the elaborate rituals detailed so painstakingly in texts like "Practice Period" and "Guidelines for the Practice of the Way," which can so easily sound hopelessly arcane to the modern reader. To translate them, one virtually has to reconstruct maps of medieval Japanese monastic compounds, so detailed are they and so dependent on the physical layout of buildings and the texture of particular customs. How can such stuff be useful to us in our daily practice as twenty-first-century people?

One of the great casualties of modern life is the sense of coherent community. We all need to feel we belong to each other somehow, and when we do not feel that, our lives can feel broken, lonely, isolated, lacking in support, friendship, and love. The traditional structures for community (extended families living in close proximity to one another, an economic and social system that supports people to stay close to home on a daily basis, an agrarian or crafts-based village life) are almost gone in much of the Westernized developed world and are probably not going to come back. But I think it is possible for us to construct new forms of community that can replace or augment whatever remnants of this old community remain. Such new forms of community will require that we establish and maintain specific and sacred ways of doing things and of being together, ways that bind us closer and more profoundly than any casual or personal contact ever could. Although it is probably not possible or even desirable that we raise funds to construct detailed Japanese monastic establishments as Dogen describes them (as far as I know, none of the Western Zen monastic enclosures, even the major ones, have attempted this), we certainly can, through a lived understanding of the essentials of the monastic lifestyle, find ways to participate fully with each other in a sacred way. Once we train in such ways of conduct, we can apply the insights we have gained from them to our whole lives. In my own case, having spent a number of years living monastically, I can bring the deep structure and feel of that life to my daily life in the ordinary world. This training has helped me a great deal to learn how to include others in what I do, and to feel that I am joined by others, even in my solitary acts.

For monastic life is fundamentally a life of participation with everything, and of kindness. Monastic renunciation is, in essence, letting go of the self-centered life. As Dogen says in "Regulations for the Auxiliary Cloud Hall," we should all be together "like milk and water," as grateful to each other for our mutually supportive practice as we are to our parents for our very life. It is this sense of communal sharing in gratitude that characterizes the monk's life, and that stands behind all that may strike us as archaic in Dogen's monastic writing. This inspired life of sharing and gratitude is also, in the final analysis, the essence of Dogen's understanding of meditation practice.

# Introduction to *Opening to You: Zen-Inspired Translations of the Psalms*

*As this essay indicates, I became interested in the Hebrew Psalms at Gethsemani Abbey (Thomas Merton's monastery) in Kentucky in the late 1990s. That led me to making my own translations, which were eventually published by Viking Compass under the title* Opening to You: Zen-Inspired Translations of the Psalms *(2002).*

Some years ago I stayed for a week with the Trappist monks of Gethsemani Abbey. There I encountered for the first time the Christian monastic practice of choir, which consists, for the most part, of daily recitation of the Psalms. Although I had grown up chanting the Psalms in Hebrew (a language I can pronounce but not comprehend), it was at Gethsemani that I first paid attention to what these texts were saying.

There are many uplifting, inspiring, and soaring verses in the Psalms. But the passages that caught my ear during those early morning and evening hours in that Kentucky summer were not those. I was astonished at the violence, passion, and bitterness that was expressed. For me, whose lifelong spiritual practice has been silent sitting meditation, it seemed almost impossible to believe that intoning these disturbing and distancing words could be the basis for a satisfying religious practice. In all innocence I asked the monks about this and received many cogent and impassioned responses: that the anger and violence in the Psalms were human emotions that could find healing through expression; that these things are part of our human life and must not be left out of religious contemplation; that the suffering the Psalms express is holy suffering and that to enter into it is to become close to God; and much more. All of it made some sense to me, but I wasn't really satisfied. Nor could I dismiss the Psalms as irrelevant. I saw that these good brothers of Gethsemani were true treaders of the path, sincere practitioners, possessed of wisdom and knowledge. If the Psalms had meaning for them, clearly I was missing something. I felt I had to investigate for myself. These selected versions of the Psalms are the results of that investigation.

⁓

I call them "Zen Songs" because I approach them the only way I can: as a Zen practitioner and teacher, with a Zen eye. Yet I have not tried to rewrite the Psalms as Zen philosophy; quite the opposite, my intention has been to learn from them, to expand my own understanding under their influence. Nevertheless, although my way of life and understanding has been thoroughly saturated by Zen, I am still a Westerner, and so I have found in the Psalms a very familiar music that seems to express my own approach to enlightenment: the passionate, prickly, and lively noise that naturally seems to rise up from the silent depths of my heart.

And I do not think I am unusual. Western Buddhists are Buddhists, yes, but also Westerners. This makes a big difference. It is why Buddhism in the West is and will continue to be very different from what it has been in Asia. No matter how much Westerners try to immerse themselves in the Buddhism presented to them by their Asian teachers (and expressed in the Asian texts), they will always inevitably see it colored by Western concepts and views, and by a Western feeling for life. You could view this as a problem, a distortion of real Buddhism, and I know that many Asian Buddhist teachers feel that Westerners just don't "get" Buddhism, and that it will take several generations for them to get it. While this is a reasonable way to look at it, I prefer to see the problem as an advantage, and to view the inevitable mixing of Western and Asian Buddhist perspectives as something fresh and inspired, rather than somehow incorrect.

I have seen in myself and in my students just how deeply the Western feeling goes. It is simply not to be denied, not to be papered over with a veneer of Buddhism. There has been much written of and discussed about this in relation to Western psychology, and in many ways the Western Buddhist movement has been thoroughly, probably for good and for ill, psychologized. But I am sure our Westernness goes deeper than the personal.

Our whole sense of what we think of as human, what we think of as the world, and how we are to stand in the world, is thoroughly Western, thoroughly Judeo-Christian. Certainly Buddhism will have a powerful effect on these deeply held views if we practice it for a lifetime; for many people the change has already happened. But even so, even as quite thorough Buddhists, we will continue to stand on Western ground, and will continue to hold, in the depths of our hearts, some Judeo-Christian sensibility.

Once at a Jewish-Buddhist retreat we were leading at Tassajara monastery, my old friend and colleague Rabbi Alan Lew was asked to make the odious comparison: strengths and weaknesses, Judaism versus Buddhism. He said that the strength of Buddhism is that it really makes sense; it is clear and useful and will help your life. Judaism, on the other hand, doesn't make sense. But that is exactly its strength: that it doesn't make sense. Just like us, he said: we don't make sense. And the weakness of Buddhism is precisely that it makes too much sense.

Buddhism does make sense. It is full of practical, clear advice on how to work with anger, jealousy, confusion, and other painful emotional states, sound advice that supports in many ways the psychological-spiritual preconceptions that many of us hold. But the trouble is, our irrational and sometimes conflicted Western selves that persist somehow, even in advanced stages of Buddhist practice, waylay us now and again with deeply held emotions like longing, sorrow, loss, loneliness, unknowingness, despite all our good Buddhist practice. We find there is still sometimes a need to call out, to sing, to shout, to be heard and answered. These passions persist even though we have cleared up much of our confusion. All of this is the territory of the Psalms.

The Psalms are a fundamental text of Western Judeo-Christian spirituality, perhaps the most fundamental. They are chanted daily in Christian and Jewish services, and they contain all of the theology of both the Old and the New Testaments. For three thousand years Western peoples have been contemplating these poems, resonating emotionally their deepest feeling for life through them.

Buddhism begins with suffering and the end of suffering and the path toward the ending of suffering. This is essential and useful for everyone, not just Buddhists. But this approach can easily lead to a grave spiritual error: the notion that suffering is something to be avoided, prevented, escaped, bypassed. I have seen many Western Buddhist students suffer a great deal because of this natural error, thinking and believing they could go beyond or had gone beyond their suffering, only to find that it was there all along, underneath their seeming calmness and insight, and that because they had tried not to see and accept it, they had made it far worse.

The Psalms make it clear that suffering is not to be escaped or bypassed: that, much to the contrary, suffering returns again and again, a path in itself, and that through the very suffering and admission of suffering, the letting go into suffering and the calling out from it, mercy and peace can come (this is most poignantly expressed, of course, in the example of Jesus).

There is a crucial corollary to this point: if suffering is a path, then those who suffer are to be honored. A key theme of the Psalms—and therefore of Judaism and Christianity—is the nobility of the oppressed, and the necessity of justice and righteousness, that the oppressed be cared for and uplifted, and that there ought to be social justice for all. These ideas have not been part of Buddhism in Asia, but they are becoming an indelible aspect of Western Buddhism. So here, too, the Psalms have something to show us.

In fact, I would go so far as to say that for Western Buddhist practitioners a sensitive and informed appreciation of the problematic themes included and so powerfully expressed in the Psalms is probably a necessity.

For many, however, the Psalms remain—as they did for me when I first encountered them in English at Gethsemani—hermetically sealed. This is because their language has become opaque after centuries of use and misuse. I am sure there are some (like the monks of Gethsemani and some Jewish practitioners I know) for whom the traditional language still sparkles, illuminated by their inner experience, and the words take on added dimension with repeated encounter. But for most of the rest of us, it is not so. For those who have not made a practice of the Psalms, the traditional language communicates little, and can even be quite off-putting; for others, who read the Psalms but without much contemplation, the traditional language may still have meaning and emotion, but not much meaning that is spiritually fruitful.

So I wanted to use my own spiritual experience as my guide in reading and living with these most ancient of all poems, to try to make them fresh and lively for myself and for readers like me.

∾

And the Psalms are poems. They stand at the origin point of all of Western poetry, which is intimately connected with prayer.

I came to appreciate this about ten years ago when I went to Jerusalem and visited the Kotel, the Wailing Wall. I had never been there before and was moved by the power of the place, with all its history, with all the prayer and lamentation that had gone into it from the lips of so many people over the generations. Although prayer had never been a part of my spiritual practice, I found myself with my forehead pressed up against the cool stones, speaking heartfelt words, and then writing words on a piece of paper, and shoving the paper scrap into a crack in the wall, as people customarily do.

The feeling I had quite clearly was: language is prayer. Utterance, whether silent or voiced, written or thought, is essentially prayer. To speak, to intone, to make words with mouth and heart: where does that come from? Debased as it so often is, language always sources in what's fundamental in the human heart. The imaginative source of language-making, that uniquely human process, is the need to reach out to the boundless, the unknown, the unnamable. Prayer is not some specialized religious exercise; it is just what comes out of our mouths if we truly pay attention. To pray is to form language, and to form language is to be human.

∾

If Buddhism makes sense, because it is strong on teachings that show us how to work with the mind and heart to relieve our suffering, it is at the same time perhaps weak on the question of relationships. And although our lives are located in our own hearts and minds, they are also located, perhaps most poignantly, in the space between us. Martin Buber's thought, his quintessentially Jewish outlook, emphasizes this with a fierce thoroughness. For Buber there is no God, there is no absolute, there is no present moment, outside the profound relationship that takes place between the I and the you, between the self and the other. Within the hallowed reaches of that ineffable experience (which is not an experience, Buber insists) our true life takes place.

Relationship is the theme of the Psalms: specifically that most difficult of all relationships, the relationship with God.

What or who is God? Clearly the word "God," with all of its synonyms and substitutes as they appear in the Psalms, presents a serious problem for many. I find it meaningful, and use it freely in my teaching where it seems helpful (although it is absent in Zen language, and Zen is agnostic on the subject of God); but for many people the word "God" evokes parental and judgmental overtones, and even worse, false, meaningless, or even negative piety associated with what they have taken to be their less-than-perfect religious upbringing. In fact, the word "God" often seems to militate against exactly what it is supposed to connote: something immense and ineffable toward which one directs enormous feelings of awe, respect, gratitude, desire, anger, love, resentment, wonder, and so on.

For most of the religious seekers I encounter, the word "God" has been all but emptied of its spiritual power. Even where it is taken in a positive light, it seems often reduced and tamed, representing some sort of assumed and circumscribed notion of holiness or morality. For me, what is challenging about "God" is exactly that it is so emotional, even metaphysically emotional. The relationship to God that is charted out in the Psalms is a stormy one, codependent, passionate, confusing, loyal, petulant, sometimes even manipulative. I wanted to find a way to approach these poems so as to emphasize this relational aspect, while avoiding the major distancing pitfalls that words like "God," "King," "Lord," and so on, create. My solution was a simple one. I decided to avoid whenever I could all of these words and instead use the one simple English word that evokes the whole notion of relationship: you.

There was a personal dimension to this choice. For some years I had been noticing that the inspiration for my own poetry comes from the fact that the audience I am writing for is not any usual sort of audience. When I write poems, I am not talking to ordinary persons. The hearer of my poems seems to be someone more silent and receptive than any ordinary human being could be. The person that I am addressing isn't a person, real or abstract. It's no one, no thing. And the fact that this nothing or no one is the one being addressed, and is even, in a way, participating in the composition, is what makes the writing of poems important to me. Otherwise I am sure I would not write at all.

Because of this experience that I have persistently had, I have for many years explored in poems words like "me," and "you" or "I." I have explored, in the light of this experience, the sounds of words, their shapes, the simple extraordinary fact of words simply being words. Many of my poems are, in fact, nothing more or less than such explorations, such flights into essential language. The whole idea of writing and speaking, what it might mean and what its purpose might be, to whom it is addressed and from where it arises, has been enormously important to me. Shakespeare's sonnets, whose power comes from the fact that they are passionately addressed to a "you" who is mysteriously never identified, have been very influential for me, and I believe the whole sense of the lyric in Western poetry (beginning with the Psalms) has its source in this notion of a writing addressed to an unspecified but somehow magnificent nonexistent or supraexistent listener.

The fact that the perfect silence of being is necessarily broken, with human consciousness, by language that calls out always to a you who is profoundly unspecified, even, strictly speaking, nonexistent, has always struck me as marvelous. If we can say that the heart of the world is silence, undifferentiated being, before the arising of a single thing (which both theistic and nontheistic traditions like Buddhism assert, more or less), then the impulse toward language is this calling out of one seemingly separate being toward all that inconceivable immensity.

For me, the word "you" contains all that process, and includes all of its sadness and passion and power.

❧

This single translation decision has made an enormous difference in how my versions read. God becomes not a distant figure carrying a received and, for some, unfriendly, load of emotional attachments, but rather intimacy itself, the painful intimacy of reaching out for something (in the act of language itself, in the act of the Psalms as the Psalms) that is at once so close to you it is absolutely hidden, and so far away you can never hope to reach it.

There is certainly a theology implied in all this, and there are Buddhist roots to it. Although classical Buddhism emphasizes impermanence and non-self, clearly denies the existence of any abiding entity, and seems quite far from any feeling for a concept of God, with all its overtones of omnipotence and eternity, the later Mahayana schools come very close to introducing the theistic. The Mind Only or Consciousness Only schools describe consciousness itself, in its profound transpersonal aspect, as Buddha Nature or Dharmakaya, ineffable, neither existent nor nonexistent, neither inside nor outside, neither different from nor the same as the world, inconceivable and indescribable. In the Chinese Shurangama Sutra, for instance, there are many passages exhorting practitioners to "turn the mind around" away from the world so that it can "revert" and realize its real nature as eternally perfect and ineffable. In the Lotus Sutra the Buddha reveals himself as an eternal principle, who only pretended to appear as a human being, teach the original doctrine, and die, for the sake of beings who were not able to understand the higher singular doctrine.

In the history of Buddhist philosophy there is an ongoing dialogue about the nature of such expressions. Since a cardinal principle of Buddhist thought is precisely that it be nontheistic, there has been continuous criticism of such doctrines, contending that they are, in fact, subversive attempts to introduce the concept of God into the Buddhist system of thought. The Mind Only adherents defend themselves by replying that their conception of consciousness doesn't violate the principle of emptiness, which states that all things are mere designations, without substance, like a mirage, so consciousness cannot be said to be a God. I am surely not doing justice to this complex debate, but the point I am making is that such Buddhist speculations (the Shurangama Sutra even includes, quite un-Buddhistically, a detailed section on the creation of the mind and the physical world out of the original primordial nameless consciousness) are not so far removed from many Jewish and Christian discussions of the idea of God.

∽

The Psalms are historical documents of a particular people whose sacred narrative stands behind every line. My dilemma in making versions that I considered useful to myself and to others like me was how to preserve the emotion of that peoplehood and historicity and yet, at the same time, widen it. Although the Jewish and Christian commentarial literature on the Psalms opens and expands them into a more universal application, still, translated versions I have seen do not attempt to fold those interpretations into the poems themselves. This is what I wanted to attempt. So: how to handle these historical and particular words?

I began with the obvious fact that words like "Israel," "Zion," "Jerusalem," and so on, originally carried meanings beyond their limited later senses. In other words, if Israel became a nation, what was the original impulse or spiritual dynamic that made it a nation? If Jerusalem is a holy city existing in a particular location, what is the content of that holiness? More often than not, what I was looking for could be found in looking closely at the etymologies of the words themselves. So Israel is literally "one who struggles," which, for me, is the ideal of a certain type of spiritual seeker, one whose faithfulness is always full of doubt, one who is forever pressing on with the practice, for new and fresh insight, for deeper experience. So I rendered the word "Israel" usually as "the ones who question and struggle." Jerusalem is, literally, the place of wholeness, the place where the soul can feel whole and complete. Egypt is "the narrow place," in contrast to the place of freedom and wideness and opening.

With these ideas to start with, I looked at each Psalm I studied for the way a particular term functioned within it, and at a number of Psalms to see how that term was developed throughout the collection. As I worked on this, I began to have a feeling for the spiritual and literary movement and shape of the terms, and they took on a depth of meaning for me that they did not have before.

In my versions I sometimes retain the original words, sometimes replace them with what I feel are their spiritual analogues, and sometimes use both. My hope is that over the course of reading several Psalms, the reader will need finally nothing other than the word, say, "Jerusalem," to hear the range and depth of meaning that the Psalmist no doubt intended. I am aware that for many readers familiar with the Psalms all of this and much more is already available in the traditional English versions. But I wanted to make versions for myself and for people like myself, who have lost the thread of the meaning of the Psalms, and need some fresh language to recapture it. Perhaps such readers will find my interpretations useful, and possibly, even seasoned readers will find their innocence and enthusiasm reinvigorating.

❧

Respiritualizing some of the political and geographical references in the Psalms brought up for me the wider question of what was behind these references. From a Buddhist perspective, Judeo-Christian spirituality is challenging indeed. As I have said, Buddhism teaches simply suffering and the end of suffering. This seems a far cry from the personal and political anguish and group catharsis that one sees throughout the Psalms. It made me wonder: what does all of this amount to? If I assume the spiritual path to be, more or less, general throughout the traditions, what could the drama of the Psalms be pointing toward?

The idea of sovereignty seems to me to be one of the key themes of the Psalms. God is the ultimate fountainhead of sovereignty. Through God, sovereignty is conferred on the kings and through them, in turn, to the people. With sovereignty, there is honor, reality, a secure place to be, the possibility of wholeness and salvation, a way to live. With sovereignty, exile in the world ends, and one comes home.

The most powerful Psalms seem to yearn for the sovereignty that only God can confer, to praise it where it is present, to lament it where it is gone, and to constantly evoke God's presence and praise God's name—all because of the potency of sovereignty. I have pondered this, investigated it for what I could begin to see of its spiritual content, and have finally formed a notion of sovereignty as spiritual authenticity—some deeply felt but almost indefinable quality of meaningfulness that is the highest potential of human experience. It is as if a human being exists but doesn't live, is physically present but spiritually dead, if this quality of sovereignty is absent.

This thinking personalized for me all of those passages in the Psalms that deal with praise and gratefulness to God, or with kingship and political tragedy, and gave me a way to understand the difficult passages, the so-called cursing Psalms. While I did not want to make things too pretty, turning outward enemies into internal demons and making curses into gentle reminders toward self-improvement, I did feel in the end that the Psalms' historical narrative and poetic drama of sovereignty were also personal and spiritual.

As I considered the issue of sovereignty, I began to see a connection in the Psalms between it and the Buddhist notion of mindfulness. In the Mindfulness Sutra, the Buddha calls mindfulness "the only way to liberation." As you read that sutra, with all of its careful instructions for training, it is clear that what is pointed to differs from the usual idea of mindfulness, which amounts, more or less, to self-consciousness: I know that I am feeling this or sensing that; I know that I am myself and not another. This is how we generally understand mindfulness. But Buddhist mindfulness is, by contrast, a resting in a level of consciousness that is antecedent to the experience of ego, or to any notion of separation from the world. It is an appreciation of all that is arising within the field of consciousness, without defining an inside or an outside.

I began to feel that the sovereignty of God referred to in the Psalms was a species of consciousness, beyond the human and yet not separate from it, a kind of settled and steady contemplation of or union with the deity constantly evoked and longed for in the poems. If that were so, I had a way of understanding concepts like wickedness and punishment. Wickedness became heedlessness, unmindfulness, egotism, off-centeredness, crookedness. To fall into such a state is to suffer alienation, to be off course and terrified. Sin becomes a question of being off the mark, of being a distance away from the unity that one finds within mindfulness, and punishment for sin is natural and necessary if there is to be a course correction. I came to feel that the enemies mentioned in the Psalms were external but also internal. Praying for their defeat could be seen to be akin to praying, as in Tibetan Buddhism, to fierce guardian deities to destroy the powerful inner passions that keep one in bondage. Certainly I do not want to claim the Psalms as Buddhist texts. But such reflections helped me to understand their passion in a new light.

Despite all of this, I do not think that the difficulty of the Psalms can, in the end, be entirely avoided or explained away. Earlier I mentioned that many of the brothers at Gethsemani offered good explanations as to why the difficulty was something necessary, and in the end positive and useful. There are, however, many other committed Christians and Jews who dispute this, and who feel that the Psalms need to be edited, that there are passages and whole poems that simply ought to be eliminated, or at least, in the case of Christian monasticism, eliminated from liturgical practice. In fact, there has been a lengthy debate about this for some years in the Catholic community.

The tragedy of this difficulty and its serious consequences came home to me recently when I was in Belfast, Northern Ireland, at a peace conference. We were listening to a group of speakers who were victims of the "troubles," as they are called. Among them were a woman who had been confined to a wheelchair for most of her adult life as a result of a drive-by political shooting; a man who had been blinded as a boy by a British bullet; even a man who had taken part in assassinations, and whose spirit had been crushed by what he himself had done. I found all of these people to be inspiring and eloquent in their presentations. In each case, the personal suffering had purified them, forced them to find a way to transcend their handicaps, and so had in the end become a source of happiness for their lives. None of them was bitter, and all of them were living good lives, doing their best in various way to try to benefit others. But there was one exception to this pattern. One man, a Protestant minister whose father had been senselessly gunned down at his own front gate in full view of his family, seemed to continue to harbor strong feelings of hatred and vengeance. He said that after many years he was now finally satisfied and had been able to put the matter to rest because he believed that the killers of his father had themselves finally been gunned down, and that this made him finally happy, to see that justice was done. His speech was the shortest of all, and consisted mainly of a quotation of Psalm 10, which includes a line about how God will "break the arms of the wicked." This strong expression of righteous vengeance, bolstered by the man's religious faith as developed through a lifetime reading of the Psalms, was chilling to me.

I want finally to mention one further influence that stands behind the efforts I have been making with the Psalms. This is my reading of the German-language poet Paul Celan, a deeply spiritual and inward writer, a Holocaust survivor, whose works are an attempt to meet the tremendous challenge to the human spirit that that event (which Celan refers to only as "what happened") occasioned. Celan uses biblical material (including the Psalms) with all the traditional feeling it evokes, yet at the same time manages to make it personal, as if the ancient lines and their echoes were coming from his own mouth for the first time, expressing the depth of all he had seen and experienced. Writing in German, the language of the murderer and oppressor, he could not help recognizing with each word how easily language betrays us even as it provides us with the emotional and religious connection to that which we need most in our extremity. In time Celan's poems became more and more terse, more and more dense, until by the end of his short life (he committed suicide in Paris in 1970, in his forty-ninth year), they were all but incomprehensible, approaching closely the boundary of what can be said.

Celan's project as a writer is the desperate attempt to find meaning in a terrible situation, one in which a return to an innocent or traditional faith seems impossible. This is why it is so important for our time, in which it is the challenge of religious traditions to do something more than simply reassert and reinterpret their faiths, hoping for loyal adherents to what they perceive to be the true doctrine. Looking back at the last century, with its devastating wars and holocausts and the shock of ecological vulnerability, I have the sense that religious traditions must now take on a wider mission, and it is in recognition of this mission, I believe, that interreligious dialogue becomes not only something polite and interesting but essential. I have come to think, after working for many years intimately with people along the course of their heartfelt spiritual journeys, that traditions now need to listen to the human heart before them as much as and more than they listen to their various doctrines and beliefs. In recognition of this I offer these tentative versions of the Psalms.

# Preface to Paul Naylor's
## *Jammed Transmission*

*Paul Naylor is a poet whose interest in philosophical and religious texts is central to his writing project. He has written several book-length poem-series that are, in effect, detailed poetic commentaries to specific texts (such as the* I Ching, Wittgenstein's On Certainty, *etc.).* Jammed Transmission *(Tinfish Press, 2009) is one such text. Paul asked me for this introduction, which I wrote in February 2009.*

Tugged on thought's
cloth and asked

what does it mean
to awaken

the original nature
of things

＆

*Jammed Transmission* is a unique text. It is poetry, but not poetry, philosophy but not philosophy, religion but not religion. It probably relates, wittingly or unwittingly, to ancient writing practices that were considered to be spiritual exercises; shorthand verse-form takes on scripture, composition as devotional exploration. Such forms of writing were commonplace all over the world at a time when religion—conceived as the process of ultimate encounter with the limits of human thought and being—was not, as it is now, divorced from the literary arts. In fact, in ancient times, long before religion learned how to become as effectively repressive and oppressive as it later became, there was no distinction whatsoever between these two fields of endeavor. All religion required forms of writing, all writing was sacred writing, and all writers were, of necessity, religious people, because it was only within monasteries and religious enclaves that the esoteric arts of reading, writing, and calligraphy were practiced.

Specifically, *Jammed Transmission* is a poetic encounter with a four-teenth-century text of Japanese Soto Zen, Keizan Jokin's *Denkoroku* (usually translated as *Record of the Transmission of the Light*), a spiritual genealogy of the Soto lineage, beginning with the Buddha and ending with Koun Ejo, Keizan's immediate predecessor in the lineage, fifty-two generations later. The fifty-three stories, named for the succeeding masters (as are the poems of *Jammed Transmission*) each include a short biography emphasizing the enlightenment encounter between present and preceding master. These brief and cryptic tales are meant to serve as koan (teaching story/meditation object) for the illumination of the reader. Thus the text is meant to be practiced, personally dealt with, subject to dialogue, just as its content highlights Zen's essentially dialogic nature, that the full experience of the tradition can be grasped only through dynamic personal encounter.

Insofar as *Jammed Transmission* is itself a cryptic encounter with the original text, it is a literary exploration of the process of dialogue that the original text explores, and that subsequent practitioners furthered. What interests me is the nature of this literary encounter. It is neither commentary by a devotee, which necessarily takes the original text at face value, nor a "writing against," employing the usual strategies of satire, irony, and various forms of erasure that have become standard procedures in postmodern poetry. Instead, it seems to be a serious attempt to grapple with the original text personally and openly as a piece of language that may or may not be about something. *Jammed Transmission* is thus something new, as far as I can tell, which is to say, as I have already said, that it is probably something old. It opens up for both religious and writing practitioners new fields of possibility.

In Zen and Buddhist practice, and in contemporary spirituality in general, it has become commonplace to refer to "enlightenment," or "awakening," as though this were a distinct psychological or metapsychological state about which we could make sensible and definite propositions, that one, say, "has" it or does not, has "experienced" it or has not. One might then "be" or "not be" "enlightened." According to this commonplace notion, enlightenment is "not intellectual," and it is certainly not literary. In fact, enlightenment and thought are held to be nearly opposing functions, enlightenment being a species of experience "beyond word and thought." However, any serious reading of the works of Dogen, the founder of Soto Zen in Japan (Story 52 of *Denkoroku*, Poem 52 of *Jammed Transmission*) would dispel this notion as woefully crude. Dogen sees Zen enlightenment not as opposed to words and thought but as a profound possibility within words and thought. It's not that one would think or explain or even express enlightenment as if it were an object subject to scrutiny; rather, that the processes of thinking, explanation, and expression (as well, of course, as all other human functional processes) could be enlightened as such in the practice of them. In this sense, Naylor's text can be understood as an instance of what Dogen would call "the practice of enlightenment."

*Jammed Transmission* is, however, written both within and outside of Dogen's tradition. Though Paul Naylor does practice Zen, and certainly his practice of thinking and writing in general, and this work in particular, grapples with Zen teaching and experience, he writes neither as one who "is enlightened" nor even as a formal student of Zen. Instead he unself-consciously takes on Keizan's text as a religiously interested practitioner of the art of poetry, "tugging on thought's cloth" through the medium of the poem to ask "what does it mean to awaken to the original nature of things?" He has no answers, and is compelled to constantly subject the question itself to the pressure of his procedure.

I am grateful to Paul for having invented or uncovered or remembered or discovered a fruitful literary/spiritual practice.

# Afterword to *Training in Compassion, Zen Teachings on the Practice of Lojong*

*My book,* Training in Compassion, Zen Teachings on the Practice of Lojong, *published by Shambhala in 2013, is my Zen-style commentary on a traditional Indo-Tibetan text on generating compassion. The short piece below is the afterword to the book, expressing its intention—and also, probably, the intention of my writing and spiritual teaching.*

In *Soul Mountain*, Gao Xingjian's great novel of contemporary China, there's a powerful passage about the death of a Buddhist monk in a remote mountain monastery. A great holy master, this monk had been preparing to die for a long time with special mediations and observances. When the day finally comes, the mountain passes are thronged with pilgrims coming to pay their last respects. They listen respectfully to the old monk's final sermon (a brief paragraph in Gao's book), but it's incomprehensible to everyone, including the thousand or so monks who live in the monastery. However, this seems hardly to matter: so renowned was the old monk, and so deep was the people's faith in him, that they push forward in the thousands for a last glimpse, and somehow, as the funeral pyre is lit, the crowd gets out of control, causing a conflagration that burns down the monastery completely, destroying many lives in the process.

This is an image of religion at its most lurid and most powerful. Its mysteries inspire great faith, great passion, and great destructive force. The holy saint's sermon is incomprehensible. Even the monks can't understand it, and the monastery burns down to the ground. The master's miraculous powers becomes a memory, since there is no one to whom he could pass them on.

In old China (and in the Western World, too), religion was like that: a precious and arcane tradition guarded by sacred elites. The people didn't understand it and didn't expect to. Their lives were crushingly difficult, and it was faith and devotion to their religions that gave them hope for a better world to come.

Now most of us want and expect better lives. And we aspire to develop greater understanding of ourselves and of the universe. We don't want to abandon hope in this world for hope in a world to come.

My life has been dedicated to finding a way to practice religion, serious religion—at least as serious as that practiced by sages of old—that speaks to our contemporary condition. If we are now facing hard times ahead (as human being always have), much better to face them with patient compassionate hearts than with fear and panic. We have always needed one another. Our love for one another is both natural to us and something we need to strengthen through cultivation. We need sermons we can understand and use. We need reminders and encouragements. I hope this book has helped.

# On Stephen Ratcliffe's *Portraits & Repetition: Seeing / Hearing / Writing*

*Stephen Ratcliffe lives in Bolinas, California, a few miles up the Coast high-way from my home in Muir Beach, where he surfs—and writes—every morning. In recent years he has been writing impossibly long poem-series, some of them up to 1,000 pages in length—inherently unpublishable, but feats of historical proportion. Steve (along with poets Bob Grenier, Etel Ad-nan, Simione Fattal, and others) has been for years involved in a Heidegger study group that I have had the privilege of sometimes attending. This essay was written for* Jacket2, *for its tribute issue on Ratcliffe, published October 20, 2011.*

The epigraph to Stephen Ratcliffe's long poem *Portraits & Repetition* is a quotation from Gertrude Stein's essay of the same title:

> I began to wonder at about this time just what one saw when one looked at anything really looked at anything. Did one see sound, and what was the relation between color and sound, did it make itself by description by a word that meant it or did it make itself by a word in itself.

Steve's book is a painstaking exploration of or experiment in exactly what Stein might have meant by this. What happens when you look at anything, actually, over a period of time (say, a year and a quarter) every day, carefully, quietly, without many preconceptions as to what that thing is, and then at the same time (at the moment of looking, or just after—or as the moment of looking) you are writing this, what happens, what do you see? Is there a sort of rhyme between the seen and the heard (what if you hear the sound of a bird at the same moment you are looking at a distant ridgeline in fog) and what about meaning—is "ridge" something seen, or something heard, is the word you are using at the same time you are seeing already always there in the seeing, and so the sound of the word must be there, in the experience of the seeing? Does the word "ridge" describe what you are seeing so that the seeing is primary and the word comes later as a label or tag pasted onto it, the experience of seeing (by now it is having seen) or does the word, the faint prethought of the word, come simultaneous—or even before—the perception, so that there's no perception without the word, and the word and the perception are the same or nearly the same? And then there is the writing of the word, later the reading of it, so that the experience in time is repeated in another time in another mind. A portrait repeated as the portrait as repetition is the portrait. As words are things seen and heard, and things seen and heard merge with words.

༄

## SHAPING

Each day for a year and nearly three months—February 9, 1998, to May 28, 1999—Stephen Ratcliffe wrote a ten-line poem that consisted of five couplets, the first line of each couplet always three characters longer than the second line. The words of the couplets appear in their published form in Courier (which was originally a typewriter font), making the words appear oddly old-fashioned or anyway informal and handcrafted in a removed sort of way. The impression is that the words are not printed words in a book: that they are somehow more abstract and at the same time more intimate than words one usually sees in books or in online writing. Spacing between the word is not standard: there is extra space between words (I am not sure whether the extra spacing is uniform throughout), which makes the words oddly abstract, the eye doesn't follow along quickly as in standard text, where you almost miss the fact that you are reading words, but here the words, in this font, call attention to themselves as words, abstractions, and the spacing seems to function to make the line visually come out to where it should come out, so that each of the poems in the book—474 pages/ poems in all—looks exactly like every other poem, each page visually— relentlessly—the same as every other page.

The title of each poem is the date on which the poem was written (7.4, 7.5, 7.6) but given in this numerical way, the dates appear after a while as freestanding numerals, abstract numbers; they do not seem to stand for days on earth but rather as a mathematical series—somber, calm, laconic. Within each of the couplets there always appears a word in parenthesis—it might appear in the first or the second line, it might appear toward the beginning of the line or the middle or end, it might be underlined (Steve does not use—and typewriters did not have—italics). Sometimes the parenthetical word is not a word at all but a letter (*p*). The effect of the parenthetical word is to distance or interrupt whatever is going on in the line. Though there is occasional enjambment, the couplets appear to be independent of one another. None of the first lines are capitalized. There is punctuation, but none of the couplets end with a period. They are all double spaced, giving each line and each word that much more attention as such.

The couplets seem to include a variety of subject matter that appears again and again as the long poem evolves, day after day, poem after poem. Fog over a ridge. A pot of flowers in a glass vase. Stones on a windowsill. Birdsong in the distance. A tobacco plant. Words, language, abstraction, relationship between objects in a visual field, the negative space between them. A couple, a man and a women, in intimate—if indefinite and entirely wordless—relationship. The sea in the distance and close up—swimming in the waves. Houses. People seen at a distance. Sky. Colors, the colors of anything, distinct from one another. It appears sometimes that there is drama or tension occurring—but one can't be sure. A poem of words—but everything seems quiet, wordless.

Notice how I have used, in the above paragraphs, words like "appears," "seems," "might," "as if," "sometimes." This is because the overall effect of this quite precise—almost obsessively precise—poem is one of indeterminacy. It is not clear what is being described or what is going on. Despite the luminous clarity of the words and images.

> shape of a blue flower in the window (same) which was placed
>
> there by a second person, coming back from somewhere else
>
> small white spider who tries to hide, right (angle) of stalk
>
> below which drops of water are passing from unconcealment

"Unconcealment," the Heideggerian word. From *alethia*, "truth" in Greek, which literally means "unconcealment." This was Heidegger's obsession (Ratcliffe's?): that ordinary life, conventional experience, is concealed, that truth is an uncovering, an allowing of things to come forward to reveal themselves to us, as us, so that we can return to being embedded in the world rather than standing apart from it, as we think we do, and this makes of our experience a kind of aggression, in which we consume the world, as if we were not the world and could make use of it at will, for our purposes. The drops are literally concealed before they form as drops; they are not there at all to the person, to his sight, and then unconcealed when they appear as drops that can be seen as such, and named. Every moment of time's concealed before it appears—every perception, every thought concealed in the moment before, then appears, then returns to concealment. Writing's unconcealment. Which person writes what? When words appear and disappear, to reappear later (as reader's experience), whose words are they? In this poem the words are no one's; they come from nowhere, though at the same time the locations they depict are exact.

≈

## CONTEMPLATING

Something happens when you repeat. When you repeat and repeat and repeat. First, there's the discipline involved. You do it, you repeat, whether you feel in the mood or not. The discipline, the commitment, replaces the sense of the personal, of what you want to be doing or saying. Whatever you want to be doing or saying—or whether or not you have anything you want to do or say—you repeat. There's a system, a format, a procedure, a passion, a commitment. It, rather than you, caries the process along. Something happens that you would not have intended or desired. This is poetry as practice rather than expression—or even communication. It goes beyond the idea of skill or talent. It's devotional, literally a devotional practice. Devotion to the art of poetry—and even more—or less—than this: devotion to this project, this pattern, this exploration of mind/heart/language. Because this is what emerges when you repeat this way, with this kind of relentless devotion. You find that you go deeper into what you are, how you are, how language is, how the poem is, what seeing, hearing, writing, thinking, being is than you ever would have been able to do if you based what you were doing on your skill intelligence knowledge and personality.

I have devoted many years to contemplative practice and see that poetry is or could be the same thing. My own poetry is the same thing, contemplation, poetry as practice, and I feel a kinship to Steve's project in poetry, which is the same as mine, and also the same as my Buddhist contemplative project. You do it; you simply do it with devotion. It sustains you for its own sake. You don't write to publish. You publish to write. The writing as practice—as personal sense of meaning, as salvation—is the thing. And the community of friendship and support (not only with one's contemporaries but beyond time, back through the generations of kindred writers you are in relation with, through your own practice, and forward to the generation of writers/readers now and yet to come). Writing that is both more and less than communication.

❧

## Indecipherable Realism

The poet is in his house writing. It is silent, he is alone. A lonely quiet place, not in a city, in a small town, on a quiet street, no traffic, no street noise, no one around. Wind outside, ocean in the distance. Clouds. Grey sky. A garden—simple, not lush. The poet has lived in this house many years by now, the same walls, same floor, same view. He is methodical in his habits, arises every morning same time, goes outside, comes back in, writes. Predawn. Sees, hears, thinks, remembers: writes words. Once a word is written, it is different from the moment before it is written: the word is different, the experience of the word is different. Life is different. This difference then falls away, and now there's an inner impulse, a longing, a sense of grasping or groping, then there is another word written (a word arising to hand and ear, to mind or heart) and the experience of writing, of being about to write, of having written, and then writing again, begins again. The words come out of the quiet. They come out of the long habit of having seen, heard, felt, these same things in a former time that rhymes with this time, as echo. In the process of writing (daily writing, in a strict form, which makes the time seem to be the same yet different on any given day—as any other day, the same and also different in its slight variations, no day repeats any other day, no perception—of the same tobacco plant, the same bird sound, of invisible bird, far away, the same sea seen from the same window, the same picture on the same wall, but each day slight variations) each perception, each memory, each word, mixes with every other perception, word, memory, in the depth of the quiet there's an unfolding of time and space as the present moment of writing, as the present instance of perception, as sound becomes sight, sight sound, as selfhood, personhood, merges with perception, with memory, with feeling, each perception, object, memory, in relation to every other perception, object, memory, so that the shifting relationships condition the next experiences the next words, and the strict form holds it all in a kind of constantly shifting stasis, just as the form of night/day, life/death, man/woman, word/silence, sky/earth holds the life we are living in place, provides a format for its going on. The closer you look, the more intimate the experience of all this is, the more indecipherable it becomes. The more real it becomes. It is relentless.

∽

## Decipherable Realism

5.28 (98)
upper left corner of table (surface) slanted below the sill,
composition of yellow and pink in various stages of decay

man walking around the corner of the house adjacent to color
above which cloud brushes against the ridge, (assumption)

(*part*) missing, curve of landscape in the painting analogous
to presence of the person who witnessed it but isn't here

edge of tobacco plant leaf after which (*another*) drop falls,
all but illegible 'scrawl' that can in fact be deciphered

unidentifiable trills of notes from somewhere beyond cypress
(*single*) instead of traffic, image of grey sky above city

Outside, the man is walking around a corner of the house; inside, the table is slanted below the sill; in the distance, a cloud brushes against the ridge—which order of reality, which geographic feeling (domestic scene inside the room; man walking around outside the house; cloud in distant sky) do we focus on, and are they different orders of reality, different spaces, places, experiences, to be carefully distinguished one from the other, so we "know where we are," or are they in fact one flat (or infinitely deep) plane on which all this takes place simultaneously (in perception, in language, as consciousness)? A person witnesses this, but is no longer here: time has passed, is constantly passing (in the silence you can notice this, with too much noise it happens anyway but you don't notice) the person of this moment is never here the next, everything passing from concealment to unconcealment then back to concealment simultaneously on one flat or infinitely deep plane. The drops falling from tobacco plant leaves are writing just as much as this that I am doing now is writing or the former writing of Stephen Ratcliffe (by now more than ten years formerly) is writing: they write a meaning, as much as these words write a meaning. The meaning "can in fact be deciphered"? But not explained, perhaps. It can't be in prose. Its notes are "unidentifiable trills"; its image is "grey," and the person who witnesses it isn't here (as you read these words, no longer here).

5.28 (99) [*last of 374 poems*]
figure across the field against grey background, behind whom
feeling of a pink-white rose fills shape of window (form)

(*that*) is motion of green leaves on a branch wind approaches
and/or leaves, example imagined before it actually occurs

pale yellow petal falling to a table on the left, which (*is*)
acoustic action continued as the listener turns toward it

subject standing in front of crack in rock beyond which blue
(*position*) of noon, angle of thought coming toward viewer

surface of ridge below cloud (*c*) above which horizontal line
of final action, landscape leaning against pane of glass

"Feeling" of a pink-white rose: not seeing the rose or smelling it: feeling it. Or perhaps no one is feeling it but the rose, in being unconcealed, produces or is a feeling. A figure—which maybe is a person—is there, in the background (rose in foreground?), appearing against a grey backdrop, very quietly, as a shape, a form, rather than a subjectivity, a personality. (Person as part of the field, figure in a landscape.) Leaves on trees moving in the wind (or leaves leaving?) but this isn't actual—it is imagined by a subject before it happens, and does happen then in another moment (the next moment, the previous?). Inside (We were before this outside? Or are we inside and outside at the same time? Or is there any "we" at all, as reader, as writer, as person, to be anywhere, are "we" no longer, as "we" imagine "ourselves" to be, the central focus of any writing, any thinking, any perceiving, but just that perceiving is going on and "we" or some figure in the landscape, is present, part of the general scene?) . . . inside, a pale yellow petal falls. It is so quiet in here you can hear the petal falling when you turn toward it, or is the falling of the petal contingent on your turning toward it, it falls when and because you turn toward it, your movement having jarred the table so that the petal falls, making a sound, but can you hear the sound? The rock-hard sense of your identity then cracks open: you see blue sky opening through the crack, for the first time you can feel a thought coming toward you from a distance, the thought is a cloud above the ridge, it is seeing itself, the final line of a poem you have been writing for more than a year and now (it suddenly occurs to you, quietly, and without emotion, but with a certainty) the poem is finished, landscape like something flat and contained leaning against the pane of glass out which you are looking, a thick sheaf of pages full of uniform black lines of words on white.

# A Page for Phil

*I can find no record of publication for this piece, which sounds like I wrote it for someone. Phil Whalen's importance to my life and work has been cited in many places in this book.*

This book will change. It has to. I know I'm finally of no importance
as the promulgator of my details, because I've been so violated . . .

—Alice Notley, *Mysteries of Small Houses*

I was talking with some friends about Alice's poems about grief, which are immense. That they're about Ted's death, but also about more than that, or that you read them that way, they're about losing anything, everything, all of the time, the way the body disappears, moment by moment, places disappear, the past washes away, the present does, everyone in your life disappears. That's how time is, life is, and we're all violated by time shamelessly every day. And also—what I can gather from Phil these days—this is perfectly all right, it's normal, and there are pleasures in it, if you want to find them. Like Phil, whom she loves and admires (and the feeling is mutual), Alice has always been able to sustain great troubles, the world's troubles in her own, with a wise crack and a shrug. Surviving is a trip.

Phil and I have had the same Zen teacher, Richard Baker, a wild and crazy guy, so we're Dharma brothers, but also Phil's my teacher and mentor; I always look to him for how to be a poet and a priest at the same time, necessarily failing spectacularly at both, which means that you're staying in touch with your lunacy and willfulness, your passion, even though you are sincerely working to abandon it. For years I watched and hung out. I saw how he wrote, how he thought, read, pondered, suffered. How he put books together out of all that once in a while when he got around to it, from out of his many doodle journals, cutting and patching. He let me become a poet in his vicinity, although I'm still scared to death to read to him my poems aloud; he's so picky and hates what he doesn't like (though he'd probably now fall asleep, which is what he does when I read to him from his favorite authors, like Stein).

Phil's bedridden. He was supposed to have died a while ago but he was being so well fed he decided not to, confounding the experts and authorities, and causing his many friends much trouble and joy. Now he's not even sick; he has no known disease whatsoever, and everything (except his eyes, which barely work) works all right, only slowly, and with less power. He can't get out of bed, or do much. He sleeps, sees friends, eats with gusto (peanut brittle, pickled okra, whiskey, beer, chocolate croissants, hot dogs, and other such stuff are regularly brought to him by old friends and admirers) and watches court television. He seems fairly happy, and it's always a joy to be with him.

Like Ted Berrigan, Phil is a poet, which is something more than, though it might include, the writing or reading of poetry. More, it's a way of seeing, being, a stance, a direction, a trajectory, an aroma surrounding one's life. Now he doesn't write or read at all yet he remains a poet, is one, speaks poetry, thinks it, sees it, I am sure, full and wide, waking and sleeping, even in his reduced circumstances. There are days he grumbles, conspires to "escape." But he's never in despair, never pathetic. A poet is always wily, has resources, even in extremity. Death really isn't an issue.

# Review of Philip Whalen's
## *Overtime, Selected Poems*

*This review of Philip Whalen's,* Overtime, Selected Poems, *edited by Michael Rothenberg, with an introduction by Leslie Scalapino (Penguin, 1999), was published in* Jacket, *issue 11, 2000.*

*Overtime* brings back into print, in a new format, and with new work included, most of the essential poetry of legendary Beat poet/Zen priest Philip Whalen. I have been waiting a long time for this work to come round again, because of all the Beat writers, Whalen's work is the most relevant, holds up best, and offers the most possibilities to the contemporary reader and writer.

I am not so sure about the use of the label "Beat" (which was meant to stand for "beatific," rather than semidepressed). Other than describing a group of writers who happened to know each other well, and to have encouraged each other during the difficult and rather narrow period of American culture in the late 1940s through the 1950s, there is not so much that holds these writers together as a school. The one thread that does run through them all is their distaste for and rejection of conventional American cultural life: they are in revolt against the boredom, contradiction, and repressed violence that lies beneath the surface of the optimism of the postwar years. But beyond this, their themes and methods differ considerably.

For Whalen, writing itself, as a practice, is everything: writing as experiment, as exploration, as active assault on reality, no holds barred. This work is not mythical autobiography (Kerouac), nor is it romantic politics or personal lyricism (Ginsberg). Instead in Whalen you will find writing at its purest and most desperate: writing that feeds on writing, writing that soars and dips inside writing, writing wrapped up in the problematics of writing and struggling to get out, writing that absolutely must be written, with all the force that this necessity implies. Because of this almost postmodern emphasis on process and nonassertion, Whalen's work was and remains a source for much writing that is going on now, and in the early 1970s, when contemporaries of mine were settling out to reframe poetics in a new key, it was Whalen, among the writers of the previous generation, to whom they turned. (This was especially true of West Coast writers: there is a strong self-conscious West Coast spin to Whalen's work, in terms of theme, setting, and interests. He is, in fact, one of the first clearly identifiable West Coast writers in American literature. His serious and early interest in Asia and in Buddhism is a part of this).

And yet, unlike many postmodernists, Whalen's writing is as personal, as friendly, and as human as writing can possibly be, addressing the reader directly, without the usual obscuring screen of high poetic rhetoric. As in Whitman, with Whalen's work you "touch a man," sometimes slightly deranged or obsessed, sad or distracted: whatever is going on in the "continuous nerve movie" of language is included, with no posturing whatsoever. In Whalen, you have things straightforward and unvarnished—phenomenologically, moment by moment, as it actually is, as Leslie Scalapino points out in her fine introduction that situates Whalen's work in the present rather than in a nostalgic past. Whalen writes ("records" is a better word) what actually is going on, the mind and hand as it moves, with all their slips, joys, jokes, wit, and woe.

I remember stumbling into this work, in 1970, in the 1967 Harcourt Brace edition of his selected work called *On Bear's Head*, a thick wacky volume like nothing I had ever seen before. Here was writing that was utterly and completely free, elegant, sure. I remember going over passages scores of times, lines so simple and natural you could not quite figure out how he'd got them so completely perfect in rhythm and sound:

> but the season UNACCOUNTABLY changes, the leaves
> all brilliantly fall, thousands at a time,
> Yellow red stripey and tawny splotchy crackling
> vegetable brocade foam around my ankles
> (new cold makes them ache) the sun blares through

naked branches
wind blasted smoke of burning leaves dead twigs fallen

—From "Birthday Poem, in advance of the occasion of my next one (if
    any) 1967"

ᦸᦸ

Yet the stuff was seeming not poetry at all, because it was put together in ways poetry had never been put together before. Whalen's poems seem to be, in some cases, especially in the earlier work, a species of collage crossed with doodling, the careful and at the same time completely intuitive stringing together of writing gestures (indeed the work was composed longhand in journals that often include cartoons and calligraphic flourishes that are essential to the appreciation of the work: Whalen is one poet with whom the printed page is often a disadvantage). Some of the works of the 1950s and 1960s are many pages long, completely disconnected in terms of theme or regular structure, yet not in any sense random or shapeless. Here was poetry that was quite clearly constructed with great delicacy and skill, yet constructed in some new as yet undiscovered way: based on the shape of writing itself, rather than on narrative, theme, or emotion.

*On Bear's Head* was an instant underground classic and many poets of my generation used it, as I did, for permission to create works in a new paradigm. We had all read Williams, Stein, Zukofsky, Olson, Creeley, Ginsberg. But it was Whalen's spirit, his humor and freedom, his compositional daring, his willingness to include everything and anything, which gave us the tools we needed to create the poetry we needed to create.

In rereading much of Whalen's work, I feel as if I am revisiting my own dreams. Several things strike me this time round.

First, there is the fact of his loneliness and distance from almost any form of social engagement. While Whalen is passionately political, and often angry at things the way they are and were, his sensibility is essentially poetic: he lives in, or wants to live in, a world in which peace and beauty prevail. He is often desperate about love and yet is unable to find it in a world in which others are so annoying and difficult to get along with. Some of the most poignant moments in *Overtime* are long laments about the impossibility of living in the world as it is, and simultaneously, soaring riffs about the beauty hidden underneath things, the imaginary perfect worlds of alternative universes that just be might be this one.

I keep trying to live as if this world were heaven
puke fish dark fish pale fish park fish
mud fish lost fish selfish
Rockers and Mods
"acres of clams"

And all my friends, all the people I've known, all I'm going to know
Were mistresses and lovers, all of us with each other
All intimate with me . . .

—From "Love Love Love Again"

 ⤳

Another feature of Whalen's work is the use, following Williams, of ordinary American speech. There are numerous passages that break in here
and there of ordinary people and their everyday speech (they all sound like
they are speaking in around 1935, probably in rural or small town Oregon,
where Whalen hails from). It is almost as though in the middle of a ranting
or an elegant or a learned passage, these folks just had to show up to bring
the thing back down to the world of regular folks, from which we cannot or
should not stray for very long:

Well that's a fine how de do. Now I've got to take and hunt up
another one of them thing to go on there! One of them little
well, I certainly am put out!

—From "Native Speech"

 ⤳

Then there are the celebrated arrangements, the scattered lists of stuff that
seems irrelevant or simply odd. The obsessions with plants or minerals or
arcane studies of various sorts that are just seemingly stuck in the poems
willy-nilly, though their placement also seems to be just right. I remember
once in conversation Allen Ginsberg confiding to me that although he was
fascinated by Whalen's work (indeed, Ginsberg was one of Whalen's big-
gest fans and supporters and they enjoyed a forty-odd-year warm and mutually respectful relationship), he really couldn't understand it. Ginsberg,
his own work so firmly built on personal confession and subject matter,
could only marvel at Whalen's nonlinear deftness:

Nautilus.
Octopus egg cases,
eggs of shark

•

nest.
range
purple stone mountain
green purple martin

—From "The Grand Design"

If you consider the work at it progresses over time, you can see a clear movement toward calmness, simplicity, and finally silence. Whalen's need to find a sane way to live, a way that would take him out of the craziness of American life and toward something deeper and more real, led him finally, through his years in Japan, to becoming a Zen Buddhist priest in the San Francisco Soto Zen lineage of Shunryu Suzuki-roshi. He was ordained in the early 1970s and practiced monastically for a number of years (he and I were monks together at Tassajara Zenshinji monastery in the Los Padres National Forest near Carmel, California) before moving back to San Francisco to become abbot of the Hartford Street Zen Center. This period coincides with a quieting and modulating of the work. There are fewer and fewer rants in the poems, fewer and fewer long poems, and a kind of classicism (not inconsistent in style, attitude, or tone with the earlier work) begins to emerge. By the 1980s the poems have become quite short, just a gesture or two, and since then, with Whalen's failing eyesight and less frequent reading, there have been almost no poems at all. Here is the final poem of the book, written in 1985:

FOR ALLEN, ON HIS 60TH BIRTHDAY

Having been mellow & wonderful so many years
What's left but doting & rage?
Yet the balance of birthing & dying
Keeps a level sight: Emptiness, not
Vacancy, has room for all departure &
Arrival; I don't even know what
Day it is.

# Activity Is the Only Community:
# The Writing of Leslie Scalapino

*This piece was written for an edition of* Jacket2 *on the writing of Leslie Scalapino, curated by E. Tracy Grinnell, poet and editor of Litmus Press.*

Activity is the only community. . . . My focus is on non-hierarchical structure in writing. For example, the implications of time as activity—the future being in the past and present, these times separate and going on simultaneously, equally active (in reference to Whalen's writing and similar to Dogen's conception of time and being)—suggest a non-hierarchical structure in which all times exist at once. And occur as activity without excluding each other.

—From "The Radical Nature of Experience [On Philip Whalen,
Lyn Hejinian, Susan Howe, and Leslie Scalapino]," in *Scalapino, How Phenomena Appear to Unfold* (Litmus Press, 2011), p. 193

Leslie Scalapino died on May 28, 2010, after a fairly brief bout of pancreatic cancer. She and I shared a passionate interest in and fealty to Philip Whalen—both to him personally, as a friend and mentor, and to his work and its promise for a future writing—and to Dogen Kigen (1200–1254), the Japanese Buddhist priest/thinker/writer whose great work, Shobogenzo, uncovers Buddhist implications of writing practice as a practice of being in time—issues of enormous importance to both Leslie and me.

*Activity is the only community. . . .* Activity for Leslie meant deeply inward engagement, i.e. writing: writing as experience, the most intimate form of living; but writing as being not fundamentally different from any other living—writing as activity in which all times exist simultaneously, the living times as well as the writing times, of one's self, as well as others, in the place where one is in writing (everywhere; nowhere) as well as all other places—there's no logic, there is no linearity in time, occurrence, thought, no separation, no inside or outside—but each step, in living or writing (which are the same) contains all other steps. So there's enormous resonance and passion but no sentimentality, nothing personal (except insofar as *everything* is personal, there's nothing *but* the personal)—and everything's taking place in a kind of eternal present, whose most salient characteristic is that it's radically passing away even as it's occurring—so that nothing's ever exactly here in the way in which we think it is. It is here radically otherwise.

In "The Cannon" (*The Public World/Syntactically Impermanent*, Wesleyan University Press, 1999), Scalapino states:

> There is no cause and effect—the moment of occurrence doesn't exist either—in that the present moment is disjunction per se only (Nagarjunian logic, which is early Zen, rendering modern physics?). All times (past present and future) are occurring at the same time separately as that disjunctive space or moment (rendition of Dogen's and Einstein's sense of being as time). So occurrence is not hierarchically ordered. (These views of time and being are also [elsewhere] articulated as socially shared experiences.) (p. 23)

This may sound like abstract ideology, but for Leslie it was astonishingly an immediate experiential truth. It made her writing enormously challenging and interesting formally—a *non-hierarchical structure* by which she meant there were no linear connections at all, no overarching plan or theme subordinating parts to whole, etc. There was only packed intensity at all points, every point referring to every other point, so that her works hold up as coherent structured works, despite the lack of any conventionally recognizable unifying elements. This feat was accomplished through the torqued and complex yet at the same time, oddly, radically simple syntactic structures in which she wrote—without any sentence or line ever ending or leading to the next in coherent, normal ways. And this syntactical style seemed to come to her quite naturally. It seemed not to be contrived but simply a way, *the* way, she had of seeing, being, in writing. This quality was noticeable particularly when she performed her work. Her voice was clear as a bell, insistent, sincere, absorbed, without any hint of irony or smartness, as if she were speaking precisely what she was meaning at the time of speaking, her right hand clutching the air repeatedly for emphasis.

This quality of insistence and absorption pervaded her living and her personal relations as well—which could make relating to Leslie sometimes a daunting proposition. When Leslie's husband of many years, the molecular biologist Tom White, came down with a rare form of throat cancer that seemed on first diagnosis almost certain to take his life, Leslie went to pieces, not so much emotionally, but philosophically; that is, not only was she upset and fearful, as anyone would be, but also it seemed she was feeling the world around her, and her thought itself, that she felt created and was created by the world, collapsing. She rejected any suggestion that she was undergoing emotional strain that might be coloring her reactions. It was around this time that I had the only outbreak of conflict with her I ever had in our long association. It was around issues of Philip Whalen's estate (I am Phil's literary executor, and Leslie was one of my advisors and helpers in this)—and I couldn't ever understand precisely what the issue of our conflict was, though Leslie expended many words trying to explain it to me. Eventually we had to go to a professional lawyer/mediator, a friend of mine who is a master in the field, to get the issue sorted out. The mediator failed utterly, even spectacularly, his skill and decades of experience no match for the certainty of Leslie's position and her force in asserting it. He left his office after our meeting (also involving the poet Michael Rothenberg, another dear friend and disciple of Whalen, and editor of his collected works) not knowing quite what hit him. [Later the conflict dissolved; I am not entirely sure but think it coincided with Tom's cancer being surprisingly, almost miraculously, in remission after experimental treatment.]

However, when Leslie herself received her own fatal diagnosis a few years later—a diagnosis that pointed almost surely to the swift ending of her life—she was confident, optimistic, cheerful, courageous, almost, it seemed to me, carefree. The contrast was astounding. What could account for it? That she cared for others (Tom) more than herself—was almost unconcerned for herself? That she actually believed as she wrote, her experience in writing being that time was present and all-inclusive in activity, and so death was nondeath (as Dogen, Nagarjuna, and other Buddhist thinkers are constantly saying), and there was fundamentally nothing to worry about, that time was including everything all of the time so her death and her life folded into one another and nothing ever actually began or ended? *Activity is the only community.* Action in time, being in time, in time's fullness in every moment—so that one was always in an inclusive time frame and this time frame was essentially communal—so that one was never alone, possibly even in death? This despite the fact that the disease is a painful one and that she endured, before it was over, many extremely difficult procedures.

Leslie's writing was *non-hierarchical* in the sense that it recognized no authority and attempted to establish none. Her sense was that the great Modernists had established historical/cultural authority; this was the basis of their bad politics, that they were wanting to control culture they saw as having gone awry, that they were working out (Pound, Olson, Eliot, etc.) the corrective that they could figure out through their mastery—and were dispensing advice. The Beats (whom Leslie loved and identified with) were the mirror opposite of this. She called them "a populist avant-garde," which is to say leading the way not as an elitist cultural vanguard, but rather from an intuitive and common foundation, based not on knowledge and cultural expertise, but on nerve, intuition, and revolt.

In the late 1970s and beyond, Leslie had many disagreements with the Language writers, our mutual colleagues and friends, who took the Beats and associated others as precursors and mentors but at the same time had a powerful ethical and political critique of them. The Beats' romanticism was rebellious, yes, against social forces that deserved to be rebelled against, but at the same time it was essentially politically naive, intellectually impressionistic, and enormously self-centered. Generally the Beat writers (male) were sexist; often substance abusers, which made them destructive in their own and others' lives; did not establish and support community; saw writing as the province of the gifted individual rather than the locus of sharing, collaboration, and community. In other words, the Language writers were establishing collectively and collaboratively a set of values and procedures that were almost the opposite of the tenor the Beats had established. This aspect of their project has, I believe, been underappreciated— that the Language writers were, personally, and intentionally, by virtue of their theory and practice, ethical, kind, supportive individuals as I knew them, concerned for others and reasonable in their living, and personally modest if collectively quite ambitious in their goals and ideas. [I recognize here I am presenting no evidence, not naming names, and generalizing outrageously, yet let's let this stand as at least partially true and in any case something I believe to be so.] And all this was no less true of Leslie, despite her differences with them.

⁊

> In Whalen's writing, comparable to Dogen's articulation of being as time (the poetry not being a description of anything outside, but a demonstration of one's mind doing this—the syntax and structure duplicating the process that is the reader's own mind-phenomena), the nature of the present is only disjunctive; the times occurring separately are at the same time."
>
> —From "The Radical Nature of Experience," p. 194

In the present moment of writing, one is never writing about anything outside the writing; subject matter (and though there is a tremendous amount constantly going on multiple levels in Leslie's writing, there is at the same time nothing going on) is merely an occasion for the mind's patterns—writer's as well as reader's—to exercise themselves ongoingly. Time is disjunctive: the moment of writing and the moment of living or reading or the time referred to in the writing have nothing to do with one another—no connection—but are going on always at the same time.

Similarly, there's no connection between minds, actions, ideas; there can be no "schools" of writing, no shared ideologies. (Though Leslie recognized forebears, especially Whalen, and supported many related writers, myself included, as publisher and friend, she adamantly refused to see herself as part of any movement or school). Carried to a personal level, this sense of each thing's utter separateness (if also connection, since everything was happening simultaneously and all-inclusively) could make literary conversation with Leslie sometimes confusing. I noticed in my dialogues with her over the years her fairly consistent resistance to my characterizing anything of her—her statements, her ideas, her writing—as my attempting to fit her productions into my own frameworks—which was anathema to her. This despite the fact that we agreed on almost everything, and had virtually identical roots and lineage to our thought and writing. Agreement, accepting premises and assumptions and going on from there, is the very basis of harmonious conversation, but to Leslie, this style of discourse was essentially hegemonic ("Oh, I now see what you are doing and it turns out that it is merely a function of, an analogue of, what I have already been doing"), yet at the same time how else is communication possible if relating one thing to another is all but disallowed? And if your ideas/words are constantly *sui generis*, how is this not lonely, resulting in a constant effort to insist on distinction, which would essentially be alienating and painful? Or, one might say, this aloneness is a, if not *the*, mark of genius [though, of course, Leslie would have denied altogether—probably with a laugh—the possibility of genius]. A refusal to agree. A seeing of radical difference where others might more easily and less acutely see sameness. I sometimes had the impression that Leslie's feminism was likewise a function of this phenomenon. That is, that it is very "male" to collate and characterize, to explain and codify [as the Language writers were in the early years so bitterly accused of doing, with their rational, political, magisterial critical writing, which was often taken to be anti-poetical and "male"] while it is feminine—or at least resistant to maleness—to deny any of that and to insist on each thing's being what it is as it is, not fitting into someone's—anyone's—framework.

I am aware as I write this essay that this is precisely what I am now attempting to do—to comment on Leslie's life and work in terms of my own hegemonic frameworks. Squeezing her substance into containers of my own shaping (even as I try as accurately as I can to speak from and for her ideas—probably impossible). She would probably revolt at the idea of this, and disagree with everything I am saying here about her—no doubt she would. In "How Phenomena Appear to Unfold," she wrote about my work in a way that arguably did the same—and yet I was in agreement with what she said, and possibly the nonlinear way in which she approached the writing (which included probably as many quoted lines of mine as her own words about those lines), her syntax, as always in her essays as well as in her poetry/novels/plays, sufficiently inside-out to resist any paraphrasable meaning, so that one could never complain about what she meant since what she meant was never one-dimensional or clear, in the ordinary sense of clarity.

❧

The notebook method of [Whalen's] Scenes of Life at the Capital
(which is separate times compared to each other) allows all layers

to occur at the same time in the text, while being read/acted in by the reader as real-time (representation) where it is not. It's only the way the mind works making fast disjunctions and connections; it is phenomena as being one's mind. 'Seeing' is not separate from being action and these are only the process of the text/one's mind phenomena. Writing is therefore an experiment of reality.

—From "The Radical Nature of Experience," p. 197

When in 2007 Wesleyan University Press brought out *The Collected Poems of Philip Whalen*, edited by Michael Rothenberg, Leslie was furious. She and I had many difficult discussions over this. Leslie felt very strongly that Whalen's poetry (despite the fact that he usually dated his poems with very careful accuracy) was not meant to be presented in chronological order, as it was in the *Collected*. His books, she felt, were constructed as works, put together for their shape and feel—as "experiments of reality" rather than as chronological linear record of the writing of his poetry, so the *Collected* did violence to his work, completely destroying its actual shape and intention. She proposed various scenarios for correcting this—republishing the book in other formats (online?) that could restore it to its rightful form, undoing the damage that had been done, distorting Philip's achievement for all time. Both Leslie and I had had the experience of witnessing Philip's methods of composition and collation, so she felt pretty certain of this. (Leslie through an interview she did with Phil, included in an essay on him she wrote for *How Phenomena*, and me through helping him, when he and I were living together at Tassajara monastery, put together one of his later volumes—which was done by spreading various notebook pages from various periods over the floor, and putting them together intuitively [not chronologically] to make the sorts of shapes he felt were wanted for that particular poem or poem-sequence, though he usually had no rationale—other than his feeling at the time—for why he did what he did). I remember at the time, under Leslie's passionate onslaught, consulting with many poets who knew and depended on Philip's work (Alice Notley, Clark Coolidge, Gary Snyder) about this. Leslie was so convincing and so determined in her point of view that I needed backup to figure out what to do. None of them completely shared her perspective. In her preface to the *Collected*, Leslie wrote of Whalen, "He was the first American poet to propose or work within this terrain of free-fall in the Buddhist sense [as in previous paragraph of preface: "which recognizes all supposition, perception, and phenomena as having no actual order of occurrence except that imposed by the mind as its own context."] . . . Of words being merely labels, language itself as the material of investigation" (p. xxxix).

❧

Writing not having any relation to event/being it—by being
exactly its activity. It's the 'same thing' as life (syntactically)—
it *is* life. It has to be or it's nothing.

—From "The Radical Nature of Experience," p. 201

Writing is "the same thing" as life? This could be monstrous—the writing taking over the life, substituting for the life, as, one might imagine, could have been so for the Romantics, down to and including the confessional poets and the Beats. But I think not so in Leslie's case. Difficult as she might have sometimes been, Leslie was not self-indulgent or self-centered; in fact, quite the opposite. She was enormously caring, making efforts to help others, and engaged and concerned with political and social problems around the world. Passionate for her ideas and beliefs but not, so it seemed to me, with a sense of defending or identifying with them, but rather because they were for the purpose of protecting and sharing with others. Oddly, she was at the same time the most inward and the most socially concerned, political, of writers. So it must have been not that writing covered life, blotting it out, but that the reverse was so—that writing was so transformed by the living, the way of living as seeing, as knowing that events were simultaneous, all-inclusive, and disjunctive, that there was a powerful presence in living, not seeing persons and events as linear and connected, that was a felt experience—a particular kind of passion in living that was the same as the passion in writing. So that writing became for Leslie in a sense a contemplative practice, a process of being in her living, thinking her way through it. She lived: wasn't living *about* anything any more than in writing she was writing about anything.

In "The Cannon," she writes:

My intention—in poetry—is to get the complete observing at the same instant (space) as it being the action.

There's no relation between events and events. Any. They are separate.
Events that occur—(regardless of their interpretation—). (But also that they
are at once only their interpretations and only their occurrence). (p. 16)

In "The Recovery of the Public World," she states:

Perception itself is phenomena.
Beginning and disintegration are devoid of inherent existence as being
in perception (appearance).
For that reason the way they appear and the way they exist are
dissimilar, and they appear in a deceptive way to, and in, the world. . . .
    As no phenomena or events/constructs can be single, in that they
spring from other contingencies and are these, they do not exist in that
perceived form (single)—only appear to exist 'at present,' which also only
appears to exist. (pp. 53–54)

Nothing exists singularly, in an atomized way. Everything exists within
context, contingency. So there's nothing single and nothing actually present; all only appears to exist but really doesn't. If you took this seriously, it
would solve a lot of human problems. What had seemed heavy and troublesome would now seem lighter, not nearly as problematic (since problems
only appear to be problems, are not actually that; knowing this would potentially have the effect of lightening the burden). This explains how it was
possible for Leslie to be so engaged and involved (emotionally involved) in
the world's problems, especially in Asia, where she'd grown up, and seen the
brutal fate of women and girls in poverty-stricken areas. This explains possibly also the laughter and lightheartedness she exhibited at the time of her
illness (at least when I visited during that time) and the little spontaneous
laugh when she described to me over the years, in response to my constant
inquires about it, the pain in her neck and back that she suffered most of
her adult life, a severe disability that caused her to go through numerous
unsuccessful desperate operations, that often made the condition worse,
and forced her to sit in a chair with special cushions and pads, that she'd
bring with her when she went to readings.

In "The Recovery of the Public World," she goes on to say:

Impermanence—I wanted, in the structure throughout and in the
minute unit [only one or two words on a line] as order of perception
[past and present reverberating back into the "past" of the structure at

any one point at the same time as into its future—disrupting—serene at once] occurring in the line breaks to have impermanence, to seek this—positively—as a gesture in the world, outside of oneself, not 'about' one.

And that minute "duplication" as events simply go out and out, not recurring as prior known shape. (p. 58)

Impermanence is built into the structure of Leslie's writing. Every line disappearing as it comes up. So that there's no sense of forward movement—every element of the writing dissolving in your mind as you read it, though every element is intensely there as you read it, so that reading the disappearing text you feel as if you'd been through something enormous, though you couldn't say what it was. *"Duplication"* (why that word, and why the scare quotes?) causing the events to go *out and out*. Nowhere is this truer than in Leslie's last two books, *Floats Horse-Floats or Horse-Flows* and *The Dihedrons Gazelle-Dihedrals Zoom* (the titles themselves defy any sense of permanence—they seem to slip out of your mind as you read them; most writers want to choose memorable title; I find Leslie's to be impossible to remember, I have to look them up almost every time). These works, called novels, are written in a prose whose syntax is, as usual with Leslie, immensely twistedly complex sentence by sentence. I have characterized these books as multiple terrifying sci-fi novels whose plots—involving human and nonhuman characters who appear and disappear in and out of bizarre landscapes through enormous time frames—unfold randomly and simultaneously within each sentence. Both books employ a technique Leslie invented for them called "alexia, word blindness." In introducing this technique in *Floats*, she says, "'alexia', word-blindness (but not arising as nervous disorder) unknown words create a future/In the morning a new rose juts in the morning." In *Dihedrons*, there's a longer prefatory page which says in part:

Dihedrons and Gazelle-Dihedrals are human-like creatures. Profoundly injured, they roam jetting space in the form of vertical severed halves. *The Dihedrons Gazelle-Dihedrals Zoom* was written by leafing through Random House Webster's *Unabridged Dictionary* choosing words by process of alexia, not a mental disorder but word-blindness: trace-like stream overriding meaning, choice, and inhibition. The intention to bring about an unknown future was changed by this action of alexia making as it happens sensual exquisite corpses—leading to the discovery that there *isn't* any future, isn't even any present. Such an exquisite corpse, read, is in an instant yet not even in a 'present.' Outside's events unite gluing to each other a single object. That which had already existed is by chance. Dysaphia: as if people can have no sensations, the writing becomes the sensations that are then felt by everything.

The exquisite corpses are physical as if one such is flesh-butterfly-other occurrences (real time events such as the exploding of Mumbai), each event-cluster internally hybrid rather than being separate presentation as idea. That is, the writing is not the idea of the whole framework of occurrences after without its existence ever being.

—From *The Dihedrons Gazelle-Dihedrals Zoom*, (Post-Apollo Press, 2010), p. vii

Both works include visual elements: in *Horses*, multiple photographs of a sculpture of a horse's head by Amy Evans, as well as other photographs; in *Dihedrons*, reproductions (in color) of works by Kiki Smith, Jess, and Masami Teraoka.

ᥱᢆ

Astonished and deeply impressed by these works, which seem to me (and to Tom White) to be a kind of shimmering culmination of Leslie's lifetime writing project, I decided to write a memorial work to her (which, in keeping with all I have said above, was less for her or to her than an actual present-tense communication with her after her passing), which I called "The Strugglers" (and which later became the title poem of a collection published by Singing Horses Press in 2013). The method of composition was reading, in several sittings, *The Dihedrons Gazelle-Dihedrals Zoom* and then responding to each reading with my own words. Included in my writing (written, of course, as Leslie would have understood this, simultaneous with her work, and also at a different time historically) are reports/images of the many disasters that were occurring in the world in the "real time" of my writing, as well as events/images from Leslie's work and some of the words she had randomly chosen through the process of "alexia." I conclude this essay by leaving off whatever cogent explanation may have been perpetrated above and responding to Leslie respectfully and directly through my poem written to/with her. Here is one of the many titled poems that make up the single work "The Strugglers":

# CLADOGENESIS

No action having an ending but its effects [no action apart from effects
    fore & aft, its substance optical illusion necessary] continuing
    endless
Pullulating cancrine readings criss-cross time's luminal lintels as limen
    & thus events occur as they seem
In echolalia, speaking words of others in striated orders of transfection,
    caducous, so ground's [i.e. Occurrence's] littered with pages
    incessant and meeting requires less physical presence than one
    would have thought [absent reflection in/of material world]
So this is written literally as cladogenesis, source remaining as light
Gazelle-diehedrals sliced with deliquescent organs glistening, halved, so
    opened up as tender meat can't take world's fetid winds thus they
Die, some taking own life as sacrifice [Jesus not knowing he stands in for
    them, suicide-saints] & killings in Juarez
50,000 gone in bullets, knives, beheadings, kidnappings ending badly in
    mere six years
So terror rules as ever there, here, but no single event ends, not existing
    at any rate it's paradise
To wake in morning after decisive event/dream with feeling of
    gratefulness, so impossible
[Literally exactly that] to be alive this way [not as seems; that doesn't
    make sense]
That the dead're not gone for never was as is [was, thought to be so]
This cacography makes it all illegible, reality's cribriform seeming-solid
    metastasis
Deliration of fear-encampment where there's tiger, cobra there
Wraps around him seven times, spreads wide head of protection is
    actually single event in time
Not possible other than the saying [here/together/simultaneous/solitary]

# On Hank Lazer's *Elegies and Vacations*

*This essay was originally published in* Talisman, *28–29, Winter 2005.*

Contemporary poetry seems inescapably to be about poetry; the writing is of words and the problems they pose. But what happens when life's events press down hard? Is a poetry concerned with its own meanings capable of dealing with them? This question illuminates Hank Lazer's collection *Elegies and Vacations* (Salt Publishing, 2004):

> [ . . . ] to
> test poetry in the face
> of the worst events
>
> if the words have value
> they have value there too

In his critical writing and his poetry, Lazer has argued for the language-centered poem. In *Elegies and Vacations* he seems to have been forced by circumstances to question his poetic beliefs and strategies and, without abandoning them (he's come too far), to bend them in the direction events needed to take him. "Deathwatch for My Father," the book's longest poem, is a brave, sad, and moving work (adjectives that ordinarily cannot be applied to language-centered writing), a diary poem whose subject is the poet's confrontation with poetry's possibilities in the midst of his father's last months. It's difficult to write about the death of a loved one without sentimentality or manipulation. What can poetry, as poetry, say? Lazer holds this question steadily, writing into it with simultaneous attention to language's bones and death's rude machinery.

a
precise nature
of dying
is that it doesn't
seem
to be going
on

The book consists of eleven poems, some with long meandering sentence-based stanzas, others with Eigner-like lines spread all over the page, still others with two- or three-word lines in short stanzas, like the one above. Lazer uses the variety of modes fluidly to strike different pitches of a single more or less calm, sober, patient, and searching voice, whose fundamental confidence (despite numerous doubts) in the ongoing exploration that poetry is, manages to confront life's disasters with honest feeling, and without flinching.

# A Short Note on the Visual Poetry of Whalen, Grenier, and Lazer

*This piece appeared in* Jacket2, *May 24, 2014.*

From the beginning of my writing, I have been concerned with (floored by) the fact of a word, or a letter, as a thing, a physical, elemental thing—and the act of contemplating such a thing. In the late 1960s I noticed the poems of Aram Saroyan—one word—say, "crickets"—printed repeatedly in a single column, in Courier type, down the page. My first works were less poems or writing per se about something than memorials to the fact of words, that they appear and seem to signify.

Three poets who have been, over many decades, important to me have developed this material aspect of writing considerably: Philip Whalen in his doodle poems, Robert Grenier in his poem scrawls, and Hank Lazer with his shape poems.

Whalen studied traditional calligraphy with Lloyd Reynolds at Reed College. Accomplished with specially nibbed fountain pens, and written in traditional alphabet styles, such calligraphy is an art form itself, originating in the Middle Ages, for hand-copying sacred texts. Whalen used the pens and the alphabet styles, but was never serious about fully developing his hand—though he did spend many hours, over years, in repetitive practice. An inveterate doodler, he couldn't help himself from fooling around with pen and ink and paper. Many of his printed poems are doodles of the sort someone might make when talking on the phone or waiting in a doctor's office, full of curlicues, little drawings, various sizes and styles of lettering. Most of this is lost in the printing, although almost all his books make an attempt to indicate the feeling of the actual notebook page with the use of capitals, various sizes and styles of type, etc. Several of his books reproduce pages in facsimile, and there are many such pages in his *Collected Poems*, edited by Michael Rothenberg (Wesleyan University Press, 2007). Whalen's original notebooks are available for viewing at U.C. Berkeley Bancroft Library, and Brian Unger is doing a scholarly edition of some of the notebooks.

Robert Grenier has long been exploring the minimalist poem. Since the 1970s, he's been straying, wandering, or maybe zigzagging away from the notion of a poem printed on a page secured in a book. He's made giant poetry posters with clusters of tiny poems printed here and there on them (one I have is tiny white typed words on black paper), and his famous "*Sentences*" is an elegant box of cards with little poems of a few words, or even one word, or part of a word on each card ("*Sentences*" is now also available online). In the late 1980s he began to make what look like poem scrawls. Consisting generally of actual words (though they are often hard to make out), the works—which are shown in galleries—are quite beautiful. They are made with various colored fine-point pens (green, blue, red, black), not, as with Whalen, with calligraphy equipment in decorative alphabets. Precise thin lines bend, spread, and crisscross on large-format paper, building up a dense forest of lines in a pleasing if seemingly casual, though gorgeous, array, which only eventually resolve into words when you look at them for a while. Sample texts:

AFTER
NOON
SUN
SHINE

or

I saw it
where is it
(or it might read I saw/ where/ it/ is it)

. . . deliberate, lovely, if simple, or even simple-minded, phrases, unlike Whalen's offhand unintentional words ("B, a beard . . . B is just because. . . . Don't mention the Arizona Biltmore. . . .")

Hank Lazer's shape poems are, again, something completely different. The words are handwritten in notebooks, one poem to a page, in series. The notebook is the aesthetic unit here, as, perhaps, with Whalen, though Whalen's notebooks are what he referred to as "goofing," while Lazar's are quite deliberately in a series. (Grenier's scrawls are complete stand-alone poems.) The handwriting of Lazer's shape poems is not particularly elegant, as in Whalen, nor does it emphasize, as in Grenier, the emotional and visual primacy of letter and word. Using ordinary ballpoint pen, Lazer's hand isn't particularly distinguished one way or the other. Just words written in an ordinary way, the writing somewhat chunky, not flowing. Their distinction comes in the shapes they trace on the page—spirals, squares, circles, various complex irregular forms. The twenty or so notebooks I am aware of begin with fairly ordinary stanzaic shapes on the page and evolve as they go into these more elaborate shapes, each page unique. Whereas Whalen's word-content is rather haphazard and free-associational, and Grenier's is precise, imagistic, or emphasizing grammar and syntax per se, Lazer's words are discursive quotations. In the course of the twenty notebooks he reads through Heidegger's *Being and Time*, and later, several works by Emmanuel Levinas, and most of the words in the poems are citations from these works, with Lazer's comments and occasional other words added. The tone is philosophical and ruminative, a record, from inside language, of a person's thinking, about words, in words, in and about time, space, life, death—not thinking's products but thinking itself, as process. The poems are improvisational and immediate—the form allows for no revision. In fact, improvisation—its delightful freedom, playfulness, even joy—is characteristic of all three of these poets' visual work. [The most accessible example of Lazer's shape poems is found in his *N18 (Complete)*, Singing Horse Press, 2012.]

What's interesting and sustaining for me about the possibility of writing is that one could live in the intimate midst of words as such—as thinking in a shape, feeling, and form—as being in the world that's illuminated through human mind and language—simply dwelling there, with all the wonder and serenity that that dwelling brings. This seems to me to be the case with any writing that I find truly worthwhile, and the more you appreciate this, the clearer it is that its pleasures come fullest at the level of the word in hand and eye and mind—as you find in these works.

# A Note on Charles Bernstein's
## *Attack of the Difficult Poems*

*This short piece originally appeared in my blog and was reprinted in* Jacket2, *May 2011.*

*attack of the difficult poems* . . . is a great book! you must read this book! it will provide you with an education about what is happening, has been happening, in the world of postmodern poetry and why it is important for everyone to pay attention to it, important socially, personally, religiously. also very funny (the book is funny) and brilliant and a pleasure to read. i was sad when i finished it, but well, isn't this always what happens.

charles is always so funny and so astute about the poetry wars, who is up, who is down, and who is controlling the game. in fact, as he says, no one is paying any attention to poetry—at least to the poetry charles and i would value. a nod is given in the press and in the public to something called "poetry" and i guess it actually is poetry of some kind but mostly limited to sincere and personal statements of grief, beauty, query, etc., a little vignette, a moment of epiphany.

of course there's nothing wrong with this! but more interesting to me is a poetry that problematizes everything—the poet, the poem, the language itself. because if you are actually looking closely it becomes clear that all these things really are problems and what's a poem to do if not look closely? anyway, this is my theory. actually it's not a theory. i just can't help it. i have never minded that no one is paying attention to the poems i write.

a few are and that's all right. but charles is a professional culture warrior (and worrier) so he pays attention to that and fights for his (our) place in the sun, so to speak, and complains about it, makes fun of those who seem not to have a clue about what he and the rest of us are up to. of course it's more than merely about him/us. it's also an argument for another world, a more human and humane world, with more honesty and humor, more love, less self-centeredness. moving away from what he has for years called "official verse culture" to that. great interview with the astute marjorie perloff. between the two of them in this interview i think pretty much everything in the literary/cultural world is covered and known. also hilarious.

# On the Heart Sutra

*A version of this piece was originally published under the title "Love and Emptiness" as a review of* The Heart Attack Sutra *by Karl Brunnhölzl (Snow Lion, 2013) and* Thunderous Silence: A Practical Guide to the Heart Sutra *by Dosung Yoo (Wisdom, 2012) in* Shambhala Sun, *January 2013.*

All dharmas are empty: no eyes, no ears, no nose, no tongue,
no body, no mind, no form, no sound, no smell, no taste,
no touch, no object of mind.

I was thunderstruck the first time I encountered the words of the Heart Sutra. Somehow, no eyes, no ears, no nose made sense to me in a way I couldn't explain, and I felt great relief. As a child I had always suspected that the world I was raised in didn't hold up to scrutiny, and on hearing the Heart Sutra for the first time, my childhood confusion was suddenly acknowledged and addressed, even if I couldn't explain how. It seemed intuitively to me that the sutra was affirming what I had always felt: that the world was indeed not the way I had been taught it was.

Shocking as it is on first hearing, the Heart Sutra won't go away. You wonder and ponder, perplexed and fascinated. "No eyes, no ears . . . nothing to attain . . . no hindrance and no fear . . ." How? Why? It has taken me many years of practice and study to begin to appreciate and understand the Heart Sutra's words and put them into practice in my life.

At one page, the Heart Sutra is probably the briefest of all Buddhist sacred texts, and the most influential. Foundational to Mahayana Buddhism, it is prized in all schools of Tibetan Buddhism and in Zen, where it is chanted every day in most temples and monasteries. But what does it mean? Can it really be denying the existence of the very nose on our face? And why is that so important to a religion that prizes compassion over all other virtues?

Because of its central importance to so many schools of Buddhism, the Heart Sutra has inspired a number of commentaries in English from scholars and teachers of almost every tradition. Both the Dalai Lama (*Essence of the Heart Sutra: The Dalai Lama's Heart of Wisdom Teachings*) and Thich Nhat Hanh (*The Heart of Understanding: Commentaries on the Prajnaparamitta Heart Sutra*) have taught it, and a number of younger Western-trained teachers, probably many more than I know of, have also written commentaries.

The sutra's key term is the Sanskrit *shunyata*, usually translated into English as "emptiness." As the sutra says in its opening lines, "All dharmas [things, phenomena] are empty." Eyes, ears, noses, tongues, bodies, minds; all external objects—and all Buddhist teachings—are empty. In fact, the Heart Sutra is a brilliant one-page summary of the entire edifice of Buddhist psychological, epistemological, and soteriological teachings, which are listed in turn and then denied. A devout Buddhist, seeing the text for the first time, may well read it as a dismantling of Buddhist orthodoxy, a nightmare of antinomianism. Judging from the defensiveness you find in other, longer texts of the shunyata literature, of which the Heart Sutra is said be the pith or "heart," many early Buddhists probably did object to the sutra on exactly such grounds. But in fact, the Heart Sutra does not deny Buddhist teachings. It merely shifts the ground on which the teachings stand—which, of course, changes everything.

The word "emptiness" is a fair translation of shunyata, but it has the drawback of sounding negative, even despairing. In English the words "empty" or "emptiness" sound bleak. An empty life is not a happy life. It is flat, meaningless, hollow. Nothing inside. Alienated war-weary characters in Ernest Hemingway's short stories often had "a hollow feeling." T. S. Eliot, in the same period, wrote "The Hollow Men," describing the lost spirit of the times. Hollow is empty, flavorless. To be empty inside—of faith, of values, of enthusiasms—is to be nihilistic and despairing.

But the emptiness of the Heart Sutra is something else. It's good news.

It's freedom, ease, liberation. Commentators on the sutra often ask the question, "Empty of what?" and answer, "empty of separate self, empty of weightiness, empty of burden, empty of boundary."

The Chinese, searching for a word that might translate shunyata, used the character for sky. All dharmas are empty like the sky—blue, beautiful, expansive, and always ready to receive a bird, a wind, a cloud, the sun, the moon, or an airplane. The emptiness of the Heart Sutra isn't the emptiness of despair—nothingness—it's the emptiness of all limitation and boundary. It is openness, release.

The Heart Sutra is not denying that the world we live in exists. It's denying that it exists in the sticky intractable way we think it does. It's denying the ultimate reality of the basis of our suffering—our separate, burdensome self and all that seems to exist apart from it, all that we think we need and do not have. No eyes, no ears, and so on, doesn't deny the physical; it redefines it. Things do exist—but not as our possession or lack of possession—as stuff. Things exist freely, fluidly, and without boundary, ungraspable, evanescent. Which is why, strictly speaking, they can't be said to be or not to be. And when the sutra lists and negates basic Buddhist teachings, it doesn't mean the teachings are false. It means that the way we have understood them is false. The teachings are true—only in a freer, more expansive, less literal and crabbed way than we thought. The Heart Sutra showed me from the start that I could hold and practice the Buddhist teachings in an easy, flexible, openhanded way. I didn't have to be pious. Piety is empty, the Heart Sutra says. Buddhism is empty. And that is why it liberates us.

The other side of emptiness, or, one could say, its content, is connection, relationality. When I am bound inside my own skin and others are bound inside theirs, I have to defend and protect myself from them. And when I place myself among them, as I must, I better do that carefully, which is hard work, because I am often hurt, opposed, and thwarted by others. But when there's openness, no boundary, between myself and others—when it turns out that I literally am others and others literally are me, then love and connection are easy and natural.

Nagarjuna, the most influential of all Buddhist thinkers, seized on the emptiness teachings as the cornerstone of his Madhyamika, or Middle Way, approach. It's not that things "exist" (heavy, hard, and isolated) or "don't exist" (in despairing nihilism). The truth is in the middle: things are empty of both existence and nonexistence. There are no "things" at all and never were. There is only connection, only love, only flow. This, Nagarjuna argues, is not a new doctrine; it's what the Buddha was pointing to from the start.

This is why the emptiness teaching of the Heart Sutra, which seems to be rather philosophical and dour, is the necessary basis for compassion. Emptiness and compassion go hand in hand. Compassion as transaction—me over here, being compassionate to you over there—is simply too clunky and difficult. If I am going to be responsible to receive your suffering and do something about it, and if I am going to make this kind of compassion the cornerstone of my religious life, I will soon be exhausted. But if I appreciate the boundarylessness of me and you, and recognize that my suffering and yours are one suffering—which is empty, weightiness, and ultimately not tragic, however much we might think it is when we're smothered by it—then I can do it. I can be human and caring. It's not so hard. To be sure, living this teaching takes time and effort. And maybe we never entirely live it perfectly. But it's a joyful path worth treading.

In Mahayana Buddhism, compassion is often discussed in terms of absolute and relative compassion. Absolute compassion is compassion in the light of emptiness: all beings are empty, all beings are light, all beings are, by virtue of their empty nature, already liberated and pure. As the sutra says, suffering is empty, so relief from suffering is also empty. Everything is inherently all right—even the pain. Reality is inherently merciful. It's okay to suffer, because through the suffering we find release. The old adage "Time heals all wounds" is more profound than it sounds: time—every moment—actually is release, freedom, and healing. In the light of absolute compassion, reality *is* compassion.

This point of view sounds good, but could also be monstrous. Taken to extremes, it might inspire us to ignore wars, natural disasters, illnesses, and deaths: since everything is perfect and empty, why grieve, why cry? Why help? But this is one-sided and distorted. Relative compassion—human warmth and practical emotional support—completes the picture. Absolute compassion makes sustaining the endless work of supporting and helping possible; it grounds us in joy and ease. Relative compassion connects us heart to heart with others in their troubles. Either view by itself would be impossible, but both together make for a wonderfully connected and sustainable life. Two sides of a coin, two wings of a bird.

This is what I sensed without knowing it on first hearing the Heart

Sutra. (And I am not the only one: many others have told me they, too, have experienced this uncanny sense on first hearing it. Its matter-of-fact strangeness, even absurdity, seems to invite such a response.) It's what I sensed as a child was missing in the world around me. Life simply couldn't be as small, as difficult, and as dull as it seemed. Somehow there must be something else.

But the Heart Sutra is more than an inspiring vision or understanding. It is also a practice, a course of action that relieves suffering and transforms lives. Practicing the Heart Sutra is training in the feeling for life that you have when you fully internalize its teachings into your body and emotions. The emptiness/boundlessness of all dharmas is not only something we would like to believe; it is also a way to live, a texture of reality that can be palpably felt as a quality of awareness.

Bodhidharma is the legendary founder of Zen. Once his disciple Huike begged for his help: "My mind is in anguish, please help me find peace." Bodhidharma replied, "Bring me your mind." After some time of practice Huike said, "I cannot find my mind." Bodhidharma said, "Then your mind is at peace." Once you feel in your bones and throughout your awareness the emptiness of your mind, you are at peace. Even when problems and difficulties arise, there's still the thread of peace woven in at the heart of them.

In Zen practice, zazen (sitting meditation) is training in emptiness. The practice is simply resting alertly in the feeling of body and breath, letting everything come and go, without denying or latching on. Sitting this way day after day, retreat after retreat, year after year, Zen practitioners learn to hold things lightly: respecting them, appreciating them, attending to them when the time for that comes, but also letting them go as they naturally will—because they are empty. Everything exists in time; time is existence. And time is empty: everything comes and goes—so much so that you could wonder, "Was it ever here at all?" Sitting, you feel the truth of this as your own immediate experience of body and breath.

Emptiness teachings internalized become a way of being fully and easily present with what is—a passing, flowing, empty, ongoing stream of living and dying. At my first long Zen retreat, in the deep snows of upstate New York, I wandered for hours in the woods above the retreat center as snow fell, my tracks disappearing as I made them, until everything disappeared into a soft uniform whiteness, the trees, the ground, the sky—no eyes, no ears, no nose, no tongue, no body, no mind.

The Heart Sutra is also practiced by chanting. Since it's so short, it's easy to memorize, and anyone who has lived in a Zen temple for any length of time will automatically have memorized it. Having such a text, as they say, "by heart," is an experience increasingly rare in our culture, which makes it all the more precious. A mind that can, at any moment, begin vocalizing, in trancelike fashion (the syllables tumbling out of the mouth even before the brain registers them), the familiar words of the Heart Sutra, is a mind that has at its disposal the means for its own pacification and expansion. I remember many dark moments of confusion or despair when I chanted the sutra over and over for comfort, the words lifting me out of the rut I was in, opening up new vistas.

Once, long ago, visiting my parents in a crisis moment when my life seemed vague and directionless and I didn't know what to do, my mind raged with troubled thoughts I couldn't share. It was autumn, leaves were falling from the many oak and maple trees that lined the streets of the small Pennsylvania town where they lived. I walked through the leaves for miles, chanting the Heart Sutra over and over, until the thoughts dissolved and joy arose, my ears full of the sounds of crunching leaves underfoot, and my heart grateful for the strangeness of the passing of time.

Sutra chanting went in deepest of all at my mother's hospital bedside, just after her death. Everyone had gone and I was alone with my poor be-wildered mother's body. Not knowing what else to do, I chanted the Heart Sutra again and again as tears filled my eyes. I was sad and not sad at the same time. The words of the sutra never seemed truer or more comforting.

# On Dogen's *Shobogenzo*

*A version of this essay was published as "Rigorous, Pious and Poetic: Comparing Different English Translations of Shobogenzo," in* BuddhaDharma, *Fall 2010.*

Shambhala's recent publication of Kazuaki Tanahashi's two-volume translation of the complete text of Shobogenzo (*Treasury of the True Dharma Eye*) marks a watershed moment for Western Buddhism. The master work of the founder of Japanese Soto Zen, Dogen Kigen (1200–1254), Shobogenzo has been legendary for centuries. At first known only to adepts and disciples, the text was later brought to light and venerated, but for centuries almost never read. During the Tokugawa period the text was unearthed, edited and published, and used as the basis for a radical reformation of Soto Zen. In twentieth-century Japan, secular Japanese philosophers touted it as their answer to the great philosophies of the Occident. In the West, Shobogenzo stands almost alone among Buddhist writings as a work that philosophers and intellectuals with or without Buddhist affiliations take seriously. Its notorious difficulty and startlingly modern themes (like language, being, and time) have caused it to be compared in scholarly essays and books to Heidegger, Wittgenstein, and others. Naturally, contemporary Soto Zen practitioners, both here and in Japan, have embraced Shobogenzo as the basis for their practice.

With all this, it is no surprise that Shobogenzo has been amply translated into English. In addition to many volumes of selections, there have been three complete translations of the text (that runs usually to several volumes) into English: one by Nishiyama and Stevens, one by Nishijima and Cross, and one by Rev. Hubert Nearing, a monk from Shasta Abbey. All three of these works, impressive though they are (translating Shobogenzo is justly considered the feat of a lifetime), have remained fairly obscure, published in small editions, and generally only studied by specialists. With the Tanahashi two-volume version, we now have an edition that will receive the sort of attention this great work deserves.

Tanahashi has been at work on this project for fifty years. In 1960 he began a translation into modern Japanese of Dogen's difficult medieval Japanese text, and within a few years had produced (with the late American Zen teacher Robert Aitken) the first English translation of what is probably Dogen's most well-known essay, *Genjokoan* ("Actualizing the Fundamental Point"). Since then he has been translating steadily, working with dozens of Zen teacher-collaborators from around the country, from several Soto Zen lineages, and producing several volumes of selected works, the first of which, *Moon in a Dewdrop*, (published in 1985), has become in its own right a contemporary Zen classic. The present full version draws together all the previous work and adds considerable material that had not before been included.

Tanahashi's version, compared to the others, has two key advantages: first, the long time frame and the sheer number of collaborators, almost all of whom have been practicing and/or teaching Zen in America for decades, makes for a deeply considered and deeply relevant text; and second, Tanahashi's insistence on emphasizing the poetic flavor of Dogen's prose—combined with the excellent work of poet and Zen teacher Peter Levitt, overall associate editor of the present volumes—brings to the text a beauty of tone, diction, and style the other versions lack. I have been studying Shobogenzo for almost forty years (though only in English versions), and to my eye and ear, the Tanahashi-Levitt version seems not only most accurate but also—and especially—truest to what I imagine to be Dogen's potent expression in Japanese. To put it most simply: Dogen writes profoundly, and Tanahashi, Levitt, and their collaborators have paid more attention to the quality of expression in English than any of the other translators. (Disclosure: I am one of the collaborators, so can make no claim to objectivity.)

Japanese Zen was the first of the Buddhist traditions to make big waves in the West. In the 1950s the Japanese Zen scholar-practitioner D. T. Suzuki taught at Columbia University in New York, where his lectures were attended by many of the leading cultural players and avant-garde artists of the day. Through them his influence spread to the Beat writers, who popularized Zen as a form of aesthetic improvisation and passionate present-moment awareness. With the cultural space for Buddhism opened by Zen and the arts, many other forms of Buddhism rushed in. By the 1970s, what we now call Vipassana, as well as Tibetan Buddhism, was well established, and Western Buddhism moved beyond its original Japanese basis, with a strong emphasis on the aesthetic, to a more psychologized perspective, in which personal transformation and "the science of mind" became most important. From today's vantage point, it is easy to forget how important Japanese Zen and Japanese culture were to the original establishment of Buddhism here.

Contemplating this new translation, I find Shobogenzo inspiring and important exactly because of the Japanese spirit that Dogen brings to his rereading of Chinese Chan. Two Japanese cultural concepts that seem to me to be major influences on the general mood and tone of Shobogenzo are *yugen* and *aware*. *Yugen* means, roughly, "mystery." It refers to the fact that this human world that we see and hear and take completely for granted is, in fact, deeper and more mysterious than we can ever know. Yugen was an aspect of Japanese court poetry even before Buddhism arrived, but in Dogen's hands it becomes conflated with the Far East Buddhist doctrine of Tathagatagarbha, or Original Buddha Nature, as taught in the Lotus Sutra. In this text, of single importance in China, though noncanonical in Theravadin countries, and barely read in Tibet, the Buddha reveals that his practice, enlightenment, and Parinirvana, as taught in the Pali suttas, were an illusion, a tale told for effect, because human beings were not capable of grasping the shocking and more mysterious truth. But now, in the Lotus Sutra, this truth at last is revealed: the true Buddha was in reality not born, did not attain enlightenment and enter Nirvana; in fact, he has existed, exists, and will exist everywhere and in everything, and all practice is nothing other than the manifestation of his True Illumination, all pervading and everlasting. Like a phantom city that is produced by a magician to encourage weary travelers far from their destination, the earlier teachings of a historical Buddha were given to aid practitioners who needed them. In truth, reality itself is Buddha, and even our suffering has its Buddha Nature. Dogen couldn't help receiving this teaching as profound confirmation of the mystery of human life that is a deeply embedded value of Japanese culture.

The second Japanese cultural concept that Dogen brings to Chinese

Chan is *aware*, "impermanence." Aware appears as a form of nostalgia and sadness, love for a fleeting world we can never grasp. Of course, impermanence is also a cardinal principle of Buddhism. In Dogen's hands the two conceptions collapse into one, so that the fleeting world and its human sadness and sense of beauty are one with the three marks of Buddhism, suffering, not self, and impermanence.

Because of these cultural roots and combinations, Shobogenzo presents a radically unique view of Buddhism and of Zen as being not so much a retreat from or a transcendence of ordinary reality, which is essentially *dhukka*, suffering, a vale of tears to be overcome, but instead the full embrace of the human world as the world of Nirvana. To be sure, this radically nondualistic approach to Buddhism is not Dogen's invention; it is a clear doctrine of Mahayana and Vajrayana Buddhism. But in combining this doctrine with his Japanese cultural sensibility, Dogen brings a poignancy and an appreciation for humanity that other Buddhisms lack. This sensibility is everywhere in Shobogenzo, but perhaps nowhere better expressed than in Genjokoan, where, after delineating the dialectic between enlightenment and delusion, Dogen concludes, "Yet in attachment blossoms fall; in aversion weeds spread." In other words, for Dogen the ultimate standpoint of Dharma is simply the full affirmation of our ordinary human words of attachment and aversion and their consequences. It is precisely through full appreciation of this vale of tears that Buddha's illumination shines in us.

I remember, as a young Zen student, being enormously moved by these words when I first read them. It made sense to me then, and still does, that the point of my practice was not to overcome my humanity, to transcend it in becoming enlightened, but rather to settle into it with ultimate depth and appreciation. This is the overwhelming point of Shobogenzo.

There's little doubt that Dogen did not intend to reread Buddhism in the light of his own culture. He apparently felt, as he often wrote, that what he was transmitting was not only not Soto Zen, and not Zen—it was simply Dharma itself, as originally taught by the Buddha. He felt that in his teaching and practice he was returning to the root of the Original Teaching, as he had received it from his own Chinese teacher, Rujing.

Nevertheless, his reenvisioning of the Zen tradition is clear throughout the text of Shobogenzo. Quite often he will comment on a traditional Zen story in a way that seems quite blatantly to turn upside down the typical way the story is understood. Usually the key to this reinterpretation has to do with the fact that whereas in the usual view of the story someone is enlightened and someone else is not, in Dogen's version everyone in the story is equally enlightened from the start, no matter how much this would seem not to be the case. For example, there is the famous story of the First Zen Ancestor in China, Bodhidharma, who calls his four disciples together for a contest, to see which of them has the best understanding. He poses a question and they each answer. To the first he says, "You have my skin," to the second, "You have my flesh." The third has his bone, and the fourth, Huike—clearly the winner and in Zen's sacred history the Second Chinese Ancestor—has his marrow. But Dogen reads the story as if all four equally possess the full measure of Bodhidharma's truth, using expressions like "the skin contains the skin, flesh, bones, and marrow."

Such a rereading of the tradition, on such radical principles, connects to the perspective that Shobogenzo is most famous for, and that becomes almost a fixed doctrine in Japanese Soto Zen: that practice and enlightenment are one phenomenon. This runs completely counter to the normative Buddhist view (that dovetails fully with our conventional materialistic and psychological view) that one practices in order to achieve Nirvana or enlightenment, which comes after the practice has been accomplished, as a consequence of it. After all, what would be the point of practice if it weren't a process leading to a positive result? This is what we all want, and it seems to be exactly what the Buddha's teaching promises. The Four Noble Truths seem to point to this: suffering, cause of suffering, end of suffering, path to bring this about. To explode this conventional view in as many ways as he can, Dogen takes on many fundamental questions in Shobogenzo: Time (Uji), Space (Koku), Practice (Gyoji), Compassion (Kannon), Meditation (Jisho Zammai), Language (Mitsugo), Enlightenment (Daigo). In essay after essay he is at pains to show that the way we conventionally understand the teachings is not in accord with what the Buddha actually taught. The view that time is sequential, yesterday coming before today and tomorrow coming after, is incorrect, Dogen tells us. Time is nonexistent, and simultaneously eternal: so the thought that practice leads to enlightenment is wrong; it is a superficial view. Practice doesn't lead to enlightenment: a moment of practice is a moment of enlightenment. And enlightenment, to begin with, is not a state in contrast to delusion; it is "delusion throughout delusion."

Given this, one might wonder, why practice at all? For Dogen this is a question that could only come from ignorance. To ask why one should practice if practice doesn't have a payoff in enlightenment is for Dogen to completely miss what practice, enlightenment, and human life actually are. We practice because of enlightenment, which is the key to our essential human nature. Shobogenzo is a powerful argument, made in many ways— from the deeply conservative to the wildly radical—that the only thing that counts for Dharma, and for human life in general, is continuity of practice. Ongoing practice that is inspired by and is a manifestation of Original All Pervading Enlightenment.

For Dogen, this radical fact of life pervades everything. Because of it, we can't talk or write about practice as if practice and enlightenment were objects or states we could examine and comment on: our talking and writing are necessarily a form of practice. This understanding accounts for both the beauty and the famous difficulty of Shobogenzo. It's not that Dogen is obscure for the fun of confounding his readers. It's simply that we do not find in Dogen's writing what we expect to find. His insight is that explanatory teachings will always be misleading because they will reinforce delusional concepts of cause and effect, time and space, enlightenment and ignorance, and so on. Therefore speaking and writing about Dharma must avoid explanation in the ordinary sense and tend toward the poetic, suggestive, and all-inclusive statement. Thomas Cleary once collected a group of his Dogen translations under the title *Rational Zen*, to make the point that, unlike almost all other Zen masters, Dogen did not consider Zen to be a mystical teaching "beyond words and letters," but rather something that could and should be discussed. But the word "rational" is misleading. Dogen's painstaking discussions of koans and other traditional Zen and Buddhist material are not rational in the usual sense. They are essentially poetic. Shobogenzo has been prized over the centuries and especially now as a text whose religious and philosophical insights are perfectly matched by its form of expression. Dogen's literary mastery is impossible to bring over into English. No translation will do justice to it; all translations will be essentially incorrect. But as far as I can tell, no better attempt in English for a general audience has been made than this present version.

# Rethinking Ritual

*This essay is a review of* Zen Ritual: Studies of Zen Buddhist Theory in Practice, *edited by Steven Heine and Dale S. Wright (Oxford University Press, 2008), published in* Buddhadharma, *March 2008.*

Buddhism was first introduced to the West as a rational, iconoclastic, psychologically oriented form of spirituality. So different did Buddhism seem from Western religions that there was even some question as to whether it was a religion at all, considering there was no God, no revelation, and no supernatural element whatsoever. Educated Westerners who held this view of Buddhism had a strong Protestant, anti-magic, anti-ritual bias and an enthusiasm for the new science of psychology, which more or less debunked religion as a product of the primitive human mind. While other religions were full of superstition and mumbo-jumbo (the very concept of God as a punishing father being entirely dependent on blind belief and fear), Buddhism, in the view of these Westerners, was sober and balanced. It was an essentially rational approach to spiritual fulfillment, based on personal effort in meditation to reach exalted states of human perfection. The British scholars who translated the early Buddhists texts were predisposed to see them in this light, and the Asian Buddhists who supplied the texts to the British were quite happy with this view as well; it's nice, when you are a victim of colonial rule, to be praised by your masters for the superiority of your religious culture.

In Japan, the twentieth century saw the advent of a generation of Buddhist scholars who depicted Zen as all this and more: Zen was supra-rational, that is (in line with Heidegger and other Western philosophers of the time who were critiquing rational Western metaphysics), it possessed a reason beyond reason. Clearly aware of the challenge the West posed to their own traditional culture, these Japanese scholars wanted to show not only that Zen Buddhism was the best of all possible religions, but also that it was a religion beyond religion. The rough-and-ready, spontaneously enlightened Zen master, beyond all piety and doctrine, was a creation of these scholars, who depicted Zen as essentially antinomian, iconoclastic, and beyond all categories. This all sounded very good to postwar Western artists and cultural entrepreneurs, who were looking for a spirituality that fit in with their needs and preconceptions. In fact, though, these scholars were blinded by their heavy agenda. Their version of Zen, although skillfully turned out and based on brilliant textual scholarship, was never the way Zen in China or Japan had been understood or practiced—or at least this is what I learned from T. Griffith Foulk's impressive essay, "Ritual in Japanese Zen," presented in *Zen Ritual*.

All the scholars represented in this important collection of essays share a point of view: they cast doubt on the Western view of Buddhism as rational and sensible, as a path to individual spiritual fulfillment and personal growth. Buddhism in Asia, they say, has never been understood like that. In fact, Asian Buddhism has always functioned the way religion in the West has, with just as much ritual, magic, and irrational exuberance.

There's no doubt that if you read Buddhist texts—from the Zen masters' sayings to the Pali canon materials—you will find a basic philosophy and recommended practice that does lend itself to the idea of Buddhism as a sort of rational self-improvement religion. And Zen and early Buddhist texts do express, to some extent, the notion that ritual, faith, and sacrifice are to be rejected in favor of personal ethics, meditational cultivation, and transformative insight. So the early scholars, however blinded they were by their own cultural biases, were not making something up out of whole cloth. They had texts to cite.

But the essays in this book are not based on the study of sacred texts. These essays are valuable because they reflect a crucial sea change in the contemporary study of religion: a shift away from the study of what religion says it is about (as explained in sacred texts) to what religion is actually about (as discovered in historical records and sociological observation). And this turns out to be one of the most astonishing and salient facts about Buddhism and religion in general—that there is always a huge gap between what a religion says and thinks it is about, and what it is actually about. And the question of ritual, why and how it is practiced, and how important or unimportant it is lies at the center of this gap.

The contemporary Western Buddhist movement tends to be anti-ritual. Most Western Buddhist converts [I use the word "convert" to distinguish between Westerners who have taken up Buddhism and Asians living in the West, also Westerners, whose cultural background is Buddhist—but the word "convert" as understood in Judaism, Christianity, or Islam doesn't actually apply] rejected the ritualized religions they grew up with, religions in which people "just went through the motions." They come to Buddhism because it's essentially not about ritual, it's about "experience," usually identified as meditational experience. In the Vipassana movement, ritual has been eliminated altogether. In the Tibetan and Zen Buddhist movements, ritual is more likely to be practiced, but by and large only as a supplement to meditation, which is viewed as the real practice. Or if ritual is not seen as supplementary, it is practiced as another form of experiential practice; that is, practice that will "change the mind."

In thoroughly exploring the question of Buddhist ritual, both in theory and in historical practice, the ten essays in this book reject such one-dimensional views. In his introductory essay, "Rethinking Ritual Practice in Zen Buddhism," Dale S. Wright explains the "performative theory" of ritual that sees ritual as going beyond an exclusively mental or psychological orientation to transformation to one that is embodied in action of body, voice, and heart. Far from mere empty gesture, ritual can be a fuller and more developed way of practice than the personal-growth style of meditation popular among many Western Buddhists. Ritual allows for the possibility that the practitioner can go beyond merely recognizing change cognitively to practicing—manifesting—change with the whole body, mind, and heart. Performing rituals over and over again remakes the practitioner into the form of being suggested by and embodied in the ritual. Mario Poceski's essay on the Zen Dharma talk as essentially a ritual expresses this view, as does Taigen Dan Leighton's piece, "Zazen as Enactment Ritual," which shows that even meditation itself can be most effectively seen not as a technique toward a desired result but rather as the ritualized physical enactment of truth within the act of meditation itself.

The study of ritual presented in this collection brings out another limiting bias of Western Buddhism: the notion that spiritual practice is exclusively an individual affair. Though ritual is important for individual spiritual transformation, it also, and possibly more importantly, has a communal effect. Two essays in the book in particular emphasize this. Paula Arai writes of a ritual performed by Soto nuns in Japan, the *Aran Koshiki*, in which the nuns ritually offer thanks to Ananda for interceding with the Buddha on their behalf, thus establishing the original order of Buddhist women. Arai studied this ritual not in libraries, but by attending it several times (which involved long stays in nunneries) and interviewing the nuns who perform it. She found that the ritual had a profound effect on how the nuns felt about themselves as a community of practitioners, and on the position the nuns eventually came to occupy within the essentially male-dominated Soto hierarchy (they were accorded much more respect). She thus shows how ritual creates and affects community and has the capacity to influence society.

This point is further amplified in Albert Welter's essay on Eisei's "Regulations of the Zen School," a thirteenth-century document that argued for the original founding of the Zen school in Japan. The essay makes clear that the original intention behind the founding of the school was less about the production of enlightened individuals than about the promotion of the general welfare of the nation—an intention that was generally expressed in Buddhism, not only in thirteenth-century Japan but also throughout history in Asia. The idea of practicing Buddhism, or any religion, not for personal benefit but rather to promote the general welfare, sounds to me like an idea worth considering for the present.

Other essays in the book of particular interest to me were David E. Riggs's tour de force discussion on the history of *kinhin*, Zen walking meditation (its detailed textual analysis set my head spinning), and William Bodiford's discussion of Zen Dharma transmission, detailing the religious and sociological meaning that Dharma transmission has held in Zen. Bodiford also discusses a new transmission ritual created in the West in recent years and how that ritual fits in historically.

Reading this book raises two important questions for me as a religious practitioner: First, what is the use of knowing the history if what you are primarily interested in is not what religion is or has been, but rather the ways in which religious participation can give meaning to a human life? Is there any use in history at all beyond mere passing interest? There is. While one doesn't need to be an expert on religion in order to practice it, one's practice will definitely be broadened and widened by at least some knowledge of how religion has operated in the lives of individuals and societies elsewhere and at other times. Just as traveling to places or meeting people from different cultures has a direct influence on how we live, so, too, does the study of the religion of other times and places affect the way we understand and practice religion.

Second is the question of how Buddhist scholars and practitioners could best influence each other at the present time. The field of Buddhist scholarship seems to be booming in the West now. There are many good scholars, with new university programs training more every year, and these scholars are collectively building an understanding and appreciation of Buddhism that is more thorough and multidimensional than we have ever seen in history. There's a tremendous value in this for practitioners, all the more since this understanding and appreciation represents not only a fuller and more extensive view but also a completely new view, a postmodern view, that includes critique as well as celebration and that honors religion for its central place in human culture without dishonoring or denigrating—as religion has so often done—other aspects of life.

Unlike previous generations, most Buddhist scholars today began as practitioners. This gives them a real respect for the tradition, and a desire to study it not as an artifact or an absolute, but as a living thing. I have engaged in dialogue with Buddhist scholars many times, and I have always found it profitable and enjoyable. My own practice has been much influenced by these personal contacts and by my reading of scholarly material. At this crucial moment in our cultural life, in which religion is taking center stage, it seems to me that dialogue between practitioners and scholars is more important than ever, not only for Buddhists, but for all religious people. We need a sense of perspective. It is, however, unfortunately the case that there is a wariness between scholars and practitioners. Many scholars are suspicious of the historical ignorance, and therefore the naïveté, of practitioners, while many practitioners have a hard time with the scholars' sometimes too-bracing critique. This is a shame, and not good for Buddhism's possibilities as a transformative postmodern Western religion. Books like *Zen Ritual* need to be read by practitioners, especially teachers. And scholars need to be willing to share what they know at Dharma centers.

# IV

# Experience

# A Few Words About Emptiness

*This short text appears on the Everyday Zen Foundation website, http:// www.everydayzen.org.*

In Buddhist thought the concept of "emptiness" refers to deconstructed reality. The more closely you look at something, the more you see that it is not there in any substantial way; it couldn't be. In the end everything is just designation: things have a kind of reality in their being named and conceptualized, but otherwise they actually aren't there in the way we think they are. Not to understand that our designations are designations, that they do not refer to anything in particular, is to mistake emptiness.

When you look closely for anything and can't find it, you discover that although the thing itself seems to be void, there seem to be connections. You look and find nothing but everything else. That is, connection is all you find, with no things that are connected. This reminds me of a line of Joanne Kyger, something like, "I am the locus/ around which bees buzz." It's the very thoroughness of the connection—without gaps or lumps in it—only the constant nexus wherever you turn—that renders everything void. So everything is empty and connected or empty because connected. Emptiness is connection.

So, do things exist? Yes and no. Yes, in that experience does occur, and no in that the experience that occurs is radically not what you think it is. The Heart Sutra in a famous passage says there are no eyes, no ears, no nose, no tongue, no body, and no mind. This doesn't mean that the sense organs and mind don't exist; it means they don't exist as we are deeply convinced they do: as separate real fixed atomized entities. We think we "have" eyes and ears. But eyes and ears as they exist deconstructed in emptiness can't be possessed. They are inherently dispossessed, even of themselves. They exist only in action. Seeing and hearing take place. The world/self is a lived ongoing relation. Emptiness is freedom. Emptiness is belonging.

Why does any of this matter and what consequences does it have for living? Three attitudes arise as a consequence of the appreciation of emptiness:

Flexibility—since nothing is real, fixed, separate, or possess-able, what's the point of resistance?

Kindness—since everything is nothing but connection, kindness is natural.

Humility—who is going to feel like he's master of all this talk?

# Light(silence)word

*First delivered as a talk at a Jewish meditation retreat, a slightly differ-ent version of this essay was published in* Radical Poetics and Secular Jew-ish Culture *edited by S. P. Miller and D. Morris (University of Alabama Press, 2010).*

1. Light is mysterious. Both a wave and a particle, and therefore neither, light is a universal constant; neither medium nor content, light is strangely all-pervasive. Seeing anything is not so much seeing that thing as seeing the light that falls on and reflects from it; and it's not even the light that we see; we see only the light's afterglow. Light itself, per se, cannot be seen. Light activates eye and consciousness only after it has disappeared, its faded radiance bouncing off objects. Uncanny in these ways, light is in almost all religious traditions associated with the divine, the supernal, with God, with Consciousness, so much so that it seems possible that light actually is consciousness or a form of consciousness, matter a coagulation of light, light's grosser form. In Heaven, in Nirvana, in Pure Consciousness (or whatever other ethereal realm anyone would conceive of) objects with all their stubborn messiness and grossness fade away and there is only light, sheer luminosity, in its pure state.

The word "Zohar," title of the great thirteenth-century Spanish Jewish mystical text attributed to Moses de Leon, translates as "radiance." The Judaic scholar Daniel Matt has for some years now been working on the definitive English translation of Zohar (the Pritzker edition, of which four volumes have so far been released by the Stanford University Press). Volume

I of the text includes an introduction by Rabbi Arthur Green. What follows is my digest of the historical context of the text, as discussed by Green:

Kabbalah, though existent in various disorganized forms probably as early as the second century, remained a secret tradition until the twelfth century in Spain, when Kabbalistic works went public in reaction to the influence of the work of Moses Maimonides, the great physician and rationalist, probably the most influential rabbi in history. The whole of Judaism as it exists now, East and West, bears the Rambam's (as he was called) stamp. Inspired by Greek philosophy (particularly Aristotle), as mediated through Islamic culture, Maimonides thought of God as an abstruse entity, logically necessary. Like Freud (though, of course, unlike Freud, not an atheist), the Rambam saw ancient Judaism as essentially childlike and felt that with him Judaism now came to its mature form as a path of religious contemplation and ethics. The purpose of Jewish observance, according to the Rambam, was not to honor or appease God (who, it seemed obvious to him, had no need of this) but to educate, tame, and improve human beings, so that we would be capable of coming into line with the divine plan, which foresaw universal goodness and the final perfection of the world.

The Kabbalists opposed this view so bitterly they felt compelled to go public to attack it. To them, the Rambam's concept of Judaism as a gradual path of human self-improvement trivialized the tradition. In contrast, they saw Jewish daily observance as a desperately urgent mechanism for revolutionizing the cosmic order, which, in its fallen state, was perilously close to endlessly being lost, without possibility of redemption. For them, God was not an impersonal philosophically necessary entity; God was intimately, even personally, wrapped up within the world and within human contemplations, actions, and language. Especially Jewish actions and language. So that Jewish religious acts were constantly crucially critical to the fate of the universe. The burden of the Kabbalistic mythology and practice is the mysterious and direct correspondence between the world below and the world above, between human action and the divine plan. Creation had gone terribly awry from the beginning; the divine sparks had broken through their vessels and plunged into the darkness of the world; it was up to Jews to raise the sparks up on behalf of the entire human race and the cosmic order. Where the Rambam and his followers were patiently and wisely hopeful, the Kabbalists were constantly urgently grasping at straws.

In discussing this historical background to the Zohar, Arthur Green writes: "to know God is a necessary condition of proper worship—on this the Kabbalists agree with the philosophers [ie. Rambam and his followers]." Of course the two camps differed radically as to the significance of the phrase "knowing God." The philosophers understood intellectual contemplation of teaching and creation as the path to knowledge of God; for the Kabbalists knowing God meant mystical union, achieved mainly through language-based ecstatic concentration practices.

The Kabbalists were obsessed with language. They were not interested merely in analysis, contemplation, and interpretation. Study for them was not a rational act. Instead, every word of text masked hidden depths that revealed operations crucial to the salvation of the world on a moment to moment basis; and every word was related not only to every other word of text but to everything else throughout the whole of the mundane and supernal realms. Things of the world were, in their essence, also "words" (in Hebrew *devar* means both "word" and "thing"), because God had, after all, in the most hidden of all parts of the Bible, *Bereshit* ("In the beginning" the Jewish name for Genesis, and the main subject of the Zohar) created the physical universe exactly by uttering words. What was the nature of God-speech, God-word? And how did it relate to human speech, in which it lay hidden?

The Torah, it was said, was written in light. Every letter was light. And within this light all mysteries were contained. The Book was the world, the world was the Book. To those who then and now complain that the Torah is a primitive text, full of the violence and vindictiveness of a terrified people and a terrible God, the Kabbalists had little to say; they knew otherwise, but how could one explain, for without faith, spiritual practice, and intimate knowledge, what could be understood? They knew that certainly the Torah was not saying only what it seemed to be saying, what the black letters on white seemed to indicate; it was saying that and everything else, in multifaceted, ineffable ways. The words, the letters, were fire; the page was burning. (In an essay on Buber's vision of Chasidism, Kenneth Rexroth, who felt that the Bible was the most destructive text ever written, said that the Chasidim had managed to read the Bible in such a way that it said exactly the opposite of what it actually did say; Rexroth was seemingly both right and wrong about this.) Behind every letter of the text, every infinite pinpoint of light, lay universe upon universe.

Long before the medieval Kabbalists, the rabbis of the Talmud saw the profundity of the biblical text, which they had fashioned into a substitute for the cult of the now-destroyed Temple. Judaism had for centuries been a cult of ritual action; it now became a cult of the book, into which all the mysterious efficacy of ritual action had disappeared. The Talmudists saw that the book therefore could not be merely what it seemed to be. Words could not merely be words. Each was subject to infinite interpretation, and there were infinite approaches to interpretation. Within these infinite approaches, the tradition delineated four: *Peshat*, the plain meaning, what the text seemed to be saying on the surface; *Remes*, the level of linguistic correspondence and textual operation through which completely unexpected meanings could be derived; *Drash*, the vast literature of legends and stories that purported to tell incidents and details (many quite anachronistic and clearly manufactured to suit situations long lost to history) that had been left out of the highly elliptical original text; and *Sod*, the level of mystical vision, trance, dreams, visitations, etc. (There are various interpretations and glosses on these four levels; the foregoing is my own, based on reading in various sources.) Together the four (PRDS) spell the Hebrew *pardes*, "garden," or "Paradise."

PARDES

The trees bear fruit, the book
Binds
Like water brimming in the pitcher's
Poured out steady till no drop's left
By a firm hand, an outstretched arm,
The book bears them on through the storm
Tree tops twisting, stripped debris shattered
In the violent nights
Though the fruit's sweet lingers on the tongue
Like melody—
That's the plain meaning

Beyond that and embedded in it
Like seeds in a winter earth
(Officially only a thin layer
Atop a hard dark mystery below
Exactly as deep as the plow turns)
The meaning-fingers splayed forth

Like hairy roots laterally
Entangling other letters, heterodox tales, bits and strands

(The third level now)
Of lives, songs, opinions, certainties
Wild stories, rewordings, revisions
Attempts to harmonize or humanize
Upheaval, sickness, fierce mistaken force
The worm in the infinite, how sky
Reflects the turmoil of the sea
The soul's own sequential poisoning
In its reversing desire to crawl out
Of its own skin, like the famous snake
That spoke for it in the orchard
That had no hands to touch with, to grasp

Then the inner turning
The quiet of snow falling on rock and twig
With a hush beyond speculation and thinking
A meaning pressed only into breathing
Or illuminated by the speechless waters
That suck underground
Into the capillary rootlets opening beneath the feet
In the winding uncharted journey of footsteps
From one point of darkness to the next

—Norman Fischer, originally published in *Five Fingers Review*

The Zohar is a Kabbalistic commentary on Torah but also a fiction, a novel, the adventures of Rabbi Shimon bar Yochai, a second-century rabbi from the Galilee, and his small band of disciples who offer the commentary in discussions that take place as they wander around the Holy Land meeting various people. They usually discuss sitting outdoors by a brook or in a garden. A feature of the text is their constant delight in one another and in the various interpretations that they espouse. Almost certainly there was in thirteenth-century Spain a similar group of disciples surrounding Moses de Leon. A key theme of the Zohar is light, light and darkness: the disciples arose for study at midnight, a thin thread of light going out into the world emanating from their words and feelings. A "thread-thin ray of love" (Matt) that reverberates seven centuries later in Paul Celan's holo-caust-inflected "thread-suns," thin light rays of hope, that leak out of books and words even still.

The symbolic edifice of Kabbalism is prodigious and esoteric, and I don't know enough about it to say much here. Suffice it to say that the system references the stage by stage emanations from *Ayn Sof*, the beyond beyond the beyond, into this world below through many supernal stages, the descent of the ineffable through light that illuminates this world: phys-ical light, but also the light of human divinity and human goodness, which is a reflection of the divine. Ayn Sof ("without end") is beyond light and dark; it is endless formless unknowable indefinable, beyond being and non-being. Yet within Ayn Sof, for no reason, there occurs an impulse toward light. This impulse creates an energy that leads to the first of the ten *Sphi-rot* (emanations), which is *Keter*, "crown," "circle," or *Ayin*, "nothing" (Ayn Sof being more nothing than nothing): a point of light that is completely surrounded by darkness, and this long before the world, even before what we call God (also an emanation of Ayn Sof) had come to be; a point of light that is, essentially, hidden. This becomes a key Kabbalistic theme, conceal-ment, hiddenness. It led to theologies like those of the Marranos (Spanish secret Jews) and the Sabbatians (followers of the seventeenth-century "false messiah" who converted to Islam): to be a Jew concealed in the world is to manifest and imitate the concealed divine light. So that outward conver-sion to Islam or Christianity, while inwardly remaining Jewish, came to be viewed as the highest and most God-like of all paths.

In all this we can see germs of nearly all of avant-garde writing's chief themes: revolt against the polite, rational, Aristotelian order of things; fo-cus on language not as conduit of communication but as infinitely suggest-ible medium that writes the world; concealment, hiddenness, obscurity, exile; intertextuality; resistance to closure and the univocal interpreting self. The world is hidden within language; words conceal rather than reveal meaning, meaning as meaning being essentially concealed, the not said contained in the said, the written writing the unwritten, etc.

2. The word "Zen" is a Japanese transliteration of the Sanskrit word *dhyana*, which means meditative absorption. The Zen schools of Buddhism empha-size meditative absorption above all else. A cursory, or even a deeper, look at Zen literature and practice will surely suggest that language per se is not

only irrelevant to Zen but that Zen is dismissive of, if not hostile to, language. A common early Chinese phrase to indicate the essential and unique position of Zen is usually translated "beyond words and letters." Language in Zen is "a finger pointing at the moon." In Zen it's silence, not language's constant noise-making, that gets to the heart of reality.

The most famous discussion of silence in Zen literature centers on a koan that is actually a quotation from the Vimalakirti Nirdesa Sutra:

> Vimalakirti asked Manjushri, "What is the bodhisattva's method of entering nonduality?"
>
> Manjushri said, "According to my mind, in all things, no speech, no explanation, no direction, and no representation, leaving behind all questions and answers—this is the method of entering nonduality."
>
> Then Manjushri asked Vimalakirti, "We have all spoken. Now you should say, good man, what is a bodhisattva's method of entry into nonduality?"
>
> Vimalakirti was silent.

Manjushri's explanation that explanation, speech, representation are all to be let go of apparently doesn't go far enough, for he is still talking. Vimalakirti goes him one better by saying absolutely nothing. In Zen, Vimalakirti's silence is referred to as "thunderous," and there is much discussion about its nature. Though the word "silence" might suggest a singular experience, in fact there are many possible silences: passive silence, silence of withdrawal, angry silence, confused silence, enigmatic silence, manipulative silence. My silence is not the same as yours. Vimalakirti's thunderous silence is taken as an ultimate sort of silence, a silence which expresses, without expression, the highest, most complete, most inclusive form of truth, beyond which there is no other.

The Jewish tradition, so wordy in all ways, also has a teaching about such an all-inclusive silence. When God gave the Ten Commandments on Mount Sinai, the scene was, as depicted in the Bible, noisy and dramatic: the smoking blazing mountain, the terrifying presence, the deafening noise, thunder, horns blaring, and so on. But the rabbis of the Talmud explained that this deafening noise was actually a total and utter silence. They said that at the exact center of the noise was the most silent moment that had ever existed on earth: not even an animal stirred; there was no wind; and most amazing of all, there was no human speech commenting on the silence.

Lest we frustrate ourselves in an effort to hear such a silence (are "silence" and "hearing" even compatible?), it will be good to remember two things: first, as John Cage famously discovered, it is impossible for a living human being to experience silence (there will always be, at least, the sounds of heartbeat and nervous system); and second, that Vimalakirti's silence is a "nondualistic" silence, which is to say that it is not a silence opposed to noise, but like the silence of the Talmudic vision of Sinai, a silence which defines not a particular object of listening (or absence of object) but instead points to something essential within any listening. It is a silence, therefore, which is not opposed to, or defined as different from, sound, and therefore language. It is the silence within rather than outside words and phrases. Like the vast spaces inside atoms, without which what we call the "solid" world could not exist, silence makes words possible.

In fact, the notion that language is in this sense beyond language (i.e. that it contains at its heart, of necessity, silence) is one of the chief insights and practice pathways of Zen. What is Zen koan practice, after all, if not the practice of discerning the silence within phrases; meditating, that is, not "beyond" phrases, but within and through them to meanings unrestricted by the apparent linguistic limitations of the words. That is, what at first may seem in Zen to be a bias against language in favor of "silence," or in any case, activities (like meditation) that do not seem to be language-based, is in fact a view of language, a practice of language.

Nowhere is this clearer than in the writings of thirteenth-century Zen Master Dogen, much appreciated these days by Western philosophers concerned with language. Hee Jin Kim, in *Dogen on Meditation and Thinking, a Reflection on His View of Zen (State University of New York, 2006)*, observed: "The single most original and seminal aspect of Dogen's Zen is his treatment of the role of language in Zen soteriology. We moderns may pride ourselves on our acute language consciousness in the twentieth and twenty-first centuries, but Dogen was no less aware. He is similar to us in this regard. . . ." (p. 59). Dogen was the rare Zen master who was as much a literary practitioner as he was a religious figure, and his text Shobogenzo (*Treasury of the True Dharma Eye*), a multivolume work, is considered a key text in Japanese literary, as well as religious, history. In his writings, Dogen constantly excoriates those Zen adepts who are critical of language, pointing to "silence" or other extra-linguistic positions, as Zen's goal. Over and over, Dogen expresses his dissatisfaction with this essentially unsophisticated, dualistically unnuanced, and in his view, religiously destructive understanding. Like other Zen thinkers, Dogen saw language as the prison from which we seek freedom. But unlike them, he saw that the way out of this prison (from which there is no escape) is to be found within the prison itself. In other words, language's hold on us can be loosed only by language itself. For Dogen, human beings must live within language, which is, as Heidegger put it, our "house of being," the constituent of essential humanness. The way out of the house is the full occupation of it, with awareness of its nature, so that in the end resistance is transformed into celebration. Kim quotes Dogen as saying, "The monastics of future generations will be able to understand one-taste Zen (*ichimizen*) based on words and letters if they devote their efforts to spiritual practice by seeing the universe through words and letters, and words and letters through the universe. . . . How pitiful are they who are unaware that discriminative thought is words and phrases and that words and phrases liberate discriminative thought" (pp. 60, 62).

In his discussion of Dogen's view of Zen, Kim delineates seven literary techniques with which Dogen endeavors to deconstruct conventional Zen and Buddhist language, so as to turn restrictive pious understandings inside-out. Like the Chasidic masters, who make liberal use of linguistic sleights of hand (reference to word-roots, gematria, etc.), Dogen employs strikingly postmodern operations to produce texts so dense that they are from time to time incomprehensible. The seven techniques are (1) transposition of lexical components (an almost mathematical mechanical shifting of words or phrases in repetitive sentences, so that all possible, if sometimes apparently nonsensical, syntactic combinations are played out); (2) semantic reconstruction through syntactic change (often making use of the differences in grammar between Chinese—into which Buddhist texts that Dogen read had been translated—and the Japanese in which he was writing, to yield unique meanings); (3) explication of semantic attributes (making often punning or contraindicated use of the multiple meanings possible within Chinese ideographs); (4) reflexive, self-causative utterances (in which statements and their opposites are identified, or the bald assertion of nonsequiturs upon which arguments are based); (5) upgrading commonplace notions and using neglected metaphors (using obsolete meanings buried in contemporary words, leaning on ordinary expressions to yield surprising correspondences, emphasizing commonplace throwaway words); (6) use of homophonous expressions (not unlike Zukofsky's *Catullus*); and (7) reinterpretation based on the principle of nonduality (in which clearly dualistic statements in the tradition are interpreted as though they were not dualistic). Through these and other methods, Dogen relentlessly deconstructs the Zen and Buddhist traditions—as he believed they had been meant to be deconstructed—for the purpose of restoring to language and ordinary everyday reality the potential, dignity, and sense of wonder he believed they deserved. Dogen's project as a writer and religious teacher was to work against the perennial distinction religion (and language) inevitably wants to make between "holiness" and "the everyday." He believed this erroneous distinction to be the root of all human anguish. Kim explains:

> Language thinking and reason constitute the key to both zazen and koan study within Dogen's praxis-oriented Zen. The koan's and zazen's function is not to excoriate and abandon the intellect and its words and letters, but rather to liberate and restore them in the Zen enterprise. In short, enlightenment is not brought about by direct intuition (or transcendent wisdom) supplanting the intellect and its tools, but in and through their collaboration and corroboration in search of the expressible in deeds, words, and thoughts for a given situation (religious and secular). (p. 78)

3. Where does all this leave language's capacity to describe reality? And where does it leave the possibility of a soteriologically efficacious understanding? That is, recognizing the silence of words, are we left speechless? And recognizing the impossibility of going beyond words, are we doomed to mouth them to our continued distress and confusion?

In a world in which we are all "dim-sighted" (Dogen's phrase), nothing could be more dim-sighted than to assert that one is not dim-sighted; and such an assertion could be none other than a projection of the very dim-sightedness itself. The way out of this trap would be to make use of the dim-sightedness (language, human perception) to see the nature of the very dim-sightedness, and in doing so, to proceed, with full appreciation of the process of becoming human, which always involves the practice of language.

It has often been remarked, and written about (I myself have written about it), that Jews frequently find themselves practicing in Buddhist centers, and that Buddhist centers are disproportionately Jewish. The foregoing understandings of language, light, and silence might provide a clue: that Jews (or at least some subset of Jews) have been spiritually and culturally immersed in language in a particular key—language whose tonalities bear the ineffable senses of light, of silence, of depth. Most modern Jews, long removed from traditional Jewish educational systems, can only dimly hear these tonalities, though they are echoed perhaps most strongly in postmodern literary expressions, which, as we have seen, seem to be so basically Jewish in character. But for the average Jewish person, the tradition's riches are, so to speak, a closed book; deep and personal familiarity with Jewish texts and the sensibilities behind them have long been lost; and in any case it is likely that there never has been a deeply satisfying way of Jewish life and learning that was not inherently incompatible with modern cultural life, which is to say a way of Jewish life that was not of necessity cut off from the dominant culture in which it found itself. It is an odd historical fact that Buddhist meditation practice, appearing as it does in the West all but divorced from its Asian cultural contexts, and therefore to some extent a tabula rasa, to be filled in with whatever soul-stirrings may be vaguely felt by those who access it, carries echoes of those ancient Jewish tonalities, so that the essentially Jewish linguistic moves can be activated within the "silence."

Silence is no weakness of language.
It is, on the contrary, its strength.
It is the weakness of words not to know this.

—Edmond Jabes, *Book of Shares*, p. 31

# The Violence of Oneness

*This essay, here updated, was first published in 2002, in* Enough, *a magazine edited by Leslie Scalapino and Judith Goldman.*

In his book *The Theory of Religion*, translated by Robert Hurley (Zone Books, 1992), Georges Bataille analyzes the arising of human consciousness as it emerges out of animal consciousness and shows how religious sensibility necessarily develops from this. His argument goes like this:

The animal world is a world of pure being, a world of immediacy and immanence. The animal soul is like "water in water," seamlessly connected to all that surrounds it, so that there is no sense of self or other, of time, of space, of being or not being. This utopian (to human sensibility, which has such alienating notions) Shangri-La or Eden actually isn't that because it is characterized at all points by what we'd call violence. Animals, that is, eat and are eaten. For them killing and being killed is the norm; and there isn't any meaning to such a thing, or anything that we would call fear; there's no concept of killing or being killed. There's only being, immediacy, "isness." Animals don't have any need for religion; they already are that, already transcend life and death, being and nonbeing, self and other, in their very living, which is utterly pure.

Bataille sees human consciousness beginning with the making of the first tool, the first "thing" that isn't a pure being, intrinsic in its value and inseparable from all of being. A tool is a separable, useful, intentionally made thing; it can be possessed, and it serves a purpose. It can be altered to suit that purpose. It is instrumental, defined by its use. The tool is the first instance of the "not-I," and with its advent there is now the beginning of a world of objects, a "thing" world. Little by little out of this comes a way of thinking and acting within thingness (language), and then once this plane of thingness is established, more and more gets placed upon it—other objects, plants, animals, other people, one's self, a world. Now there is self and other—and then, paradoxically, self becomes other to itself, alienated not only from the rest of the projected world of things, but from itself, which it must perceive as a thing, a possession. This constellation of an alienated self is a double-edged sword: seeing the self as a thing, the self can for the first time know itself and so find a closeness to itself; prior to this, there isn't any self so there is nothing to be known or not known. But the creation of my me, though it gives me for the first time myself as a friend, also rips me out of the world and puts me out on a limb on my own. Interestingly, and quite logically, this development of human consciousness coincides with a deepening of the human relationship to the animal world, which opens up to the human mind now as a depth, a mystery. Humans are that depth, because humans are animals, know this and feel it to be so, and yet also not so; humans long for union with the animal world of immediacy, yet know they are separate from it. Also they are terrified of it, for to reenter that world would be a loss of the self; it would literally be the end of me as I know me.

In the midst of this essential human loneliness and perplexity, which is almost unbearable, religion appears. It intuits and imagines the ancient world of oneness, of which there is still a powerful primordial memory, and calls it the sacred. This is the invisible world, world of spirit, world of the gods, or of God. It is inexorably opposed to, defined as the opposite of, the world of things, the profane world of the body, of instrumentality, a world of separation, the fallen world. Religion's purpose then is to bring us back to the lost world of intimacy, and all its rites, rituals, and activities are created to this end. We want this, and need it, as sure as we need food and shelter; and yet it is also terrifying. All religions have known and been based squarely on this sense of terrible necessity.

Religion wants to find a way to do this work without destroying the human world, for religion is a product of human communication, and therefore human society. Its job is to preserve the tragedy of our humanness, our selfhood, while at the same time comforting it and bringing it to wholeness through a direct encounter with the divine. It does this through carefully proscribed rite and ritual, which was all over the world in earliest times the same: the ritual of the sacrifice, which is the hieratic return to the world of intimacy, beyond time and self and other. To sacrifice is to take something that exists in the world of thingness and duration and bring it back to intimacy, to erase it from the plane of thingness and return it to the plane of immediacy. Sacrifice is conceived of as gift, gratuity, a paying back to God or the gods of what had been primordially given so that the world of thingness, of which all individuals are a part, could come to be and will only continue to be as long as the rite of sacrifice is reciprocally maintained. In other words, sacrifice involves evoking the intimacy of death, which only appears as such from the standpoint of the world of thingness. From the standpoint of the world of intimacy and immediacy, there is no such thing as death; there is only the eternal presence, which includes all absence. Only when there are things can there be their absence, and in their absence they return eternally to the world from which they came.

(This is more or less what Bataille says. I have probably shaped his argument to my own ends, but I am sure he would not mind. As he says in his introduction to *The Theory*, literary productions are not edifices, they are construction sites.)

I am evoking all of these thoughts to make the point that religion is inherently a dangerous and tragic business, a tricky business. Efforts to domesticate it have not been successful, as far as I am concerned; all attempts to make religion into something nice, something good, something harmless and polite, rob it of its vitality. It soon becomes irrelevant and uninteresting; other things look more compelling. So no, religion's difficulty is removed only at the cost of its very life. Instead of this very natural effort to make things easier (which accounts for the history of religions over the last few hundred years), we should rather admit that there is tremendous anguish in the human heart, that it goes with the territory, tremendous senses of loss and violation, grief and longing that will not be overcome by peaceful sweet means. It will take stronger medicine.

In the light of all this, I think of the terrorists of September 11, 2001, only the most extreme in a long line of religious warriors in various traditions who saw their own deaths and the deaths of their enemies as holy events, events of purification and intimacy, ultimate religious moments. We all understand rational war, as much as we don't like it, the strategic deployment of troops and materiel to defeat an enemy whose interests oppose our own and who can't be negotiated with or persuaded in any other way. War employed as a last resort by strong nations when they can't find any other way to further their necessary agendas. But 9/11 was not that; it was shocking exactly in its seeming irrationality: the obscene and sudden dramatic destruction of innocent lives for no discernible reason. (Yes, of course there were strong grievances, but rationally speaking, at least from the point of view of normal Western logic, how could the terror of September 11 realistically affect any of that?) So this act was impossible to understand from any coherent point of view. It can only be understood as a religious act, an act that strikes to the heart of religion's essence—the sacrifice of life, the hurling of it into the abyss of timelessness, toward God.

Using our own religious rhetoric (of which most of us, especially our national leaders, seem to have a crude understanding), we call these acts and their perpetrators "evil," perhaps enhancing, by some deep psychic logic, the pain and power of them. Calling them evil, however, doesn't really mean that, because we don't know what the word "evil" actually suggests. What we are really saying is, "I don't understand such a thing. A human being as far as I know what a human being is could never do such a thing. Therefore, these people are not human, they don't exist." To view the September 11 events in that way, that is, without any understanding of them, is to strengthen the energy that caused them to happen in the first place. Aside from the cultural, political, and economic factors that gave rise to them, but do not, in my view, explain them, there is their religious power—in making the sacrifice that these men made, they were returning to Oneness, and in doing so, affirming the power and ultimacy of their being.

(Many have pointed out that it is shortsighted to see the actors of September 11 as "terrorists," as if the far more destructive acts of nations, beginning with our own, of invasion, intimidation, bombing of innocent civilians, and so on were not also terrorism, and a worse form of terrorism. This might be so, and yet these political acts appear to me to be different—not worse, but different—from those that are so spectacularly religiously motivated. And as a religiously committed person, I am more disturbed by destructive religious acts, and have a greater need to understand them. Acts of atrocity that are committed by nations rationally for their own self-interest—which usually means the self-interest of those social classes that control them—seem fairly easy to understand, at least superficially.)

In honoring these acts by calling them "religious" (and I do not even say "fundamentalist"), I am not condoning or excusing them but only pointing out that they are not far from the actual brilliant heart of what is important, even essential, about religion. This is exactly what makes them so disturbing to me. It is also why, we have to admit, much of the Islamic world, though it may condemn the acts, understands them and appreciates them as we cannot. These acts have profoundly affected us not so much because of the numbers killed, and not even because of the lurid symbolism of their target, but precisely because they were religious acts, committed at a time when religion is more important and more problematic than it ever has been. Just at the moment (with globalization and the technocritization of the planet) when secularism and universal materialism seem completely on the ascendant, these acts blaze across the sky the ultimate religious message: that life, certainly one's own, and others' as well, is more than the sum of its parts, more than the body, more than the physical, more even than the psychological—that life, the ultimate reality of human life, spills outside the boundaries of life, and that it must be seen that way if it is to be meaningful.

What I am saying here is that Osama bin Laden and the Islamic thinkers whose pronouncements and interpretations back him up, have to be heard and appreciated on their own terms. It's crucial that they be, for they are saying something that all of us need desperately to hear: that the world has gone wrong, is blind and out of control; that we need to emphasize less what we have and want, and more what we are and aren't. Only by hearing this message and honoring it, looking deeply into it with our own souls, will we be able to see precisely how the so-called terrorists are wrong and why they are wrong. They believe in eternal human truths that are reducible to texts and doctrines that can be understood literally. They believe that it is permissible to sacrifice life in the service of these eternal truths. They believe (although their religion is modern) that it is possible to return to ancient faiths in apparently ancient ways. But all of this is wrong. It won't produce the results they seek. It will only lead to the deification of violence and therefore to the strangling of the human heart—it won't produce Oneness, submission to Allah; it will make more separation, more anguish, more greed, more confusion, more uncertainty—as the events and historical currents of the decade since 9/11 have shown.

It is now necessary, I think, to find a spirituality that isn't merely synthetic or polite, that is committed, difficult, real, perplexing, costly, and satisfying. This spirituality may or may not be based on ancient traditions, but if it is, it has to be those traditions understood anew—deeply anew. In the conclusion of his book, which he calls "to whom," Bataille calls for "the positing of a religious attitude that would result from clear consciousness" and would be a necessity for people "*for whom human life is an experience to be carried as far as possible. . . .* And if we raise ourselves personally to the highest degree of clear consciousness," he says, "it is no longer the servile thing in us, but rather the *sovereign*, whose presence in the world, from head to foot, from animality to science, and from the archaic tool to the non-sense of poetry, is that of universal humanity."

# On God for Sue

*When Sue Moon was guest-editing "the God issue" for the Buddhist magazine* Inquiring Mind, *she asked me for a piece. I told her I had nothing to say on the subject and she said, "Well, suppose I ask you some questions, would you answer them?" I said I would, and the piece below is the result, published in the fall of 2003.*

SUE: *When you were a child growing up in an observant Jewish home, how did you feel about God? Was God important to you?*

NORMAN: My impression of belief in God in Judaism—at least the way I grew up Jewish—is that it isn't a question. It was never discussed because it wouldn't have made sense to discuss it. It was just assumed—deeply assumed. The ideas of "belief" and "faith" seem to be inherently Christian concepts—because Christianity does have a complicated and interesting doctrine of faith. And "belief" is an important word in Christianity. But growing up, we had no such idea. Judaism was identity and praxis—that is, you *were* Jewish whether you liked it or not: if you tried to escape being Jewish, eventually you'd be found out, so there was no use denying it. It was for better or worse a fact of life. Like being a man or a woman. And then if you *were* Jewish, you *did* Jewish, that is, you went to synagogue, observed kashrut, and so on. So God wasn't an issue; God was just a basic assumption that had to do with being Jewish. You were you; ergo God was God. Something like that. To tell the truth, this still seems true to me.

As a child, the way it seemed true to me (and still does!) had to do with the strangeness of the experience of being alive: literally perceiving, feeling, thinking, and so on. The world just seemed strange. This must have to do with God, was the reasoning. So, for instance, walking to synagogue holding my dad's hand, seeing the sparkling substance, whatever it was, dazzling in the sidewalk as we glided by. How else would that be possible if not God?

In Judaism as I knew it, there was no theology: there were just stories. You read the Torah every week in shuel and you knew the stories. These were stories about God and about people trying to engage God—not because they believed but because God was involved in their lives as a fact: experientially. Clearly these were stories. Not exactly historically true: more true than that. There was no end to trying to understand what they meant. This was obvious. The stories assumed God. It all made sense to me at the time. I remember being very small and listening to a recording of Bible stories. God spoke in a booming baritone male voice—very intimidating, very frightening. I used to hide under the table. On the other hand, it was thrilling, and I listened to this record again and again.

SUE: *How did your sense of God change when you were a young man?*

NORMAN: As I grew up, my sense of God didn't particularly change. I studied religion and philosophy and of course became sophisticated in my way of thinking and speaking about God. I no longer believed (but I don't think I ever did) that God was watching over and protecting us in some spatial and anthropomorphic way. But somehow this increased sophistication did not touch my earliest ideas about religion, God, and so on. It just seemed like I was learning more and more developed ways of thinking about what I knew all along. Now I *do* believe in the benevolent protection of God. Not in the sense that good things will always come to good people whom God loves, but in the sense that something always happens, and that what happens is what it is and not something else—and that therefore there is a special virtue in it—whether or not we discover the virtue is our problem. That seems to me to be ample evidence of God's tremendous compassion and grace. We can absolutely depend on it!

SUE: *When you began to practice Zen, did you think about God? Did you miss God? Were you glad to be done with God?*

NORMAN: When I started to practice Zen it was like when I stopped going to synagogue and began chasing girls and playing sports as my primary obsessions: that is, I didn't think, "Oh this religion stuff is no good, I quit." I just went on to the next thing that naturally called to me, assuming that the religion stuff was still relevant and would still be there when I needed it. I guess I had an enormous confidence in my sense of Jewish identity, backed up by God. It seems I didn't think I needed to tend to it, that I could move on to whatever was next and it would all be okay. When I started to practice Zen, it was like that: my explorations had led me to Zen naturally and this is what I was going to give myself to—with the same kind of full-on hysteria that I'd given myself to the great American triumvirate of baseball, football, basketball—and girls. Now it was Zen. But I didn't miss God or wonder whether I was abandoning God or God was abandoning me. I figured (or rather, I didn't figure, I just assumed without thinking about it) God would always be around. Because when you think about it, if God is, as I had assumed, simply embedded in the strange and uncanny fact of existence, then how could God *not* always be part of the equation? The fact that God is officially not an issue in Buddhism—or is, in some forms of Buddhism, apparently denied—didn't trouble me at all. Different language game. No problem. Anyway, Zen seems not to be invested in denying the idea of God. Suzuki Roshi mentions God several times in *Zen Mind, Beginner's Mind*, with apparent approval.

SUE: *Did you return to your Jewish practice after you were a Zen practitioner/ teacher, or was it always there?*

NORMAN: I didn't practice Judaism much when I began doing Zen. I was living in a Zen temple and it was a very full life, no time for it. But when our kids were old enough, we did seders and other stuff, and then when my mother died in 1985, I wanted to say Kaddish (prayer for the dead said in synagogue for eleven months after a parent dies) for her so I went to a synagogue in Tiburon, the nearest place to where I lived at Green Gulch, and told the rabbi who I was (a Zen priest by then) and why I wanted to be there. He said okay; he was a very nice man. And I got involved with regular attendance there, with my mother in mind. Then in 1990, my dear and now departed friend Rabbi Alan Lew returned to the Bay Area, and from then on, I began doing a lot of Jewish practice with him. We started a Jewish meditation center, Makor Or, that I still direct and teach at. I learned a lot from him, a tremendous opportunity, and he got me to study a lot, which I still enjoy. Judaism is so great, so fascinating. So I actually have quite a lot to do with Judaism.

SUE: *How does your Jewish meditation practice frame the idea of God? Is there any conflict with your Zen practice? Do you speak about God freely in the context of Jewish meditation and Makor Or?*

NORMAN: Our Jewish meditation theory is that God is presence, presence both within and beyond your life (within and beyond turn out to be completely mutually implicated, when you look closely). And that while Judaism knows this and Jewish practice is meant to foster it, in fact most contemporary Jews do not have access to the richness of God-encounter that Judaism contains—even often those who are observant. (Because a major motivation for Jewish observance is to strengthen the community—which is not only reasonable and salutary; it is also self-protective conditioning from a long history of oppression.) This is where the meditation comes in—it is easy access to God-encounter—through encountering your own body, breath, mind, and presence. I speak of God all the time at Makor Or—and sometimes at Everyday Zen, too.

SUE: *What, if anything, did you tell your children about God?*

NORMAN: I communicated to my children what my parents communicated to me—God is obvious, necessary, and ubiquitous. It is not a matter of belief or faith. And you don't need the word "God" if it seems to cause you problems. After all, does it make sense that God would be limited to positive feelings about a three-letter word in the English language, and that if you had a problem somehow with that word (because maybe where you live it is socially unacceptable) that God ceased to exist for you? No, this makes no sense! There is no doubt there is more to life than meets the eye, more to being alive than the material world. In fact, there is more to the material world than the material world! What is this "more" if not God? It's also fine to call it something else. As to the question of God as personal: as the French Jewish philosopher Emmanuel Levinas once said, "Of course God is personal, because we are persons."

SUE: *Do you pray? To whom do you pray?*

NORMAN: I pray all the time. To God. I am asking God to help out with this and that, mostly friends who are ill, people who have died, the crazy messed-up sad and foolish world. Please help with all this, God, as I know you will. I am never disappointed with God's active response. Because I know what to expect. And I am thanking God a lot for almost everything.

SUE: *Have you had moments of feeling directly connected to God?*

NORMAN: I usually feel directly connected to God. I'm alive and I can tell I am alive.

SUE: *What is God like?*

NORMAN: God is like being alive—like life, like being, which of necessity involves death and not being—which is where the God part comes into it.

SUE: *Do you think about God in connection with death? Do you think people go to God when they die?*

NORMAN: I think that, yes, death is the mother of God—or vice versa. So of course when you die, there's nothing left but God—no more resistance.

SUE: *What is your responsibility as a Zen teacher in talking to students (like me) who yearn for God, or to other students who come to Zen relieved that at last they don't have to "believe in God"?*

NORMAN: I try not to think too much about my responsibility as a Zen teacher. As you know, I resist the idea of myself as a Zen teacher. It seems like such a trap—for me and for anyone else who practices Zen with me. I always think of the old koan "There are no teachers of Zen; I don't say there is no Zen, just no teachers of Zen." There are roles to occupy, and I have mine; everyone has his or hers. I am interested in responding honestly to anyone I meet, as far as I can understand that person, and the life I have lived, in the practice. I hope it helps but I never really know. If it does help, the reason is not my wisdom and brilliance; it is the luck (you could also call it karma) that will produce some fruitful encounter between two people meeting in the middle of a dazzlingly complicated world. Since I am sensitive to language because of my long-standing poetry habit, I usually do not get caught up in debating with someone about their choice of words. I think useful truth is in the meaning, not the words. The art is to find the words to indicate something to this person now. Speaking of which, I'll close with a poem from my 2004 collection, *Slowly But Dearly*.

## HOW GOD GETS INTO IT

God arrives in the transitions—
the times between before and after
the shatterings, bendings, breakings
moments of devilment and blasted pose—
The feeling then arises, a draft in the system
tiny shaft of light in the visual field
which, when noticed and affirmed,
opens out to an aura on the screen of eclectic ineffability—
One's arms open in quietude and perplexity
There's nothing to say, do, or think

# Hank Lazer–Norman Fischer Interview, July 2010

*Hank Lazer has been a colleague and friend for some years. This interview, conducted via e-mail, was published in* The Argotist Online *at http://www. argotistonline.co.uk/Fischer%20interview.htm.*

HANK: *I'd like to hear, Norman, about your experiences in the San Francisco Bay Area in the 1970s, particularly your friendships with various Bay Area Language Poets. What I'd like to explore is the story of your early involvement in poetry, from your schooling at the University of Iowa's MFA program, to early Language days in the Bay Area, to your turn toward intense training in Zen Buddhist practice. Did the training in Zen take you away from the Bay Area poetry writing community for a period of time? Did you continue writing poetry during your early training in Zen?*

NORMAN: Good question. This would be a 500-page memoir about my life and the lives of my friends in San Francisco in the early 1970s (see *Grand Piano*). But I could never write that memoir because most of this stuff I hardly remember; it is mixed up in my mind. I seem not to have much of a sense of history, personal or otherwise, though I am very interested in history, and the past, as a proposition. The 1970s: those were the days of tremendous freedom and so tremendous change. We did not know what we were doing, and the possibilities, and the various necessities, were almost endless. People coming and going all the time so that I think now it is nearly impossible to keep track. I graduated from college in 1968 and went immediately to Iowa City, where I was a student in the Writers'

Workshop. I had written prose in college. Poetry was not that interesting to me; I found it difficult to understand, and it struck me as overelaborate. I did not come from an educated background; I had a very commonsense view of reality. So poetry was odd, but prose made sense and that is what I wrote, under the influence of my undergraduate writing teacher Frederick Busch, who was a good young writer at the time and continued to write well. I always appreciated Fred and stayed in touch with him for a while. I had a lot of theories about writing, and Fred would always say, forget the theories, just write something. I found out, just this year, that Fred had died a few years ago. I was reading something and it referred to "the late Frederick Busch," so it was a bit of a shock to me, realizing I had never got around to reconnecting with him and that now I never would. Howard Fineman, who is always on television (he is a political pundit for MSNBC and senior Washington editor of *Newsweek*) was also, as I recall, writing prose in those days, and was one of the small circle of us around Fred. Anyway, all this explains why I went to Iowa City and was a fiction student. But it didn't work out very well. I came to Iowa City with the idea of participating in a community of serious writers who were interested in language, in experimentation, in meaning, in thinking, and so on. But no one there seemed to be interested in any of that. They were almost all older than I was, and what they were interested in was finding agents and making connections. From my present perspective, this doesn't seem so bad or so surprising. It makes sense. But at the time I was completely bewildered by it. To me a party was a party; you went there to see your friends. At Iowa there were a lot of parties whose purpose was not to see your friends but rather to network and so on, to get someplace. People were very experienced with all this, very worldly; I was a small-town kid, very ignorant, out of my element and my depth. I was baffled by it all and never got the hang of it. On the other hand, though, the poets at Iowa made sense to me. They were doing much more what I was trying to do. So even though I was officially a fiction student, I mostly hung around with the poetry gang. It was the time when Ted Berrigan and Anselm Hollo were both at Iowa, and there was a marvelous scene around them that I became part of. I met Barrett Watten and we became good friends. I met Alice Notley then, when she was first getting together with Ted, and I was close also to Sandy Berrigan, Ted's first wife. I know all these people still, though I don't see them as much as I wish I did. They are family friends. (Well, Ted, of course, died in 1983, and I only run into Anselm when I go to Naropa [Amselm Hollo died in January 2013]; Alice is in Paris but I always see her when I am there.) Bob Harris was a great star at Iowa then. He was Ron Padgett's cousin and, like Ted and Ron, had to do with Tulsa, Oklahoma, and the very hip New York school. I had heard of none of this stuff before coming to Iowa, so I was fascinated and amazed. Barry was up to something very different and I really admired his work and his intelligence, though I am not sure I understood it. Bob Perelman was there, too, but to tell you the truth, I can't remember if I knew him then; maybe I met him later. In any case, he and I remain close and see each other with some frequency. So I learned a lot in Iowa City but not what I expected to learn. I figured I would write novels and win prizes (how this would come about was very vague in my mind), but it turned out that I actually was not made to do this. Instead, a whole new world opened up, baffling, but baffling in a positive way. The one prose writer there with whom I resonated was Gina Berriault. She was a wonderful person, quiet, emotional, and deeply sincere. We became quite close. I was finishing up at Iowa and another hot summer was coming and I didn't know what to do, because I hated the hot summer and I figured there was no escape. As far as I knew, all places on the planet are too hot in the summer. I was used to being miserable in the summer. But Gina was from the Bay Area and she told me that it never gets hot there in the summer. San Francisco is never hot. I found this an astounding fact. So for this reason, and because I heard you could study Zen meditation there, and because it was 1970, and because I had no idea how I was going to become a famous writer, I moved to San Francisco. Maybe I knew that Barry and Bob were there, maybe not, but they were there, and I made contact with them, and pretty soon their friends became mine, and it was a tremendous group of people, as everyone now knows—Barry, Bob, Leslie Scalapino (a very close friend, who just died, sadly with so much more great work to do), Lyn Hejinian, Carla Harryman, Steve Benson, Kit Robinson, Ron Silliman, Erica Hunt, Tom Mandel, Rae Armantrout, Norma Cole, Jean Day, Laura Moriarty, Jerry Estrin, Alan Bernheimer, Bob Grenier, and many more; it was really something. All kinds of writing and experimenting, events, readings, an explosion of it. As usual, I was dazzled and bewildered. I always felt as if I was on the margins of all this. For one thing, I was married and had children, very unusual at the time. (Lyn had had children.) For another, I was seriously involved in practicing Zen, and probably most importantly, I felt (and still feel) as if all these people were much smarter and more knowledgeable than I was, certainly about writing and poetry and the arts in general, but also about everything else. They read Wittgenstein, Saussure, and so on. I learned about all that stuff through them, and came to read a lot of it myself because it seemed to be really interesting and important. I was drinking it in, washing my mind in it, whereas they were actually able to explain it and make use of it and even to criticize it. I say "they" as if they all shared a point of view. That's, of course, too simple. But there was some shared ethos. We were self-consciously another generation—we were not the New York poets (because we were from San Francisco, and that must be different) and we were not the Beats. We were not going to be the heroes of our own Romantic picaresque novels and poems, and we were not going to drink, beat our wives (or be beaten), and run naked in the streets. Thanks to the Beats, who did that for us. No, we were going to think about things and read and write—also we were going to be ethical and political, thinking about society and culture in a serious way.

I've referred to my study of Zen; maybe I should say a little more about it. Zen was an important part of the intellectual scene then, from the late 1950s onward. D. T. Suzuki had been in New York and had had a profound influence on the arts scene, Cunningham, Cage, Kline, and many others. The whole idea of performance art, of improvisation (which was at the heart also of the be-bop jazz players' work) of immediacy, which was seen as anti-traditional, anti-conventional, was related to Zen. So Zen was in the air. It was read as more or less existentialism without the angst. It was natural for me as an undergraduate then to find Zen interesting. There was the arts angle, but also (as I later came to realize) the religious angle. As a boy I had been obsessed with death, and all religion is about death. So I was pretty religious as a kid. I grew up as an observant Jew, I prayed regularly, I led prayer, I was a kind of child prodigy in this. Though I always valued it, and never rejected it, as soon as I left home, I was on to other things. But it turned out that these other things led me back to religion. So when I found that you could actually study Zen in San Francisco, there was a meditation practice, I instinctively wanted to do this. I had a real drive and passion for it. It was much more than a passing interest. I had a lot of suffering that needed to be addressed—even though I had no actual reasons to suffer. I was a romantic, though, and also very vague in my thinking, so I had no plan to go to a Zen Center and become a student. I thought I'd learn how to meditate and do that on my own until I became enlightened, just like in the books. I didn't like gurus and Zen masters. I didn't imagine that I needed them. So that's what I did, living as a hermit in Northern California for a few years, meditating intensely and regularly, going on hikes, backpacking in the mountains, writing, working as little as possible, being alone a lot. But after a while I got tired of doing odd jobs to earn a living and decided I should use the rest of my Danforth Fellowship (which had paid for my Iowa MFA) studying Buddhism in Berkeley. It was then that I became active in the Zen Center there and later went to Tassajara Zen Mountain Center. I never wanted to become a Zen priest (God forbid!) or a Zen professional but I somehow got forced into it. Many of the other poets in that time and place were also influenced by Zen—maybe all of them. Leslie Scalapino was a serious Zen person who practiced and based much of her thinking on Zen; Steve Benson and Kit Robinson practice now; Bob Perelman did for a while; Barry's cousin Martin was a major Buddhist, and a close friend of mine. But I was the only one who took Zen on thoroughly, and this made me different from the others; I think it diminished the effort I put into poetry, though I was always writing. (My teacher would tell me not to write, and I would say certainly, but then I would always write, though not so much, because the monastic schedule is very demanding.) So I had a double focus. I was writing, and I was also not writing, I was silent. One of my favorite writers, since Iowa, was Philip Whalen. So I was astonished one day when I went to the Zen Center in San Francisco to have the door opened for me by him. I recognized him right away from his picture on book covers. Phil and I became very close from then on until the end of his life in 2003. I am his literary executor. We lived near each other both in San Francisco and at Tassajara. He was enormously important to me, giving me permission, as a poet, to become a Zen priest. So all this Zen stuff was going on, but I was also always staying connected to the writers. My connection to writing and those writers in particular, whom I love still, saved me from Zen, which could have been deadly. And my practicing Zen saved me from what might have happened if I had pursued poetry only (because I am sure my romanticism and stubbornness would have made a life of poetry ruinous for me). So I am extremely lucky to have survived more or less intact.

HANK: *I'm curious about your sense of the relationship between meditation and writing poetry. Has your sense of their relationship been an evolving, changing understanding?*

NORMAN: In the 1980s, I organized two very different conferences on this topic, one at Green Gulch Zen Temple in California (where I was director) and one in New York, when I was living at the Zen Community there. The one in California was a big public event, with an extravagant performance at the end. (I remember Gary Snyder was there, Anne Waldman, many others—an issue of Andrew Schelling and Ben Friedlander's magazine, *Jimmy and Lucy's House of K*, memorialized this event, an important document.) But in New York we had a private convocation. People delivered papers and gave talks. My friends from San Francisco must have given me the names of people to connect with because we had quite a remarkable group that included Charles Bernstein (this is how I first met Charles, whose talk included a statement about why he would never meditate). Armand Schwerner was there, as was Jackson MacLow. I remember Jackson arguing that there was no connection between meditation and writing, they were like apples and oranges, and that it was dangerous to mix them up. He used the word "chary," which to me is a great word. That he was "chary" of bringing the two practices together. I think this is because meditation is associated with authority, with religion, and the writing he was interested in (and we were all interested in) violated authority and always aspired to be wide open. Jackson was so sincere and intense! I loved him dearly; he was a great man. Anyway, to me there was some relationship between meditation and writing. Not necessarily theoretically but in my life. There was an anthology that came out in the 1980s called *Beneath a Single Moon* that included writers who were Buddhists, and everyone made a poetics statement; mine was about meditation practice, I think. The gist of it was that meditation practice was wild; it cleared the mind of preconceptions and opened the mind up. Then you could be more ready to write. Certainly this was and is true for me. Before I was practicing meditation, I had a hard time grappling with my mind in writing. I kept getting in my own way. It was pretty frustrating; I didn't have so much joy in writing. I suffered a lot. But meditation practice freed me up from myself and made it much easier and much more joyful to write. It helped me to release my grip on myself. I could be a lot more spontaneous and expansive. And fearless. Jackson, by the way, meditated almost every day of his life. And his whole project as an artist was to free himself from himself.

HANK: *How and when do you go about writing poetry? If we take your most recent book as an example, you have a strong commitment (as I do) to exploring ways of writing poetry that differ considerably from one another. How do you go about deciding how to proceed?*

NORMAN: I write when I can. It used to be daily, but in recent years my schedule has become more demanding, and now I can only write in the margins. This isn't good, isn't sustainable for me, so I am going to have to figure something out. Like probably all poets, my writing comes out of reading, and reading may be a form of writing and vice versa. So I am reading something important to me and then at some point in reading I am drawn to writing. It is a nearly physical sensation that I have come to be very sensitive to. And along with it comes a shape, a sense of form, which doesn't so much "come along" with it as much as it is it, so that the writing begins with a shape or a form, which constellates a sound and a subject matter, so to speak, if my writing does have a subject matter—anyway a tone, a tone of voice. It all seems to be there already, to have grown out of the unconscious (let's call it that, though I am doubtful of that term, as if the mind were a container, with unconscious at the bottom, whereas I doubt the mind is contained) and I begin to write it. Sometimes I do have a vague sort of plan that goes along with all this, augments it. For instance, the idea of filling a particular notebook (you know this one, Hank), or of writing long prose sentences, or short lines, or using certain kinds of words, or not using certain kinds of words, and so on. My plans tend to be very simple-minded. Whatever I do, when I begin, there is always a sense of exhilaration to it and a joy. It is not difficult at all. This is not to say that I am a "first thought best thought" guy. Not at all. I do lots of rewriting and shaping. And even more throwing stuff away that doesn't work—that was just a bridge to get me to the next thing that would work. And I am always trying to think about how to write. As if starting over again. So that I am using different modes all the time and seem to resist doing what I know how to do, resist using modes I may think I have gotten good at. In some visceral way, my feeling is that everything I have written is unsuccessful, and that now, today, as I write, I might find out how to do it right, in a completely different way. Of course, I know I never will. Still, I have that feeling—that writing is essentially inexpressible and mysterious, and one is always trying to figure out how to do it and never quite getting there. That there is something absolutely essential to be expressed but one can't ever quite express it. So it always feels like finding a new way to write, starting completely over again on a new tack. It reminds me of the first Zen bodhi-sattva's vow, "Sentient beings are numberless, I vow to save them." First, they don't need to be saved. Second, if they are "numberless," how could I save them all? So with writing. First, no one needs me to write; there are enough great writers already. Second, I must do this, and will always fail, yet this doesn't matter. I will continue to believe that I will get it right the next time and this belief will keep me going. It strikes me that writing (at least writing as I view it, experimental—if that is the word, though I am sure it is not—writing) is a faith. An irrational faith. Really, it is a religion for writers, writing. Writing, you feel whole. Not writing, you feel sinful, unholy, incomplete, guilty, not right. Even if no one is paying money or attention, and you are not getting anywhere at all, you have to do it. I was thinking this the other day, talking to the many good friends, poets, who were at Leslie Scalapino's funeral, a full-on Zen Buddhist funeral at which I was officiating: that religion is essentially an imaginative practice. As writing is. It's not "real" in the sense we commonly use that word. Writing is also not real. And yet it is essential.

One more thing about rewriting. I do not have a theory or an intention about a work. As I said, it comes out of a feeling that is almost physical and some kind of vague or spontaneous plan. But once it comes out, I have a sense of the integrity of the work. So I rewrite to enhance the shape the work has taken of its own accord. I have learned to discern that shape and then I know how to improve it, knocking away extraneous bits (that usually come too much from my personality or my habitual stupid ideas) and adding fresh bits that will help. I write works in notebooks and then a lot of time goes by before I type them onto computer. I rewrite then. Then I set the work aside and rewrite again, probably several times. Refining. This could go on indefinitely. But at some point I stop. I was lucky enough to have helped Philip put together some of his later books, and I learned a lot from him about how to be picky and to refine and to cut and paste things together, as he always did. I have noticed, though, over the years—and this has come to me as a sort of surprise—that despite the radical non-intentionality of my works, and the fact that I have never been interested in expressing myself, or putting my personal stamp on what I write, nat-urally my works have my personality all over them, and my thoughts and feelings and so on. It is obvious that this would be so, and probably a good thing, since writing is not machine talking to machine; it is people talking to people about what people are concerned about. So, of course, although I have avoided writing about religion and meaning and death and language and so on, my writing is all about these things.

HANK: *If words for a poem arise during meditation, what do you do? Do you set the words aside?*

NORMAN: This almost never happens to me, maybe even never. I am not thinking about writing when I am sitting. In fact, I do not think about writing that much if I am not directly engaged in it. But if something did come into my mind, I would just ignore it and keep on with my sitting. For me, sitting is about abandoning everything and just being present. I trust that completely—and I trust that if a thought that is important crosses my mind, it will come back to me when I need it. I don't ever worry about preserving anything. What I need will come—otherwise, I guess I didn't really need it. After all, my literary career isn't much. No one is paying me or living and dying with my works. So I should have a good time writing them, and not worry about anything. I should be having fun, I should be joyful, in my writing, and I am more or less. And I hope that I am communicating that, cheering the reader up. Not by writing cheerfully about cheerful things, but by writing with some sense of reality, and without any worry or fuss or angst about reality.

HANK: *What kinds of reading nourish your poetry?*

NORMAN: I read poets that matter to me, and there are very many of these, and always more to discover. It impresses me that in a way, over all these years, I have read a lot, and yet actually I remain pretty ignorant, fairly unlettered, not so much different from the way I was when I got out of high school, having read almost nothing, and blinking my eyes looking out at the world, as if I had been in a cave for a long time. It feels the same now. Part of it may be because I seem to read like a caveman: I more or less eat what I am reading, I chew it up directly, for its sound and basic sense, I don't seem to have much capacity to be critical, to understand how the work fits into the cultural conversation, what it means, what the point of it is, and so on. It's as if I am completely mesmerized by what I read. And then I forget it almost completely, except for a general impression, which has indelibly changed me, but which I can't explain. I read contemporary poetry, all the writers who are my friends, and others; people send me books, I read them; I read American and one or two European poets that I keep coming back to: Stein, Whitman, Dickinson, Hopkins, Williams, Stevens, Zukofsky, Reznikoff, Oppen, Creeley, Ashbery, Celan, Mendelstamm, Whalen. I read Dante and Shakespeare. I read Miyazawa Kenji. I read lots of Buddhist stuff and Western philosophy. I read in Judaism, Buber, Scholem, Heschel, Sfat Emet. I keep coming back to Heidegger, who always stimulates me. I read contemporary theory. I read fiction sometimes, but not often. I like to read Dickens, Balzac, and the nineteenth-century Russian novelists. I like Saramago and Sebold and Murakami. At the moment, for instance, I am reading Etel Adnan's *Paris, When It's Naked*; Leslie Scalapino's *Considering How Exaggerated Music Is*; Charles Dickens's *The Mutual Friend*; and Hegel's *Philosophy of History*. (I usually read several things at the same time and mostly finish books I begin.) Two things usually are going on in my reading: I am getting a sound and a sense of things, a shape, a flavor, a voice for things. And there are some ideas that are important to me.

# For the Poem Itself—A Language View

## An Interview with Norman Fischer
## by Monica Heredia and Denise Newman

*Monica Heredia and Denise Newman are Bay Area writers and friends. They interviewed me at my Muir Beach home in December 2010. A version of this interview appeared in* Zen Monster 3, *Fall 2011, edited by Brian Unger.*

MONICA: *In your essay "Are You Writing?," you open with a kind of apology about how you are a Zen priest and writing for a Zen priest is something that you shouldn't really be doing. The essay concludes with the idea that writing is a kind of prayer. It seems apologies or theoretical reinterpretations for the idea that Zen is somehow beyond words are easily found in the work of many contemporary writers. So what is going on here—is it that Zen is archaic and needs to incorporate contemporary understandings of language? And how is it for you to work with this idea that Zen is somehow beyond words, particularly given your background as an avant-garde poet, as well as your lifetime study of Judaism, which has a history and commitment to texts and interpretation?*

NORMAN: Well, contrary to what you're saying, I think that Zen actually does engage the question of language as a major part of what it's dealing with religiously. One of the key themes of Zen literature is how we describe the world to ourselves, how that description binds us, how we can release ourselves from it, which turns out to mean not releasing ourselves from it—which is impossible—but simply admitting to ourselves that we are bound, knowing how we are bound, stopping the struggle with that—and then we're free. So it's a paradox, but a serious paradox. A super-ficial and quick reading of Zen seems to indicate that language is our prob-lem, conceptualization is our problem, and that awakening is, by definition, completely beyond conceptual frameworks. If you are enlightened, you go beyond words, beyond thought, and so on—as if thinking and language were the enemy. So language is bad; you should stop it. But, of course, this is ironic. You can't stop language.

A deeper reading (and practice) shows you that Zen also understands that even though, yes, we do have to see through our conceptualizations, not be so tangled up in them, still, being human *is* conceptualizing; we can't not be doing that; being human is being in and with language. Dogen really hammers on this point. He argues the obvious: If awakening is pres-ent in any experience when we're disentangled from that experience, if it can be present in seeing, hearing, tasting, touching, and so on, then why not also thinking, why not language? Why would language be any differ-ent? Why couldn't we be awakened within and throughout our language? If there can be awakening in looking at the moon, there can be awakening in reading or writing. In fact, there are many Zen stories where people are awakened by reading or by hearing someone say some Dharma words. All of a sudden through the words the person lets go. Many Zen stories turn on this plot twist. The Sixth Patriarch is awakened by hearing a line from the Diamond Sutra, according to the text. And he demonstrates his awak-ening by writing a poem—as countless Zen masters have done. Expressing Zen in poems is commonplace through the tradition down the ages. Not to mention the fact that Zen has a voluminous prose literature! So it's not as if language as enemy is actually what the tradition is proposing. Far from it! Dogen's discussion of this is unique, his direct emphasis on it unique, but he is not making this up on his own. He is simply emphasizing it.

Maybe the question is what's the difference between the way Zen or Dogen would see language as a liberative tool or as part of a liberated life and the way a literary person might view language. And is there a differ-ence? Of course, it depends on what literary person we are talking about. Literature isn't a monolith—neither is Zen.

I'm looking for something very specific from poetry, and these days not all poetry interests me. What does interest me, and what always interested me about the Language Movement when it first came on the scene, and for me it wasn't a movement or an theory, it was just my friends and me and what they, in my vicinity, were doing with their writing. . . . What interested me was that it seemed to be similar to what I was and am looking for: a language that is not so bound by its one-dimensional relationship to the world that it can't be its own experience. You could argue that poetry is always that anyway. I mean, who writes a poem and is not aware of words and the experience of words, per se? No matter what you think you're writing about, it's always about the words. So although this has always been true to an extent, the more aware you are of that (of language as language, as the experience of language itself), the more you're working with language as that, the more interesting it is. Writing that is concerned with reporting inner or outer states or conditions is less interesting to me than writing that engages the act of writing itself. To me this is realism. Other stuff is so artificial; it seems all artifice. Not that there's anything wrong with artifice! But even that is different when you know artifice as artifice, rather than taking it seriously—that is, thinking it isn't artifice.

In the essay you mention, I say, well, maybe it's philosophical poetry and maybe that's what Dogen is writing not only in his poetry but in his prose. He may be writing prose that is philosophical to the extent that it becomes poetic and insofar as the more intimately you write philosophy, the closer it gets to poetry, and I would say the reverse is also true. So for me poetry is a liberative exercise. It's writing that engages what's real—that makes the question of what's real its inevitable subject and method. Nothing taken for granted. Everything up for grabs. When I write, I feel like I'm living in a more open space because I do get bound by my conceptual framework and my mind, my thought, my language, by what I think my life is. It gets to be limiting, small. But in writing I feel like I get out from under that. In language, expression. In Zen sitting, I can get free of it, too, but in silence.

MONICA: *What is the difference between religion and poetry and particularly when you take into consideration this notion of a liberative quality that they each express? Is there such a thing as a religious poetics? Would this poetics be an emanation from the poem itself or the manner in which we read or approach the poem? In your case, one might assume you are a religious poet because of your involvement in Zen and Judaism. However, and here I'd like to read a couple of quotes from two poets who are not religious poets per se but whose writing captures a kind of religiosity. Both, of course, are your good friends. Charles Bernstein writes: "The lines of an / imaginary are inscribed on the / social flesh by the knifepoint of history." And in an essay about Leslie Scalapino, Lyn Hejinian writes: "We can never see anything as it is [or per se, to use Leslie's term]. This is the case in part because reality doesn't show itself as it is, but also because, after an infinitesimal space of time, whatever perceptions we might have of reality are taken over by the distorting power of the mind, with its many preconceptions and fixations, and the conditioning force of the social sphere, which seizes, rather than observes, the world around it." Bernstein's writing reads very much like a koan which is always traversing the relationship of emptiness and the material world. Could we call his work religious? When is this work religious and when is it not? Is there a difference between Zen and avant-garde poetry or are they just different practices of the same thing?*

NORMAN: Well, first of all, the word "religion" has really become a problem. You can't say that word without it having huge associations one way or the other in people's minds that are completely obscuring—that's too bad. It's just not a good word because it conjures up limiting belief systems, obedience, close-mindedness, and so on, even though as far as I am concerned, that's not what religion's supposed to about. More like the opposite of this. So most poets and artists would really shy away from any idea of religion or using the word "religious." But yes, as you indicate, there are poetries that are, to my mind, essentially religious—if we could use the word "religious" in a more open sense. Maybe the characteristic would be a poetry whose purpose is the open-ended investigation of reality, as opposed to a poetry that assumes a conventional reality and then goes on to comment on that reality. So if, say, reality is the ground of things, there are some poets (and I would hope that I am one of them, anyway; that's how it feels from the inside, that I am one) who are digging up the ground and tasting it, playing around with it, hurling it up and around, trying to figure out what it is—and not figuring it out, because you don't figure it out. These are the religious poets. And there are other poets who assume the ground and write about something they think is going on on the ground. And that's, as I was saying, artificial. Because, in fact, it's all ground; there's no getting away from ground.

Maybe that's the problem with "religion." It's that "religion" proposes to tell you what this ground is, but it never really does tell you, it was never really intended to tell you, but it looks like it is tells you, and certainly lots of religious people imagine it is telling you, and so it becomes limiting. That's dogma. Terribly limiting, not to say destructive. Meanwhile some of us are digging, investigating, almost ignoring what goes on on the ground or maybe wanting to use what goes on as part of the investigation. Others are saying never mind about that, we know what the ground is, we're standing on it, we all agree what it is, what are you digging for? And probably most readers agree with that view. They have no time to entertain these essentially religious doubts about reality (which, besides, make them nervous and afraid); they are simply interested in being entertained and informed about what's apparently happening on the ground because it reminds them of something they think they experienced yesterday. And this is very reassuring! This received sense of coherent reality is reinforced in a high-class or not-so-high-class way by the art or culture we all consume. And the nice world goes on destroying itself.

But, of course, you are aware of, having quoted them, people that are good friends of mine, writing in another sense, with the same kinds of concerns that I have. Certainly that quote from Lyn could be written by a Zen person; it's very much the same. I think that we probably have to be careful about the use of the word "religion" or else maybe use it in a fresh abnormal way. I use it myself a lot because I think it's a shame to cede the term to people who are practicing a very limited, small religion and let them lay claim to the word "religion." I'm very aware of the riches, even if only for literary purposes and sources, of religious traditions. Brilliant people have had enormous experiences over centuries, using shared languages, technologies, concepts, practices, rituals. It would be a shame for us and a shame for art to throw that all out. So part of my whole life and argument is saying religion is not that, or at least not only that—not only the traditions and the doctrinal senses of reality they seem to be proposing. Religion is a bigger category, more lively, more exploratory, more open-ended, more freeing, more imaginative, doesn't have to be narrow-minded—and I actually think it's very important that that case be made. So I do use the words "religious" and "religion," even though I'm very aware of how they're' heard. But yes, I think any poetry that's exploring the ground, to repeat that metaphor, is poetry I'm interested in. And as for Charles—he's actually a rabbi! Everyone knows that.

DENISE: *What do you think is the stigma associated with religious practice?*

NORMAN: Well, I think that there is a sense that if you're involved in a religion—Buddhism as much as any other religion—you're taking directions from somebody, your mind is not open, you're not free to think or experience because you have to think and experience "according to the book," as Phil used to say. So if you're a Buddhist, you have to have a Buddhist view of reality; and if you have to have a Buddhist view of reality, how are you going to be able to explore reality in all the ways that your aesthetic allegiances dictate? If you're in the arts, actually it is pretty much the same. You're in a camp of some sort, or even a camp of not being in a camp, which is its own camp. And how can you have allegiance to that camp and also have allegiances to another belief system? So in that sense, art is a religion of its own even though it's unofficial and has no set scripture (though there is a canon; every writer has his or her canon—why do you think they call it a "canon?"). There is an arts belief system, arts practices, dogmas, rituals (like the workshop, the reading); there's clergy, saints, sinners, and so on, and it would be a violation of that tradition to hold to another tradition—like a religion. I do think that's the way people see it, though I don't think this is thought through because it's so much about fashion and desire and social groups and about how you position yourself within the needs of your career. All this I find very troublesome and discouraging.

DENISE: *Writing seems to be the place where you are free of any kinds of constraints.*

NORMAN: Yeah, that's right. And audience is a constraint. I mean it's a constraint that is not painful; it's not like I give a Dharma talk and feel resentful of the people who are listening. Quite the opposite; I feel very tenderhearted for those people. But I'm writing my talk for them and am constrained by my sense of what they would benefit from hearing. I don't want to offend or upset them if I can help it. That's not a problem for me, but it's very different, as you're saying, from writing in an open space. This reminds me of a panel I did once down at Stanford, with Leslie and Michael McClure. It was some sort of forum on writing and Dharma, and I remember that somebody asked the three of us who our audience was and what was our relationship to our audience, and the three of us said, each in our own way, exactly the same thing—that we're not writing for an audience. We're glad somebody's listening, we appreciate that, we know that that's part of the process. But when you come down to it, we're not writing for others, or for ourselves particularly, to express ourselves; we're writing for the poem, we're writing for the writing, there's an imperative there, and being true to it seems to be the main thing. Somehow we step into the poem and the poem has its own necessities and it's that that we're writing for and it's an encounter with the ineffable or an encounter with God or something like God, and that's who our audience is; that's who we're writing for; that's the pleasure of it and the importance of it for us. And I remember Carl Bielefeldt, who was there—he's a Zen scholar and an old friend—got upset about this. He thought it was irresponsible or narcissistic. I'm thinking about this because the other day Merwin, who is now the poet laureate, was on the radio, and he said exactly the same thing. People who are engaged in this activity have a bond with one another; poets who are writing with that understanding are all facing a very lonely, very full and complete, but essentially lonely, project. But they recognize one another in it and that makes a wonderful community of those who are all fumbling around in the dark quite intently, each one alone, and by virtue of that, together.

DENISE: *I want to talk about your latest book,* Questions/Places/Voices/ Seasons *[Singing Horse Press, 2009]. The different forms and voices you take on here seem like a departure from previous books, and I'm wondering how that came about.*

NORMAN: I'd like to think that I'm always departing; everything I'm doing is departure. I mean I'm getting now old enough to have certain tried-and-true modes that do keep coming back. Nevertheless, what gets me energized is trying something, however slightly different it might be, oh, I never did that before, what would that be like? So I feel like I'm departing from book to book. Here's the way that came about: After I did *I Was Blown Back*, well, to go further back, you see, I really didn't have any business being a poet to begin with. I was really being a prose writer and actually at Iowa I was in the prose writing department. But I found it distressingly boring, the people were not lively, and the people in the poetry department were much more lively, so I was hanging around with the poets. But I was always in awe of them. They were far more astute than I was; to me it was much more difficult to write poetry, you had to be smarter, literary, whereas writing a short story or a novel seemed more like my speed.

But when I started doing Zen, I didn't have time—to write prose of any sort takes a lot more time, you have to sit down for hours at a time—as I used to do. But you can write poetry quickly, at least I can, it's usually a shorter form so it takes less time and it was living a Zen schedule and that forced me to write poetry. But even in the beginning of writing poetry, I was always writing a poetically inflected prose. I was scared to write in lines, it seemed like wow, I don't know how to do this. And in fact, when I studied literature, I mostly studied prose. I studied some poetry but not very much so I didn't know poetry and I didn't feel competent. When I began, I was writing a poetically inflected prose and I was always trying to learn how to write poetry, which was a big challenge to me. And I felt that I could never figure it out. So you've noticed that all my early books have long works in prose and some poems and I never felt that I could write a book that didn't have long works in prose because I felt like every poem was an attempt to write a poem and I never really wrote one until *I Was Blown Back*. I felt like, with that book, which was a long process of exploration, I'd finally figured out enough to be confident to write poems. Oddly, by the way, although I didn't pay too much attention to this, I was so obsessed with how I couldn't write poems, all the poets were getting past poetry and they were writing prose. Most poetry was being written in prose by then. Barrett Watten, Lyn Hejinian, Ron Silliman, all my buddies, the great language writers— all were writing prose. They had figured out that poetry was too limited. Too pretty. Meantime, never mind that, I was finally figuring out how to write poetry in *I Was Blown Back*. There's no prose in that book. So at the end of that, and also, there was a lot of deaths, it's a memorial book for people who died, a lot of deaths in it, a deep reflection about Judaism and the Holocaust and my own past and my own heritage as a Jew, all that is in the book. So I thought, well, that's the end, I can't write anymore probably because there is nothing else to do. And I thought, well, that would be okay, I don't have to write anymore. But, of course, I kept thinking about writing and somehow hit on the idea of writing in somebody else's voice because although there was nothing else I could do personally but maybe somebody else could write if I couldn't. And that's when I did the Caeiro poems, which were the first things I wrote after *I Was Blown Back*. They just began, rather unintentionally—and I found that getting into somebody else's voice enabled me to write again. The Saigyo poems are older unpublished work that I put in the book because I had a section about voices and they fit. I had written other poems in other voices, the Rabbi poems, and then I was back to writing after that. That's how that happened.

I do take care to put books together as books. You write good poems or poems you like and they don't fit into any books, which is a shame. I like to cram in as much as I can and stretch the container so much more than you do, Denise. Your books are very tight, very well put together. I'm much looser, but even so, there's a limit. There are always poems that don't fit. Usually—not always—I put a book together after I've been writing works, not books, maybe long works, and out of the corner of my eye thinking about how these works can be fit together in a book—so the works might relate to each other in some way. I got that from Phillip because I was able to work with Phillip, putting some of his books together, and I saw how he did that. He didn't write books, but he put books together very carefully but from disparate materials. So that's how I do it and so, yes, I have never put a book together in this particular way before, with many thematic sections, each complete in itself. I don't know how I hit on that way of doing that, but somehow or another, it just fell into these sections and that's different.

# Sixty-Five

*This long prose poem was written as an elegy for my friend Rabbi Alan Lew (November 10, 1943–January 12, 2009), who died suddenly on a meditation retreat for rabbis. Alan and I met on the first day of classes at Iowa, and remained close friends for the rest of his life. In 2000 we cofounded Makor Or, a Jewish Meditation in San Francisco, which I have continued with since his death. "Sixty-five" was first published in the online magazine* Sybila *at http://sibila.com.br/english/norman-fischer-4/4575. It was posted on January 18, 2011, and appeared in my book* The Strugglers *(Singing Horse, 2013).*

1) I can't walk across the room without forgetting why I wanted to do that, what I was after. I arrive at the other end of the room, I don't know why I am there, I can't tell in what precise sense I am there, is it some sort of trick, an illusion?

2) I am upstairs, I don't know why. Finding myself at this new level, I wonder whether I ought to be here, whether I actually am here, whether it actually is another level in relation to the previous level, or whether my sense of having changed levels is accurate, since I seem to have been on this level continuously.

3) Sometimes I recover my purpose by stopping. I leave a space for thinking. Something occurs to me, something new. It is not my original purpose. So I have new purposes.

4) I am caught in the daily, physical, specific detail of my life. But I can't tell what this means to me. To what extent is all this a theory, fruit of

contemplation, artifact of language, training—the chair, the table, the refrigerator, the pencil, the impulse to wipe the counter.

5) I made a video of that, I sent a link. It went everywhere, all over the world, though not to anyone specifically. So far no one has responded. Maybe they could not open the link. That happens. Maybe the video was devoid of images. Maybe it had duration, it began, it ended, but no images.

6) Nothing is repeated. Each moment is new. When you are here you are here. When you are gone you are gone. Does that count? Does absence occupy time, is absence a new moment? Does it have its own sort of presence? How intelligent the aggressive others, who live in great cities, who write books. Who know facts. Have opinions that matter to others who have opinions that matter to others. Tonight I saw moonlight on the patio. I saw blooming plum trees like white clouds against the grim background of darkened buildings.

7) The computer screen's depth. Switched on, it glows, cool and detached. The underlying binary structure of everything. Formless and void, and then: let there be light! Words dividing the chaos. Life, death, so simple, so clear. Or is it just confusion, wishful thinking, finger in the dike?

8) Thirty to forty minutes and it's done. Then I can begin. Travel is broadening. Your life story, a frame around a picture, a basic mood or thrust. Blink your eyes and . . . a life gone by. Just like that, as they say. The flowers are breathing too, in the same rhythm.

9) It's so difficult to come up with something. Nine gateways to the body, guarding inside from outside. Yet you always take things in, give them out. There's no purity. There's no integrity.

10) The gangly rosebushes bristling in the wind. It couldn't be any more austere than that. How you put a world together, by will and idea. Until you can cut it with a knife.

11) I'm not sure. Why be sorry? As if what happened didn't, or, having happened, has always been happening, that everything inexorably leads to it. That this can be said—at all. The actual insists on itself, its tyranny. It crowds the unbeing out. Why not imagine a world? You would still be in it, or are. To enumerate the ephemera. Living is painting. People won't stop getting older, won't stop dying, because I can't imagine it.

12) Where's the argument? The rug's edge comes up to the wall. Then the wall—just a wall. Stunning clarity. Designing a genre. It envisions a life. Gone is gone.

13) There is no sense of completion, things just come to a halt. Our reasons are stupid, our poverty poor. I become my opposite, and already am. Reason is emotion. I say and do the opposite of what I wish I believed. I was taught that way. I do not believe myself. But I believe the others. I believe they are me. Reason is illusion, though it worked well enough when I first arrived. Dark impulses abound. My cage has depth.

14) Let's talk about our structures. They do not include the absences, and only then do I look for a word. But I am excitable. I don't know what to say. Like an amoeba.

15) Having stumbled onto something firm, it seems doubtful. Even the doubtfulness seems doubtful, because, doubt about what? Yet it is taken so seriously. Is so upsetting. Everything is replaced anyway, the substantiality of the world a gross exaggeration. Words are as fickle as they are clear. You can count on them to make you up. They have stubbornly remained in your absence. Those, and memory, feelings, a painting.

16) When the decisive moment occurs it's hard to say whether anyone holds a pivot or a purchase on it. The rule reads, you can't touch money, ever. Everything's removed suddenly with a flourish, a turn toward the actual, and a life's undone, it was never what it is. All that twaddle that comes after— grasping at straws, trying to love the indecipherable, the incommunicado. Counting, cleaning up.

17) A hardness of the soul, like a diamond. Can anyone understand these words? Can the world we recall be improved? Where do you stand? All right, and where do you stand now? What's the value of the obstructed, the obscure? What if I am always overheard by hostile others, and that is my body? Gone is gone. Impervious to the senses, the only game around.

18) The aperture is injured. The gulling fragments open. Things cluster around their concepts like moths round a flame. One thing not real is as illusion, but illusion is just as real, it counts for something, things do follow, a constant. Thinking of imaginary words with faulty meanings. Real words, but as illusion, because the meanings are not the ones agreed upon.

Each thing its own. That's not here but was/is fissure, it's dizzying, like at the narrow top of a precipitous cliff in very bright light. You are unable to recall what you are doing in this room. Where are you now?

19) And so the famous music plays, note by blasphemous note. Beyond the window the hills muted by the fog's smudging. Fading. I've gone upstairs, come back down. Moments loaded up like pens or guns with ink or bullets. Written, killed. Time is dangerous, the violence that goes with it, tearing everything apart. Passing this note to you through the veil quickly, indicating something. I talk to you as though absence were a medium. It is. I cannot put my hand through it.

20) It follows that existence—being here as a function of doing, perceiving, giving, receiving, communicating—comes to a sort of dither. It is neither here nor there. People talk to the dead all the time. The dead have the best information.

21) The rabbis don't argue about this, because they are duty-bound to be certain about something. The rules are not made up. As I spread my arms wide I sigh, I weep, releasing a host of assumptions. Life turns on its head. I make culture, I know how to do things. I have memory, I respect the past. I follow the rules, I am the one who is alive. I will not be undone with too much doubt.

22) When I come downstairs a telephone is ringing. An intruder on my pure subjectivity. How can I know myself if I don't know the one at the end of the line? Experience is alienating. Misleading. Being a person always is. It constellates another. And in another's absence, the revision is in the beginning, always was. The past darkens. The grass illuminates. A beginning includes an ending. Why God must be my good friend.

23) So I came here to let something fall from my grip. It's in the drawer, a world I can improve. Passion's twist, my childhood, my parents. Here they are. We danced. We never sat down. We coaxed the wallflowers into dancing too. I'm here on the couch, water dripping from the eaves. I'm a person, beyond artifice, beyond genre. I am my own genre, template, limitation, what I say is what needs to be.

24) Orchids in a vase, ceramic dishes. Underwater invertebrates, surpassing strange. Little whirring fins, a delicate locomotion. All genres express love. All love exfoliates death. People kill as an improvement technique? Is that

what this has been about? Whatever needs to be is, by being that, all forms end at their edges. So I keep on listening to the tale. At the wall—the wall.

25) The urge toward dominance, or more of the same, is a feature of language. Held in comforting arms.

26) At the other end of the room the white rug, as expected. Time marches on. Spending it, wasting it, losing it, gaining it. All the world's diseases. A horse falls down and gets up. A cat stretches. An engine turns over. A telephone answered: Hello? Is it really you?

27) I open the drawer, remove a notepad, write a note to myself, this note, so I'll be sure to remember. I promise. I am depended on. So will remain the same person, at least till then. At least to that extent. As long as there's limitation, and time hasn't run out, I will act.

28) Sun, blue sky, wispy clouds. Fuzzy, faded, cirrostratus. Trees, shrubs, flowers, quiet grasses, mosses. This can't be a city, yet city is a relative term. But what terms aren't relative, and what relatives don't come to terms? How does God know God if, as the Rambam suggests, in God there is no known or knower for these are one in God who is One. This is at the limit of thinking. God's beyond the limit, God doesn't think. Or is thought, without anything being thought. So there's no knowing. God is ignorant? Innocent? This explains a lot. Maybe the angels know more. At least a little.

29) Say a lot and keep on saying, frequently, repeatedly, differently. In this way you become convincing. Then yams, trolley cars, baby blankets, annoying bugs, paving stones, hatchets, front yards, lilies, stovepipes, digits, ideas, and ramifications all become inevitable.

30) A storm blasts across the plain sucking up houses, a swirling funnel of debris. When the physical world asserts itself all thinking is suspended until equilibrium returns—temporarily. Disaster is a feature of journeys, and though we try to prevent it we never do, it always redefines the landscape like a bomb. You search everywhere for a metaphor. Collect data until there's only data, and every tiny feeling has its ramifications. Pulse, pulse, pulse, pulse: do I ever get beyond this? Up and down, left and right, cold and hot, me and you, land and sea—does anything exist in its own right?

31) If everything dies anyway, why not kill? Isn't killing just moving the place-holder in time? Which happens. If I see another in myself or myself in another what's the difference who will live or die? Angels fall from the

sky for the same reason. The rabbis ask, what was Akiba's reward? God answered, To be ripped apart with combs, flesh torn from bones. God said, Get used to it, don't try to understand. This is the way I think things through. Cheerfulness and peacefulness operate on a much larger time scale and may not match their dowdy theoreticals. Two steps forward one back. The medium's shifting, going in and out of business.

32) It's the richness of the proof that matters: how much you know of this checkered world, and can throw into the stew. Pain, lets say, or grief, is just an experience, gone in a flash, subject only to a little bit of consciousness. If a tree falls, and nothing's there, did it fall? If the door's locked no one escapes.

33) I'm losing my religion—or yours. Who decides? There are as many senses of this as there are forces that can seize it, religion is everything and nothing. We need a new religion, let's make one up the way we like it. But then who will rule us, who will forbid us from the things we love, who will shepherd our guilt? The dialectic's reactive, it pacifies the opposites which otherwise would howl. I want what I want but I'm not sure what that is. I've got a million friends, I haven't got time for this. I'm subject to the weather.

34) Persistent dream of an idealized past or perfect future. The wisdom of crowds—the sum of our lunacy yields the best results. Bad results. Numbers always add up to zero. Hope and nostalgia are functions of language, thought is hopeful and wistful, to tie two twigs together with soap. I think the green hills, they think me. Who knows whether they are there, depending on my being here. Hardness, softness, color and shape. A currency of ideas. We can't all be crazy in the same way or at the same time.

35) A symbolic system engages me with the ultimate conditions of my existence. A set of notes, metaphors, rituals and rules. I used to like it but now I don't. I used to be one but now I am many. I used to be you but now I am me. Then I fell when the sun melted my wings. Plunged into the sea. And the farmer wiped his brow, the dray horses plowed on, the little girl drank cream and brushed her hair away from her eyes. The world rolled on.

36) The need to know—or at least imagine. How have dealings with you if I don't know who you are and who I am and what we are dealing in. It seems to be insufficient simply to get though the day. Does utilitarian individualism free us from bondage? Which is what, to what? Finishing the hat.

How does the smoking mountain play out its drama if not through force of sound, melody of demanding words. Do this, don't do that. Is love the drama implied in wine and bread, lilies of the field? Lay down the law—in both senses. Sigh and move on or fight and gasp till you drop. It comes at the end of an era that the one you love is cancelled. The feeling of losing everything is worse than it seems. Even the landscape weeps for want of meaning. It needs a reason to bloom.

37) In the recognition that all forms fade in the dark, we sleep, dream, and fail to make account of ourselves. Sooner or later a sigh illuminates the horizon and the world as we know it caroms back into view. In cartoons you are blown to bits yet return in the next frame. How hard it is to count the days. At dawn everything seems gray.

38) Silence seems to float things, they bob, weave, and eventually fade. What we say of silence breaks it. Chirps, crackles, grunts, rustlings, bumps, crashes, all arrive at a distance. In it. Which is moist and proximate, enables it, ennobles it, covers its shame. You are in that whistle, that hiss.

39) Fortuitous dilemma, to be alive now and is there more? A flash of a flash of an ephemeral flash. I need more words now, where are they when I need them? The end is proximate: the heart has its reasons. The urge to spell—or quell. To enunciate very clearly so you can understand. Watch my lips as I say this.

40) How wondrous the conclusion—popping out of your head and hovering above with little angel wings. You see light at the end of the tunnel, headlights of a truck speeding toward you. The altercation remains. Fruitful and amiable discussions were held—the conflict festers. Here, there, impossible locutions. Now, then, rudimentary promontories. Consider the real, the not.

41) Years slipped by then circled back. Or were already encircled by their circles. Illumined by those quiet grasses more silent than before, another quagmire, that things repeat. But—now—if—and then: where are you? I think I know?

42) I recall. Recuerdo. A man down by the boat. Bobbing, getting in, pushing off, going forth. Big ocean out there. Not a memory, I can't remember anything. I'm losing my past. An old box of memorabilia, misplaced it.

Someone threw it out. I've only got now. And lost that too. But remember everything as if now. What would you say to that? What if it hadn't ever really happened? Like an actor in a role I find a memory someplace, a feeling for now. You live in my memory. You're here. Your face. Where did it go, what to do next? Who talks back?

43) Poppies for remembering. This new century—and the last one's history, and the one before that. We've been everywhere they didn't want us. We're the ones left out, resented for our affinities. Loyalty to the dead for whom we live. All at peace, never. You cradled them, forcing them into new eras. Their lives yours—now it runs through me.

44) Recalling you as a grassy field, each blade illumined. The rabbis taught each is remanded to its sacred place, near the chariot, below the throne. Where the light leaks out. The heavenly power, the aureole. The sacred name. Exactly the one you fled.

45) Increasingly distant with the marching time. If I came to an ending. So to speak. From beyond the wall a pleasure leaking from the words. Up in the air where you are, your wings whirring amid the sacrificial smoke, the ovens' aroma, so rational, quietly efficient, the irrational that haunts my nights, passions unbridled—that God did not prescribe, yet implies, sanctions reproduction, if with difficulty.

46) In those years a power gathered round you. Inspiration. People came in single file supplicating themselves waving fronds and citrons. A formula repeated. And time wound round you. You grew into available spaces, you recommenced.

47) I'm not sure of the prices now. Everything bought and sold is registered. Those without homes, lost to their hearts, preferring the cold. Is being outside the social norm any colder? Is being unseen less fettered? Freedom in being nowhere. Calling the rest of us out. And to account.

48) Those who are killed. The state kills them. It is rational. It is necessary. Tit for tat. Someone is satisfied. Her grief assuaged when the wall's erected, nothing on the other side, there is no other side. An orchard perhaps.

49) Dusk. Pause. Seeing slowed you down, you saw love in the others with some distance, with strong activity, forceful word. Then she picked up and

left or did not do anything. Slowly went her way. So many Jews played violins. Others told jokes, wrote the songs we sing.

50) So critically definite. The state kills, the state hurls tiny people off its back, the state growls at its borders and checkpoints. People scowl or cower in terror. Bombs strapped to them. They're looking at fences. Neighbors are persistently bothersome, out confined by in, right by wrong, the colors shift as the day wears on.

51) Smothered then by dark impulses. It had been later but began not to be. There were some decades that arrived, the pages turned. Old voices speak to you between the words of their stories, remembering they had nothing to say, nothing happened, the old story, the fierceness of their loyalty that then became yours, because it was lodged in you (as a bullet). Later on in your silence you saw that, staggered back in awe.

52) Can't have felt the purity in merely having occurred but in some ways did sense that, which propelled you, so variously in a single lifetime, a good story we can tell now that it's ended, leaves turning in the autumn's cold, driving by them in a quiet black car.

53) Always in the air, in cemeteries, drumming of earth on pine caskets, words for their tears, melodies. You were there. Wore the coat. Spoke the prayer.

54) It couldn't have meant more to anyone than it did, a community, including all, multitudes poised at the sea's edge, whether to plunge in, do not wait, do not see, do not pause. Be still. Get going. Thrown into air: ashes for the saddest seekers. Each one pathetic. Gather them in once and for all, the dream, the grandest illusion ever.

55) Nevertheless the fear of them, the need, changing continually, changed to be in that night, with that hope in the hopelessness, that it would be there near the wall, that it would be limitlessly comforting, a weight to it, not the words without, that lifting words on a tongue. Personal. Pomegranates, red and sweet. The fulsome dates.

56) A bulk to you, lumbering. On the Sabbath in the rain in a hat. When things die there's pause, now beginning to be otherwise, absence a source of rest, behind the tree across in the park, where you sat and watched the stars and worried.

57) Any arrangement of people on the pathways. Any combination of numbers. You remain fixed in my mind but the warmth diminishes as you recede into reverse distances, always coming closer. It seems to be not possible, as savannas in this room seem not to be here, until I find I go to them. Another here, another there. A sable antelope flowing by, trees rushing.

58) The bowl you built, just like the old one. Another holder of memory. The children gather there, waving their little flags. Absence refracts presence, action bounces off. Saying it seven times with the lights out. These pulsing melodies canceling time out. In a minor key. Amorphous, objectionable, identity defended though ill-understood. Harrowing implications. For a while you held that up to the light—something was seen. A river washed it away. Drops in a waterfall. Sayings of the sages, the words' revenge, return.

59) It ripened, deepened, grew more thorough in its repetitions. Fatigued, it thickened, grew viscous, a shrinkage in the carrying capacity, strain on the breakers. Always foam on those beaches. Storms dredged up kelp, and an occasional rockfish. Carrying them, more stiff-necked ones. It was costly. Sacrifice.

60) Became an evening. So much blood lost. Blood of your emotion. Coughing it up, out, in a dark clot. Not knowing what you felt, not feeling it. Moving through space, which isn't anything, carrying history, seeing shapes of clouds gazed at from miles-high windows. A chance to think. Thoughts that lingered.

61) A pressure as the wall's approached. It's in illumined grasses, you sense an aura around your words. I'm not sure how I knew. But what a surprise. Dreamed before or later. Not words exactly, not pictures or sounds, but senses of things that the named perceived thing would only dimly suggest, the things and their presences, not physical but not not. All of this is your body. Now that the wall's dissolved. And the orchard behind it. We do not have any words for that. Our words only take us this far. Here we set them gently down in the grass. But going this far we are already where we must be. We use words to say that.

62) Becoming still more unspeakable. Can't defend any action, all action brings dire result. Everything ends badly because it ends at all. The prayer shawl that wrapped you. The illumined presence, not a face anyone could

see, yet we called it a face, and we said, you cannot see the face, and did not know what we meant though we were certain when we said it. The contradictions confirm themselves, connected as they are to their absences, which are yours.

63) The rabbis spoke of God as if they knew him, they did. In sacred syllables events going on there, praising each other, speaking in each other's name, no one can, it's in the praise itself, wailing at the wall, waiting for generations there, nothing happens—and brings violence.

64) Of endings, none. Of stopping, nothing. Of evening and of morning, one day. Then seven. Then twelve. Then more. Explosions of being, which is affluent. One which is dark.

65) Not wanting to say good-bye. God be with you, you be with God in sky, cloud, field. Not wanting to hear dirt drum on pine casket, decisive, mournful, distinct, shoveling till hole's filled up, and you are tucked in earth asleep. Why insist on one? What is one? In the things that fly up and over, so many, the days the weeks the years. The secret endings begin again, what place there is seems glum, I set my jaw, am Jew, am word, and tested.

# Counting, Naming

*A version of this essay was originally given as a talk at a Makor Or Shabbat Retreat on June 1, 2012. Makor Or is the Jewish Meditation Center in San Francisco, founded by Rabbi Alan Lew and myself on January 1, 2000.*

I have been fascinated for a long time with the idea of time—or rather the experience of time. What is it, actually? What does it feel like? Does it speed up or slow down (as it certainly seems to) or does it move in a steady flow? Does it move at all, does the idea of movement, applied to time, make sense? If so, in which direction does it move? Or are we moving in relation to it, time itself being a stationary container in which events occur? Is there any way to answer these questions, or are all possible answers already so much inside of time that there's no way to know or feel what time is, or how it moves or doesn't move, because there's no place to be outside of time to scrutinize it? Or maybe there's no time at all.

We take time for granted as our master. We are constantly looking at our watch and calendar—we must be in time, on time, use time well, not waste time or lose time. As a consequence, we feel "time pressure." There's never enough time. Generations ago (as we imagine) time passed more slowly. So there was more time at any time. People had time to write letters and walk where they wanted to go. But now there's not enough time for these sorts of things, because time has speeded up, demanding more of us.

The Jewish Sabbath is conceived of as time out of time, the end of time. As the sun sets on Friday evening, time disappears and we are free of its dictates. According to the Torah, God makes the world in six days—puts in six time-driven labor-intensive days. On the seventh day, nothing: God rests, time ends, nothing happens, there's a gap. This means that Sabbath is built into creation. Time, timelessness, the mystery of creation: it's no surprise that the Jewish mystics loved Bereshit, and that almost all Kabbalistic works reference and analyze it.

According to Jewish thought, both time and timelessness are necessary features of the created world. Living things are of necessity in time, which means they constantly change. But change requires death, loss, disappearance, time's end. Nothing new arrives unless something old departs. A new moment can't appear until a previous moment disappears. This is so obvious it seems absurd to mention it. Life is time, death is timeless—yet creation—which is also the arising of any moment of time—involves both. Six days and a seventh day. God says, "Remember Shabbat and keep it holy." Don't forget time's end. Remember and keep, God says. But the timelessness isn't just there on Shabbat; it's at the heart of every moment.

God creates the world by speaking: "Let there be light." Ten utterances constitute creation. The letters of the words in the text that memorialize this are sacred and mysterious. Hebrew letters are also numbers, abstractions, eidolons hidden in the messy furniture of the created world. The ten utterances become, in Jewish mysticism, the ten sephirot, emanations of the Godhead. Language— simple human words—is also mathematics. The word *sephira* (*sephirot* is the plural form) derives from the word for "number" or "counting," which is close to the word *safer*, "book," and *sappur*, "story." The Tetragrammaton—the four letters that stand for the unsayable name of God—is not actually a name or a word. It seems to be an impossible form of the verb "to be," in past present and future tenses simultaneously. The closest one can come to actually sounding the letters with lips, tongue, palate, and larynx, is a rush of air—an exhale.

Adam Frank's book *About Time: Cosmology and Culture at the Twilight of the Big Bang* (Free Press, 2011) is about how human beings throughout history have understood, lived, and measured time, and how their understanding of the universe's origins in any given historical period is relative to their conceptions of time. Clocks are only few hundred years old. The first clocks didn't have minute hands. Time was vague everywhere and different in different places until railroads created the need for precise standard time at the same moment that mechanical clocks that could measure precisely were developed. Although calendars as we know them are older, they are not so old. Once, human beings lived in a cyclical timeless round marked by sun, moon, stars, and seasons. Now we have precise electronic instruments that can measure time in tiny increments—so we can say (instead of "let there be light"): "At the time of the Big Bang, a tiny point of mass suddenly expanded in ten-to-the-thirty-third power of a second to make the beginning of the Universe as we know it." For centuries space and time were considered eternal constants—until Einstein's math proved that space and time are flexible and elastic, relative. It was probably no accident that Einstein was Jewish.

There are many descriptions and interpretations of the ten sephirot, most of them dizzyingly intricate. Kabbalistic mysticism, as far as I have studied it, seems simultaneously precise, messy, reasonable, and outrageous. The basic thrust is this: God's unspeakable unknowable perfection (Ain Sof) emanates out as this world but remains, tragically, hidden and obscure. Various dimensions of the sephirot have their analogs in human action, which obligates human beings, through sacred action, to bring the hidden perfection to the fore. (This is the well-known idea of "*tikkun olam*," repair of the world—an essentially mystical notion that has been, in our secular time, translated as the pursuit of social justice.) So the sephirot are simultaneously cosmic and psychological forces.

There are various conceptions of the sphirot. Here is one: the three higher sephirot (Keter, or Crown; Cochmah/Binah, or Wisdom/Understanding; Da'at, Divine Knowledge) are unmanifest and ungraspable, yet susceptible to higher spiritual intuition. The seven lower sephirot (Chesed, love; Gevurah, restraint; Tiferet, harmony; Netzach, dominance; Hod, subservience or empathy; Yesod, perfectly balanced giving; and Malchut, kingship, which is all the rest combined in perfect dynamism) manifest in improvable human conduct. In practice, the system is a bit like astrology— at any moment the cosmos line up in a particular way and you should therefore watch out for this or that, behave in this or that way to anticipate and accord with the cosmic pattern—which your behavior will, in turn, affect. Another (completely different) version of the ten sephirot is as follows: beginning, ending, good, evil, up, down, north, south, east, west, which amounts to space, time, and morality.

Frank's book details developments in cosmology in recent decades. New data has cast serious doubt on the big bang theory. But doubt about the Singularity was always common sense: if something exploded at the beginning, where did it come from and what was it? Any beginning begs a question. But philosophy and language were not enough to create doubt in scientists' minds; data was necessary. Now we have string theory and its attendant conception of multidimensional worlds, flat universes oscillating independently of one another in a multiverse that's in a constant state of creation and destruction—a possibly endless series of beginnings and endings, which would be, I suppose, no beginning and no ending. So the very idea of beginnings and endings is now problematic. As is the question of whether science is capable of discerning the universe's mysterious origins. Perhaps inherent limitations in science's objective methodology suggest that solutions to the ultimate problem of origins are impossible. The physicist Julian Barbour comes to the conclusion that there is no time, that time exists only as a conceptual framework. That there is only a "now"—utterly self-contained and complete—that arises and passes away.

⨯

I often wonder what is actually happening when I am sitting in meditation. When I breathe and come back to presence—the feeling of the body, the feeling of the breathing—I return to a kind of timelessness. Time doesn't feel as if it's passing. I don't feel as if I am inside time. Or outside it either.

⨯

Fanny Howe writes in her essay "Bewilderment":

> According to some Sufis, it was God's loneliness and desire to be known that set creation going. Unmanifest things, lacking names, remained unmanifest until the violence of God's sense of isolation sent the heavens into a spasm of procreating words that then became matter.
>
> God was nowhere until (God) became present to (God's) self as the embodied names of animals, minerals and vegetables.
>
> On the day of creation Divine transcendence was such an emotional force, energy coalesced into these forms and words.
>
> Now the One who wanted to be known dwells in the hearts of humans who carry the pulse of the One's own wanting to be known by the ones who want in return to be known by it.
>
> Lacking is in this case expressed by the presence of something—the longing to be loved—and so humanity, composed of this longing, misses the very quality that inhabits itself.
>
> —From *The Wedding Dress* (University of California Press, 2003), p. 12

# Late Work

*This new piece was written in 2013 for this volume. This is its first publication.*

Walt Whitman: Born May 31, 1819, West Hills, Long Island, New York; died March 26, 1892, Camden, New Jersey.

Wallace Stevens: Born October 2, 1879, Reading, Pennsylvania; died August 2, 1955, Hartford, Connecticut.

Robert Creeley: Born May 21, 1926, Arlington, Massachusetts; died March 30, 2005, Odessa, Texas.

The barest of facts: name, time and place of birth, time and place of death. The shortest and most expressive story that can be told of a person's life. The tenor, the tune, the landscape in which the skein of a life unwinds: the field or body of space and time that shapes and evokes what's done and made.

The next event, before it happens, in the story of any living person's life, is unknowable. It is potential: it could be anything. Despite whatever consistency there may be in what's been lived through so far, one never knows what's next, because every life is at all points unfinished, tentative, until it is not. With death, a life's shape's clear, and the rest of us, the temporarily undead, try to make something out of that life that we need, telling the story in whatever way can make sense of our own tentative unfinished business. If that story is the story of a poet and his or her work, the last poems having been written, the book closed on the Collected, readers can finally examine the poetry's meaning and place in the history of the art.

I have been reading Whitman, Stevens, and Creeley (among many other intimate favorites) as voices in my head, shapers of my mind, most of my life. Whitman was a legend before my grandmother was born; Stevens was read as the late great by the time I was in school; Creeley was alive and in mid-career when I began reading him (I met him but did not, as did so many of my friends, know him) and following his books, always with a particular excitement, as they came out, until the last.

For me, as I suppose for any poet, reading is more than reading. It has the weight of religious vocation, identity—crucial and central to one's purpose. For me as for any poet, reading extends life, gets a grip on it—reading is as real as life if not more. I am an amateur poet I hope in the best sense of the word. Writing and reading have been a love, not a livelihood. Because of this I have not had to read seriously and well. I read crookedly and spottily, meandering unsystematically according to interest, need, and chance, with no point of view to support, defend, master, or attack. I have not read for much more than to keep company with poets—to enjoy a connection, different and possibly more intimate than I have had with people in the flesh, within the stream of what's written in the language that's shaped me. To encounter poets in their works at the depth of myself, as I have needed and hoped for. Such reading has made my life somehow more real. In the midst of it, I have found poets whose works struck me so startlingly that I have spent my life wishing I had written them—until I became finally convinced that I *had* written them.

That's what reading feels like to me.

Yet from the outside, in what they now call (even in reference to poetry) "the marketplace," that great give and take of ideas and reputations, poets have careers, points of view, territories to stake out among their contemporaries and in history. Generally an important poet is discovered to be important at some budding time of life, usually early, sometimes later. But certainly by the time an important poet is forty-five or fifty, his or her importance will have been noticed and proclaimed by those whose business or interest it is to notice and proclaim. This notice and proclamation then become the mark of that particular poet. Certain of his or her works, styles, or interventions are singled out as exemplary and referenced. The poet can't help but notice this—probably he or she intended it from the start—and then, if the poet is lucky, he or she will continue to build a body of work on the foundation of this reputation: a career, something useful in the world.

All this is objectively the case. Subjectively, poetry's most potent manifestation is otherwise. Important poets and their important works are important. The rest (the actual inexpressible experience of reading—and writing—its effect on the silent life we barely know we're living) is easily forgotten because it's so subjective and vague. You can barely talk about it. But what's "importance"? What use is poetry for us struggling persons? Maybe important poetry is less important than unimportant poetry. Maybe what we are looking for sometimes in a poem isn't something important but something unimportant, something private we stumble into and hear in ways we know are not so important, can't argue for, can't see any social or cultural usefulness in. Important poems are known, written about, and discussed. We know what they mean. We know why they are important. Their importance rings in our ears. My reading of Whitman, Stevens, and Creeley has been unimportant, even useless, a distraction, probably a mis-understanding—and essential to me.

Usually a poet's important poetry is written early or in mid-career. Usually late works are not so important (there are exceptions to this, of course—always exceptions—late Yeats, late Williams, others). After the important works have been written, the particular genius of the particular poet having been fully developed, there comes the inevitable self-repetition (with reduced excitement). Next comes the loss of vitality and then maybe finally the terrible whimpering sounds of poems of complaint or confusion leading to the inevitable silence. Anyway, most of us prefer life, hope, en-ergy, desire, promise, engagement (and answers) to death, despair, sorrow, grief, hopelessness (and the unanswerable)—and since this latter list is most likely to characterize late work, late work is inherently unappealing—and unimportant. Poetry's point is to build great works for great cultures—not to dampen enthusiasm. So no, late works are not important. But if po-etry, like life, is cumulative—the present always including the whole of the past—so that there's more resonance, more thickness in time as time in a life goes on—and if poetry, like life, isn't so much a building of something as the dwelling within a body in a place at a time—then it would stand to reason that late works would always be the most important works—even if they are unimportant. This in mind, I have been reading late work of Whitman, Stevens, and Creeley.

❧

## TO GET THE FINAL LILT OF SONGS

To get the final lilt of songs, to penetrate the inmost lore of poets—to
    know the mighty ones,
Job, Homer, Eschylus, Dante, Shakespeare, Tennyson, Emerson;

To diagnose the shifting-delicate tints of love and pride and doubt—to
truly understand,
To encompass these, the last keen faculty and entrance-price,
Old age, and what it brings from all its past experiences.

—Walt Whitman

Whitman was aware, as he wrote this, that his important work was done,
the many editions of *Leaves* already printed, sealed, and shipped. But the
culmination of his work in poetry, which was his life as he could live it,
end to end, was still to come: to continue to follow his experience in the
poem, darker and darker, until he came to understand poetry deeply, at its
root, where the mysteries of the reading he had done his whole life through
would at last (perhaps) become clear: "To diagnose the shifting-delicate
tints of love and pride and doubt." "Love and pride and doubt" sound to me
here, perhaps, habitual words for Whitman, words without much meaning other than to stand for everything, the whole range of human feeling
at its most basic; but "shifting-delicate tints" sounds true, something he
senses and aches for—to be able to see his life, all life, awesomely as it shifts
and changes colors, almost imperceptibly through the works of the poets
he loves; to "diagnose" like a doctor does the meanings (almost as bodily
sensations) between the words. This final and all-important task requires
a newer, keener faculty than he had hitherto been able to employ: the "entrance-price, old age." High price indeed for him, involving strokes, in-
validism, loss of faculties, terrible digestion—yet absolutely necessary to
the task. Whitman, legendary for his high spirits, spiritual wisdom, and
positive attitude, wasn't always able to keep up appearances in old age, and
couldn't help but express this in poems (despite his early decision, as a poetic strategy, to idealize himself as the Brave American Spirit Incarnate):

QUERIES TO MY SEVENTIETH YEAR

Approaching, nearing, curious, thou dim uncertain specter—bringest
thou life or death?
Strength, weakness, blindness, more paralysis and heavier?
Or placid skies and sun? Wilt stir the waters yet?
Or haply cut me short for good? Or leave me here as now,
Dull, parrot-like and old, with crack'd voice harping, screeching?

This is no "Song of Myself." The late poems are brief, plain, pure, more honestly personal, with nothing to prove or assert—not much more than a murmur. Yet all the qualities of bravado and direct statement that had been there from the beginning remain, if in distilled and quieter form: sometimes saying almost nothing because age had all but erased the colorful material world he'd been so in love with. Is the specter referred to here death? Or age itself? Approaching, nearing, so ominously—yet also curious, like a child. No way to know what will happen, more life, more stirring of the pot, or nothing but the dullness of suffering and its repetitions. In old age there is simply less strength, less vitality, so that it becomes difficult even to hold a thought long enough to see where it is going. The following three-line poem begins with the effort to see, simply, the room beyond the pages of the book he is reading, but he can't even get past the mist hovering over the page:

APPARITIONS

A vague mist hanging round half the pages:
(Sometimes how strange and clear to the soul,
That all these solid things are indeed but apparitions, concepts,
    nonrealities)

So often Whitman's late poems break off suddenly off like this, trailing off elsewhere in the middle of the poem, till the words dissipate into silence, so that the poem leaves off before it gets going:

GOOD-BYE MY FANCY

Good-bye my Fancy — (I had a word to say,
But it is not quite the time — The best of any man's word or say,
Is when its proper place arrives — and for its meaning,
I keep mine till the last.)

This is the first of at least two poems Whitman wrote to bid farewell to his "Fancy," which seems to be his daemon, his muse, alter-ego, soul, or spirit, the motivating, animating power of his living and his verse, the "Walt Whitman" who is the hero of *Leaves*. (The second poem, quoted below, is also titled "Good-bye My Fancy!"—note the exclamation point).

Not so easy to say good-bye to a good friend, particularly when he is one's essential self, confusing if not impossible (Where is he going? What is absence? etc.). Whitman knows it will soon be necessary to do so . . . "but it is not quite the time." You'd imagine that late works would be obsessively about death. But poets are always writing about death. Possibly all poems are about death, the unsayable, or at least death is lurking around their edges. What is linguistic expression, at its most challenging, if not a skirmish at the borders of the sayable—and very soon one is nose to nose with life's basic oddness: the world itself, and death. As Creeley wrote in his final essay "Reflections on Whitman in Age," "Yet even the 'world' itself is imagination, simply 'the length of a human life,' as its etymology defines" (from *On Earth*, University of California Press, 2006, p. 60).

This seems to be very much the case. That as life lengthens, the world seems more and more imaginary and weirdly doubtful. Memory fails, one notices that inaccurate memories seem often to be somehow truer than accurate ones, and it can appear equally doubtful that past and present experience is real at all. Was I ever really here? Am I here now? Did all that really happen? Daily experience, as senses lose their acuity, passions blunt, and motivation for further forward motion in living diminishes, seems somehow dreamlike. I have been reading all my life Buddhist sutras that talk about all experience as "empty of own-being, without self: like a dream, a lightning flash, a bubble, a dewdrop, a magic show." This has always struck me as true, but ever truer as I age. Time is becoming thicker, the past seeming sometimes as present as the present, the future a big question mark. The world and all there is to say and do about it is becoming essentially doubtful, and I come to appreciate that I may well have been mistaken about everything.

THE UNEXPRESSED

How dare one say it?
After the cycles, poems, singers, plays,
Vaunted Ionia's, India's—Homer, Shakespeare—the long long times'
    thick-dotted roads, areas,
The shining cluster and the Milky Way of stars—Nature's pulses reap'd,
All retrospective passions, heroes, war, love, adoration,
All ages' plummets dropt to their utmost depths,
All human lives, throats, wishes, brains—all experiences' utterance;

After the countless songs, or long or short, all tongues, all lands,
Still something not yet told in poesy's voice or print—something
     lacking,
(Who knows? The best yet unexpressed and lacking.)

How dare one indeed! The possibility that after a life lived—after all lives lived, expressed, chronicled, sung—after even the lives of the very stars—something essential has been left out. Old age as the last and most essential adventure: maybe, now, finally, we'll get to see the truth—we'll get to heaven by and by, we'll make the Ultimate Ascent. If anyone would propose such a thing, it would be Whitman, he who celebrates and sings himself, assuming what you shall assume, speaking through and beyond himself for all humankind. In fact, he does propose this, but the bravado in it seems sadly hollow, with perhaps too many exclamation points and flaunting pennants:

OLD AGE'S SHIP & CRAFTY DEATH'S

From east and west across the horizon's edge,
Two mighty masterful vessels sailers steal upon us:
But we'll make race a-time upon the seas—a battle-contest yet! bear
     lively there!
(Our joys of strife and derring-do to the last!)
Put on the old ship all her power to-day!
Crowd top-sail, top-gallant and royal studding-sails,
Out challenge and defiance—flags and flaunting pennants added,
As we take to the open—take to the deepest, freest waters.

Derring-do aside, old age brings perspective—and retrospect. One has the chance to review and interpret: what does this life come to? And to say good-bye gracefully, with appropriate words, from the dignity of one's present stature. This was something Whitman did often. He did not wait for old age. Throughout his life he was constantly looking back, revising old poems, redoing *Leaves* again and again; it was as if his original poetic impulse (which his physician, Dr. Maurice Bucke, attributed to a spontaneous spiritual enlightenment Whitman experienced, which Bucke called "cosmic consciousness") existed in eternal time, his first poems were his only poems, and he kept writing them again and again as events of his life wound on, adding, but in effect not adding, anything that was not already there in the beginning. In "Backward Glance O'er Travel'd Roads," his preface to the deathbed edition of *Leaves*, Whitman wrote, " . . . looking at the actualities away back past, with all their practical excitations gone. How the soul loves to float among such reminiscences!" (p. 365). This floating in memory, which happens with frequency in old age, when past and present swim both toward and away from each other, is indeed a great pleasure. Especially if in its midst you can sum up and reinforce your life's work, as you'd like posterity to appreciate it, as Whitman does in this poem:

L. OF G.'s PURPORT

Not to exclude or demarcate, or pick out evils from their formidable
    masses (even to expose them),
But add, fuse, complete, extend—and celebrate the immortal and the
    good.
Haughty this song, its words and scope,
To span vast realms of space and time,
Evolution—the cumulative—growths and generations.

Begun in ripen'd youth and steadily pursued,
Wandering, peering, dallying with all—war, peace, day and night
    absorbing,
Never even for one brief hour abandoning my task,
I end it here in sickness, poverty, and old age.

I sing of life yet mind me well of death:
To-day shadowy Death dogs my steps, my seated shape, and has for
    years—
Draws sometimes close to me, as face to face.

                        ☙

With the word "haughty," Whitman, for once, acknowledges the perhaps too daunting task he has set himself. However arrogant he has seemed, or actually been, in the end he has not wanted to create anything special—only to "add, fuse, complete, extend" what has already been thought, felt, and written—to celebrate what already is and has been, and to bring it forward into his own moment. And he has never swerved from this celebratory task, not even for an hour abandoned it, and now it is ending pathetically, as "Death" dogs him even as he writes from his wheelchair, breathing into his face. Reminiscence's pleasures may be considerable, but in old age, with rude reminders of the darkness ahead, they are intermittent at best.

⁓

Retrospective, too, are the poems in Creeley's last short collection, *On Earth*, because Creeley has, as Whitman, put "himself" at the center of his verse, though in a much different way (the scare quotes belong around Creeley's projected poetic self as much as around Whitman's). Whitman's heroic nineteenth-century Natural American Democratic Everyman can't be anything like Creeley's fractured post–World War II self in search of self, formed in the grey 1940s and 1950s, saturated and wrung dry in the 1960s to 1980s. In Creeley there's doubt and recrimination, a questioning of the possibility, to begin with, of being one, and the confusion and pain inherent in the prospect, whatever it proposes, of rubbing shoulders with the many others, as sadly we both love and misconstrue one another. *On Earth* includes several elegies to deceased friends, also poems of apology, regret, score-settling. "When I Think" first circulated on the Internet before Creeley's death, with a note saying he'd intended to put it into the previous collection (*If I Were Writing This*, 2003) but had somehow forgotten. I was much moved by it, and moved as much again on reading it in *On Earth*, the volume's first poem. Whereas Whitman's "L. of G.'s Purport" reads like a brave statement to posterity, a thoughtful, calculated summing up—at least until the end, when he gets personal, and even a little bitter— Creeley's poem is entirely personal, and emotional, with the problematics and confusion of a long life lived here and there, jumbled up in memory and presence and in the act of writing itself, fully embedded in the poem's rambling syntax.

WHEN I THINK

When I think of where I've come from
or even try to measure any kind of
distance those places, all the various
people, and all the ways in which I
remember them, so that even the skin I
touched or was myself fact of, inside,
could see through like a hole in the wall

or listen to, it must have been, to what
was going on in there, even if I was still
too dumb to know anything — When I think
of the miles and miles of roads, of meals,
of telephone wires even, or even of water
poured out in endless streams down streaks
of black sky or the dirt roads washed clean,
of myriad salty tears and suddenly it's spring
again, or it was — Even when I think again of
all those I treated so poorly, names, places,
their waiting uselessly for me in the rain and
I never came, was never really there at all,
was moving so confusedly, so fast, so driven
like a car along some empty highway passing,
passing other cars — When I try to think of
things, of what's happened, of what a life is
and was, my life, when I wonder what it meant,
the sad days passing, the continuing, echoing deaths,
all the painful belligerent news, and the dog still
waiting to be fed, the closeness of you sleeping, voices,
presences, of children, of our own grown children,
the shining, bright sun, the smell of the air just now,
each physical moment passing, passing, it's what
it always is or ever was, just then, just there.

*On Earth* includes Creeley's final essay, "Reflections on Whitman in Age," which is of course a series of reflections on Creeley in age (just as this essay is a set of reflections on myself in age, though as I write it, I am not as old as Creeley was when he wrote his Whitman essay, or as old as Whitman was "in age"). In her acknowledgments at the end of the book, Penelope Creeley reports that, "'Whitman in Age' was written over Christmas 2004. Robert worked at it intensely, with passion, delight, and often tears. He would disappear for hours to his desk upstairs here in Providence, peer out through the attic windows at the morsel of industrial harbor he could glimpse between the neighbors' shingled rooftops, listen to music and talk to himself. Later, after hours of work, he'd re-emerge satisfied, relaxed, and ready to celebrate with us" (p. 87). In the essay, Creeley writes of the strangeness of aging, particularly as a poet, living in a world that isn't anything one can live in until one's made of it what one can and must in the poem—which is, he says, finally the life, "the issue and manifest of its existence" not "a product . . . answering either to a determined definition or else to a use not necessarily its own." Poetry— like life—is common; it is its own justification and validation, and any external definition or use of it is necessarily terribly wrong. "Now I know, for example," he writes, "that age itself is a *body*, not a measure of time or a record of how much one has grown" (p. 60). As a body, poetry moves through a life, struggles, triumphs, grows weaker, stronger, is finally abandoned, without ever being susceptible to explanation or answerable to anything outside itself. Creeley writes at greatest length about Whitman's poem "Good-bye My Fancy!" (a second poem with this title), the final poem in the deathbed edition of *Leaves*. In the poem Whitman says good-bye (which turns out to be also— maybe—hello) to his Fancy. He tries to be as cheerful about this good-bye as he can, recounting the wonderful joys and delights he and his Fancy have experienced together: joys and delights that now must end, for the time has come to leave the world behind. Creeley writes, "Age wants no one to leave. Things close down in age, like stores, like lights going off, like a world disappearing in a vacancy one had no thought might happen. It's no fun, no victory, no reward, no direction. One sits and waits, most usually for the doctor. So one goes inside oneself, as it were, looks out from that 'height' with only imagination to give prospect. . . . In that world perhaps one's whole life is a dream, a practical, peculiarly material dream. . . . Whose persons become the same complex 'music' that Keats's nightingale evokes, a tenacious fabric of inexhaustible yearning. Is that the 'world' that has to fall away in age? When one can no longer sustain it?" (pp. 83–85). Old poets are in reality no closer to death than young poets; they simply find it more interesting because they take it more personally.

GOOD-BYE MY FANCY

Good-bye my Fancy!
Farewell dear mate, dear love!
I'm going away, I know not where,
Or to what fortune, or whether I may ever see you again,
So Good-bye my fancy.

Now for my last—let me look back a moment;

The slower fainter ticking of the clock is in me,
Exit, nightfall, and soon the heart-thud stopping.

Long have we lived, joy'd, caress'd together;
Delightful!—now separation—Good-bye my fancy.

Yet let me not be too hasty,
Long indeed have we lived, slept, filter'd, become really blended into
    one;
Then if we die we die together, (yes, we'll remain one,)
If we go anywhere we'll go together to meet what happens,
May-be we'll be better off and blither, and learn something,
May-be it is yourself now really ushering me to the true songs (who
    knows?)
May-be it is you the mortal knob really undoing, turning—so now
    finally,
Good-bye—and hail! my Fancy.

The poet looks back fearfully. He can feel his clock ticking ever more slowly and imagines the end: "exit, nightfall, and soon the heart-thud stopping." Bravely he says good-bye. . . . But wait! Perhaps the sad parting he envisions isn't as sad as it sounds. Perhaps it's not a parting at all. What, after all, is his Fancy? He'd imagined it as the force of his life itself, the source of his engagement, his poems. But what, in actuality, is that? Maybe it was always both the body and not, both life and not—in life, in the body, but beyond them. Maybe he's not saying good-bye to his Fancy but rather recognizing (possibly—he can't be sure) that the Fancy not only accompanies him toward "what happens" but has all along been bringing him in the direction of this culmination, when the "true songs" will finally been known—"may-be," as he says, it has always been the Fancy who has been turning the dials and churning the wheels of his life—toward this end he'll meet not in loneliness and isolated terror but together with his good friend Fancy. So that finally it is both "good-bye—and hail!" hello and good-bye in the same breath—as ever.

Creeley's "To think . . ." is likewise a late poem of hello-good-bye. Death, the end, advancing old age, is surely a shutting down, a gradual dimming of the lights, mediated, as are all times of life once one learns to think as a self—by thought. So one "thinks oneself again" (as one has always done, but does now more poignantly than ever) "into a tiny hole of self." Thinking, so full now of retrospect, shrinks to a nub of regret and emptiness—at which point, and through whose price, one sees the whole world, one's life in its bodily form in time—as a dream that was there even before one arrived, and remains after one's gone, an "afterthought."

"TO THINK . . ."

To think oneself again
into a tiny hole of self
and pull the covers round
and close the mouth—

shut down the eyes and hands,
keep still the feet,
and think of nothing if one can
not think of it—

a space in whose embrace
such substance is,
a place of emptiness
the heart's regret.

World's mind is after all
an afterthought
of what was there before
and is there still.

&

For Stevens, what he called "abstraction" was poetry's task—the fashioning of an aestheticizing vision, almost a sense, beyond the meaningless chaos of messy so-called reality. Abstraction *was* life in actual reality, life purified, distilled and made whole, an accomplishment of the imagination. Stevens's early work demonstrated this theme; his mature work drilled it home at length; his late work stated it in fewer, plainer, and sometimes, even (but only almost) personal words. The "he" in "The Poem That Took the Place of a Mountain" is certainly Stevens the poet; distant as it is, this "he," the contemplative recipient of poetry's redemptive grace, is as close to personal as Stevens would ever get:

## THE POEM THAT TOOK THE PLACE OF A MOUNTAIN

There it was, word for word,
The poem that took the place of a mountain.

He breathed its oxygen,
Even when the book lay turned in the dust of his table.

It reminded him how he had needed
A place to go in his own direction,

How he had recomposed the pines,
Shifted the rocks and picked his way among clouds,

For the outlook that would be right,
Where he would be complete in an unexplained completion:

The exact rock where his inexactnesses
Would discover, at last, the view toward which they had edged,

Where he could lie and, gazing down at the sea,
Recognize his unique and solitary home.

The poet does have needs. He needs (as any of us do) "a place to go in his own direction," a pristine and private place, beyond the world's excesses and confusions. To find such place he must reorganize a world, make it exact, precisely as he is inexact, but even then there's no getting there; that would be too much to hope for. At least, though, through the process of the poem (however discarded the poem may end up being in the dust of someone's desk or bookshelf), its words—he can gaze out from where he is, high up at the place to which he has climbed, down at the sea, in whose plunging rhythms he can recognize his "unique and solitary home." He may not be there, but he can see it, off in the distance. At this vantage point, at any rate, there's some peace, and at least a feeling of wholeness.

This abstract sense of home, of place, that, perhaps, one approaches with increased intimacy in late life, is expressed more directly in "A Quiet Normal Life." In this poem, itself a place to be, Stevens seems to repudiate the abstraction he praised all his writing life ("so frail, so barely lit"), in favor of what? . . . the felt sense, in the mind but also in the flesh, here, now, in his house, in his room, alone, thinking (always this solitary sense of the contemplative, which was Stevens's truest home). Yet this quiet normal place isn't somehow that. Its concrete actuality blazes with artifice. The poem's words, though they seem to describe a quiet normal evening at home, certainly don't feel like that. The world itself, after a lifetime of recomposing it for "the outlook that would be right," becomes, finally, the poem. Like Whitman's Fancy, which might not need to be abandoned after all, the world, as it is and as the poem, in the words yet not, in the living of it yet beyond that, in "the uniqueness of its sound," might remain forever as it is.

A QUIET NORMAL LIFE

His place, as he sat and as he thought, was not
In anything that he constructed, so frail,
So barely lit, so shadowed over and naught,

As, for example, a world in which, like snow,
He became an inhabitant, obedient
To gallant notions on the part of the cold.

It was here. This was the setting and the time
Of year. Here in his house and in his room,
In his chair, the most tranquil thought grew peaked

And the oldest and the warmest heart was cut
By gallant notions on the part of night—
Both late and alone, above the crickets' chords,

Babbling, each one, the uniqueness of its sound.
There was no fury in transcendent forms.
But his actual candle blazed with artifice.

"Late and alone," the poet feels "the oldest and the warmest heart" (God's? Which is also his own?) "cut" by "gallant notions on the part of night." Such notions (ironized with the word "gallant" that echoes the earlier ironic "gallant" that describes the world of the poet's own constructions) cut through even the poetry and the process of poetry that has been the life. The passions of its forms are quiet now. A lifetime of work falls away; it doesn't matter anymore; a gallant attempt to which one had remained obedient for a lifetime now fallen away. Let go, without resistance or grief. A single "actual" candle blazes. That—the sense of the poem—is enough.

Like Whitman's "L. of G.'s Purport," Stevens's "The Planet on the Table" is a summing-up poem. This is what it's come to; this is what it's all been about. In his poem Whitman can't help veering off into the personal, the plaintive, as if, after a lifetime of following his solitary abstracting path, he is now, in old age, unable (as so many are) to hold one thought in mind long enough to finish a poem in the spirit in which he begins it. Stevens is nothing if not controlled from beginning to end of any poem, all parts bending to the whole. This poem wholly affirms, as "A Quiet Normal Life" does not, the thrust of Stevens's lifetime work. The statement, for Stevens, is uncharacteristically direct: Ariel (Stevens's alter-ego, an obedient sprite) "was glad he had written his poems," that were, simply (as it turns out, after all those theoretical claims) nothing more than responses to the places and times of his life. They had made sense of the "waste and welter" of the world. He had made them, but his making did not rise above the "makings of the sun," for he and the sun were one, and his makings were no less makings of the sun. Like everything under the sun, Ariel's poems will not survive: no matter. What matters is that they have borne "some lineament, some character, some affluence, if only half-perceived" of the planet of which they were a part. Stevens's late life summing up of his life's project is, as Whitman's, both arrogant and humble: he and the sun are one, yet the value of his poems, "in the poverty of their words," has been, simply, to reflect, however dimly, the richness of the world that made them.

THE PLANET ON THE TABLE

Ariel was glad he had written his poems.
They were of a remembered time
Or of something seen that he had liked.

Other makings of the sun
Were waste and welter
And the ripe scrub writhed.

His self and the sun were one
And his poems, although makings of his self,
Were no less makings of the sun.

It was not important that they survive.
What mattered was that they should bear
Some lineament or character,

Some affluence, if only half-perceived,
In the poverty of their words,
Of the planet of which they were part.

⁓

One would like to conclude that late work—old age itself, when there is some work as mirror to reflect and contain it—is poignant and profound. But it's more complicated than that. Like any work, late work runs the gamut. And yet there is in it—at any rate, judging by this small sample—a quality of spareness and honesty simply unavailable at other times in a life. Close to the end, one knows (or at least feels compelled to have thoughts that grapple with) what one has done and struggles to—failing—express it. Late work is inevitably sad, as good-byes are sad. Full of love sometimes, gratitude, appreciation, and once in a while, flashes of transcendence, as what lies beyond the last poem (Stevens's "palm at the end of the mind") reveals itself, at least in part, at least as a frightening or a comforting illusion. But rest, peace? Probably not. Probably, as in the "hail!" in "Goodbye My Fancy" and the blazing candle in "A Quiet Normal Life," there's a sense of ongoingness somehow. Who knows what this amounts to. Some truth glimpsed through the murky lens of age and a lifetime's work? A vain hope? I am impressed with Creeley's late doggerel poems, little, simple, almost nursery rhyme poems, that somehow distill his poetic persona into thoughts so earnestly serious that they could only be expressed this way. An old guy, having written so much and so thoughtfully, honestly, having a dalliance with words. And yet. . . .

In "Here" (I wonder how many of Creeley's poems have this title—ten? twenty?), life is described as a gentle little hike—up the hill and down. Around and in—all the little directional prepositions you can think of. Out was what it was all about. But now it's done. Or is it? Quoting "someone" (Eliot) who pointed out that the beginning is in the ending (or is it vice versa?), Creeley concludes—three times—that there is no end or beginning, no in or out or upside down. You arrived, you tried to figure out what was going on, you couldn't, so you kept looking. And even now that "it's done" you keep on looking, keep on looking, keep on looking.

## HERE

Up a hill and down again.
Around and in—

Out was what it was all about
but now it's done.

At the end was the beginning,
just like it said or someone did.

Keep looking, keep looking,
keep looking.

# Imagination

*This new piece was written in 2013 for the present volume. This is its first publication.*

1. Coleridge's famous distinction between Imagination and Fancy is as follows:

> The IMAGINATION then, I consider either as primary, or secondary. The primary IMAGINATION I hold to be the living Power and prime Agent of all human Perception, and as a repetition in the finite mind of the eternal act of creation in the infinite I AM. The secondary Imagination I consider as an echo of the former, co-existing with the conscious will, yet still as identical with the primary in the kind of its agency, and differing only in degree, and in the mode of operation. It dissolves, diffuses, dissipates, in order to recreate; or where this process is rendered impossible, yet still at all events it struggles to idealise and unify. It is essentially vital, even as all objects (as objects) are essentially fixed and dead.
>
> FANCY, on the contrary, has no other counters to play with, but fixities and definites. The Fancy is indeed no other than a mode of Memory emancipated from the order of time and space; while it is blended with, and modified by that empirical phenomenon of the will, which we express by the word CHOICE. But equally with the ordinary memory the Fancy must receive all its materials ready made from the law of association.
>
> —Chapter XIII, Biographia Literaria, p. 516 in *The Portable Coleridge*, edited by I. A. Richards, Viking Press, 1950

For Coleridge, Imagination is perception. We don't see hear or taste the world; we imagine it, just as God created the world through an act of divine imagination, conjuring it with a spell of words. What we usually think of as imagination, human creativity, Coleridge calls "the secondary imagination." It grapples with the real through a process of deconstruction in perception ("dissolves, diffuses, dissipates"), taking the world's apparent fixity apart in order to bring it back to life in a more energized, fruitful way. Without this process the world would not be real for us; it would just lie there, dead meat, a source of dread. (The horror of a relentlessly unresponsive world in which we are lost.) This process of making the world real is difficult. The world resists, so "struggle" is necessary in order to "idealize and unify" experience so that we don't go mad with purposeless confusion in a "fixed and dead" universe.

Fancy (what I suppose we would now call "fantasy") is, on the other hand, a realm of wish-fulfillment, not creative is any essential sense, yet affording some relief from the constraints of space, object, and identity. With Fancy we are free for a moment, we can relax (as at Disneyland) amid the free play of the stuff of our desire. Fancy's moving parts are loosely based on our normal experiences (Dumbo the elephant is a cute version of an actual elephant; the fantasy sex object is an idealized version of the man or woman we desire), whereas the Imagination's productions are both exactly the same as ordinary objects (since imagination is the prime agent of all human perception, whatever we see, hear, taste, and so on, is essentially imaginary) and at the same time so dark and subtle that they defy depiction.

For Coleridge, then, imagination is essentially a religious function—if by "religious" one means, as I do, reality-seeking. Coleridge distinguishes poetry's reality-seeking from that of science or philosophy. These disciplines seek truth per se. Poetry seeks pleasure—not sensual pleasure, but not intellectual or aesthetic pleasure either:

> A poem is that species of composition, which is opposed to works of science, by proposing for its *immediate* object pleasure, not truth; and from all other species—(having *this* object in common with it)—it is discriminated by proposing to itself such delight from the *whole*, as is compatible with a distinct gratification from each component part.

> —Chapter XIV, Biographica Litereria, p. 522 in *The Portable Coleridge*

Truth is sober, serious, and linear. Poetry is fluid, vital, elusive, delightful, not necessarily factual or accurate in its statements or descriptions. Its pleasure comes from its communicating the feeling of wholeness that we crave but seldom experience, and communicating it through appreciation of parts, so that, say, the description of sky in a Wordsworth poem is more than sky, evokes rather the whole, the feeling of wholeness. Which is what makes it poetry. Such acts of pleasurable imagination are exactly religious in that they give us—in our sphere—exactly the sense that God would have in His/Hers: the sense of Creation. A world made new. The same exaltation and tragic satisfaction.

2. Here is Wordsworth in his Preface to the second edition of *Lyrical Ballads*:

> I have said that poetry is the spontaneous overflow of powerful feelings: it takes its origin from emotion recollected in tranquility: the emotion is contemplated till, by a species of reaction, the tranquility gradually disappears, and an emotion, kindred to that which was before the subject of contemplation, is gradually produced and does exist itself in the mind. In this mood successful composition generally begins, and in a mood similar to this it is carried on; but the emotion, of whatever kind, and in whatever degree, from various causes, is qualified by various pleasures, so that in describing any passions whatsoever, which are voluntarily described, the mind will, upon the whole, be in a state of enjoyment.
>
> —From *Norton Anthology of English Literature*, Volume II (1962), p. 90

This is Wordsworth's compositional process. He enters a quasi-meditative state in which he "contemplates in tranquility" (which seems to be something both more and less than thinking) an emotion experienced previously—in his case maybe a feeling experienced while on a solitary hike, or in response to a story he'd been told by a farmer. As he continues with this contemplation, the tranquility fades, and an actual present-tense emotion suddenly arises in him—he is now feeling something that seems to be a poetic or ontic version of the original emotion: just as real and as powerful as the original but not identical to it. At that point "composition begins"—which sounds to me like surrender to a process that has already been developing inside, rather than an intentional or calculated act. As this mysterious process ripens in the course of writing, the feeling is (as with Coleridge) inherently pleasurable—regardless of the nature of the emotion driving the poem. The poem may be sad, tragic, painful, horrific, despairing—but the experience of being carried along in composition is always enjoyable.

This description strikes me as exactly true, and familiar to my own process, and I expect all poets. It's why we value poetry despite its lack of practical value in a world of variously assigned values. Poetry is redemptive: no matter how terrible the pressure of the mood or situation out of which writing occurs, there is always something in the act of committing poetry that brings a feeling of meaning (regardless of how fractured or irrational it may be) that—at least for the time of writing and probably for a time after that—relieves whatever difficulty the writing has arisen from. As if the process, indeterminate and vague though it may be, seems to have the virtue of transforming for a time a state that may seem to be—or is—terrible—into one essentially healing and workable. And insofar as traces of this transformation can be felt in the text produced, the reader, too, can share in it, which would account for the fact that poetry is capable of evoking the most disturbing viewpoints without producing a sense of despair or terror in reader or author—rather the opposite.

3. The Lankavarata Sutra (translated by Red Pine, Counterpoint, 2012) is a key Buddhist philosophical text, generative particularly for the Zen school. Although it is not strictly classified as a Mind Only text (the Yogachara or Vijnapti-matrata or Mind Only schools of Buddhism, whose doctrines are close to, but not quite the same as, Western forms of philosophical Idealism), it references the Mind Only map of eight consciousnesses. In this system, Consciousnesses 1 to 5 are the sense consciousnesses, each with its own organ and species of object. The clear implication of distinguishing the senses from one another as distinct consciousnesses (which distinction is now borne out by cognitive scientific research) is that what we call the world is not an organized whole but is rather a cacophony of warring mental impressions, in five clusters each completely different from the other. [It would seem to take extreme meditators, as many Buddhists were and are, to figure this out: people so attuned to the subtleties of subjectivity and the processes of perception that they could appreciate how utterly different

seeing something is from hearing something, etc., and how astonishing it is that out of this confusion and utter difference we could create what appears, on the surface at least, to be a coherent world.]

Consciousness 6 is mental consciousness. It is the "organ" that creates a unified impression from data produced by Consciousnesses 1 to 5; it is also intimately involved in the process of language and thought, which is seen as integral to the human perceptual apparatus. I literally see, hear, etc., what I can conceptualize and define and not what I cannot.

Consciousness 7 is the sense of "I," of coherent subjectivity; it seems to have been conceived in contradistinction to the famous early Buddhist teaching of No Self or Non Self, which I suspect was probably as counterintuitive and baffling to ancient Asian peoples as it is to us now. ("No self? I can't help it: I keep feeling like I am here.") In fact, personal subjectivity seems to be necessary for there to be any coherent perception, will, or activity.

Consciousness 8 is "Storehouse Consciousness." It is analogous to the Western psychological concept of the unconscious, a large, primordial, and mostly unknown substrate of consciousness that seems to surface in dreams or other uncanny experiences, and that often drives experience or behavior in ways only dimly understood. Storehouse Consciousness, as in some Western conceptions of the unconsciousness, is not limited to the personal: it is universal and includes all the "seeds" of cumulative past events, whose shadows (to switch the metaphor) remain in the Storehouse, not germinating (coming to light in action or thought) until present events "water" them.

So the process of ordinary consciousness would go something like this: Suddenly a barrage of impressions arises resultant from sensual experiences as organ meets object—color, shape, noise, body sensation, etc. (Consciousness 1–5); immediately all this resolves into something recognizable (Consciousness 6) as object, experience—which I can identify, think about, color with memories, associations, feelings, with a visceral sense of my own needs in relation to it (Consciousness 7 and partly 8) as well as some basic deep structural reactions I am probably not aware of (for instance, that the object is pleasurable or not, that the person is threatening or not) that predate my own personal experiences in this lifetime, are maybe programmed into my brain and DNA from the entire human past (Consciousness 8). Something like that, though of course far more complex and subtle. Ultimately, the system proposes, there is actually no entity "consciousness," let alone eight versions of it; the system fully acknowledges, as a central conception in it, that "consciousness" is simply a heuristic device, not a really existing entity.

Buddhism, as it is often noted, isn't a philosophical system, it's a soteriology. Its first and last point is, "suffering, end of suffering," so all its doctrinal devices and conceptual systems are set forth with reduction of human suffering (mainly spiritual and psychological suffering) in mind. This applies also in the case of the Mind Only system: the eight consciousnesses are the realm of human suffering—produced by the endless destructive confusion of human experience; they are the ongoing transformation or evolution (*pravrtti* in Sanskrit) of consciousness, without beginning, ending, or escape. Bad news! But wait, there is an alternative. The Lanka proposes that there can be "personal realization of Buddha knowledge," and that this realization is the salvific kernal at the heart of consciousness that can be set in motion simply by rolling consciousness back to its root, until it is reflexive on itself, and thereby unties its endless knot. This revolution (*paravrtti*) of consciousness reverses the energy of the ongoing wheel of circular suffering, transforming it into a lasting happiness suffused with love and the desire to serve.

Such transformation is discussed in terms of the "three realities": (1) imaginary reality, which is the ordinary unreal world we live in, is a dreamlike projection of mind, and because we don't know its nature, we make it into a realm of suffering that feels all too real to us; (2) dependent reality, which is the fluid network of connection/interdependence, which is what the world really is; and (3) perfected reality, which is none other than imaginary reality (Reality 1) seen for the projection that it really is, and thus redeemed. This formulation is Indian. In Chinese Zen, the same idea was expressed in the poetry of plain imagery, for instance in the well-known saying, "Before I began to practice, mountains were mountains and rivers were rivers" (Reality 1); as I began to establish myself in practice, I saw that mountains were not mountains and rivers were not rivers (Reality 2—there are no mountains or rivers: everything swirls together in connectivity); but now that I have fully entered the path, I see that mountains and mountains and rivers are rivers (Reality 3—back to square one, but with a new feeling, a new experience, a new possibility).

4. I am, I hope, coming around to the connection between all of this and the imagination. The Lanka's system (at least as translated into English) uses the word "imagination" in precisely the opposite sense that Coleridge does. By "imagination" the Lanka seems to mean what Coleridge means by "fancy"—our confused twisted fantasy of what the world and our lives actually are. Reality as we know it is a fantasy. It is unreal. The mad rush for power and purchase, the endless distraction and destruction, the wars, the sexism, racism, fascism, unhappiness, mania for entertainment, the debased sense of personhood, the anxiety, confusion, despair, mass murder, suicide, economic dread, political madness—all a product of fantasy that we don't know as fantasy. (This analysis doesn't refute economic and political causes of social misery; it argues for underlying spiritual-psychological causes of those causes, which must still be addressed.) The revolution or transformation the Lanka's teaching is pointing to is, it seems to me, identical to the transfiguration Coleridge feels the poetic can effect in our lives and consciousness. A transfiguration that makes us more humane—and happy. If, as I take it, the world we are living in now is a failure of the imagination, then poetry—and all works of the imagination, including religion—are, potentially, a healing of it.

# Experience

*This piece was written for the present volume in 2013. This is its first publication.*

## I. EXPERIENCE

What is experience? It seems simple enough, if not self-evident. There is world. Here am I. I perceive, I act: I experience the world. Experiences are personal engagements with a world. They take place in time. There is evidence: I was at the ballgame, too, I experienced it, and I know that 42,000 others did, too—and they can corroborate this. So experience is essentially subjective, yet it can be confirmed by others. Living is experiencing. The older you are, the more experiences you have had. You become an experienced person.

Experiences are of a world. But there are also inner experiences—thoughts, feelings, sensations, moods, intentions, desires. These are less verifiable, yet I assume that everyone has them, more or less as I do. Others have brains and nervous systems, too.

Experience has an aroma, a flavor, a feel. It seems to be more than the mechanical register in consciousness of a perception. We reflect on our experiences; we savor them. This savoring of experience is itself an experience. This essay is about experience, but my writing it is itself an experience. Your reading it is an experience.

⁓

Here is the opening paragraph of Emerson's essay "Experience":

WHERE do we find ourselves? In a series of which we do not know the extremes, and believe that it has none. We wake and find ourselves on a stair; there are stairs below us, which we seem to have ascended; there are stairs above us, many a one, which go upward and out of sight. But the Genius which according to the old belief stands at the door by which we enter, and gives us the lethe to drink, that we may tell no tales, mixed the cup too strongly, and we cannot shake off the lethargy now at noonday. Sleep lingers all our lifetime about our eyes, as night hovers all day in the boughs of the fir-tree. All things swim and glitter.

—Ralph Waldo Emerson, *Essays and Lectures* (Library of America, 1983), p. 471

In our time of maximum commodification, we collect and evaluate experiences as if they were articles of clothing. Our accumulated experiences over the course of our lives make us the persons we are, bring us prestige, character, value. We have experiences. We know what they are. We can define them, refer to them, trade in them.

But for Emerson, experience is a vague, fuzzy, somnambulistic confusion. Here we are, but we have no idea how we got here, standing, as it were, in the middle of something whose beginning and ending we can't discern. And since we are half-asleep, groggy, having lost track of the point and purpose, we live in a stupor, peering through moistened eyes, out at a world that swims and glitters. Maybe your experience doesn't feel like this. But the closer you look, the more persuasive Emerson's view is: very close attention fuzzes a seemingly clear picture. In any case, Emerson says, this is how it really is, certainly how it is for him.

On the third page of the essay, which rambles, lurching between strings of aphorisms and involved diversions (as if the essay itself were for Emerson exactly the kind of experience he is describing), we learn that two years before its composition, Emerson had lost his five-year-old son. He mentions this important fact rather offhandedly, and does not explain how the death occurred or say anything about his son, other than that he cared for him. This loss might account for the disturbing picture of experience the essay paints: relationships are impossible, daily life trivial, practically everything we do more trouble than it's worth. But no, Emerson tells us, he has been shockingly little affected by his grief: "I grieve that grief can teach me nothing, nor carry me one step into real nature. The only thing grief has taught me is to know how shallow it is." (p. 472). His lack of connection to living truth, even in the face of losing something so dear, shows him how weak a grip we have on life. "I take this evanescence and lubricity of all objects, which lets them slip through our fingers then when we clutch hardest, to be the most unhandsome part of our condition" (p. 473).

The truth is, he goes on, we are so locked into our blind subjectivity that engagement with anything outside ourselves is almost impossible. Our "temperament," our self-obsessive fog, accounts for our isolation and our shaky hold on reality. This is all very bad news. Nevertheless, Emerson, a good Yankee Transcendentalist, somehow manages to find a brighter side. True, our sight is dim, our days full of trivia, our human relations vacant if not tortured. Yet at the margins of our experience (if not in it), something else is constantly at work:

> In times when we thought ourselves indolent, we have afterwards discovered that much was accomplished, and much was begun in us. All our days are so unprofitable while they pass, that 'tis wonderful where or when we ever got anything of this which we call wisdom, poetry, virtue. We never got it on any dated calendar day. Some heavenly days must have been intercalated somewhere, like those that Hermes won with dice of the Moon, that Osiris might be born. (p. 471)

This is astonishing. Despite our dismal external condition, "wisdom, poetry, virtue" pop up in our lives timelessly, on days that do not appear in any known calendar. While we agonize over our fake uneventful lives, in the background our actual experience proceeds by pulses and fits—perhaps entirely unknown to us. (I find the possibility that we are unaware of our experience—that what we think we experience is not what we actually experience—marvelous.)

Some years ago in one of my books (*Sailing Home: Using the Wisdom of Homer's Odyssey to Navigate Life's Perils and Pitfalls*, Free Press, 2008), I suggested a thought experiment (on p. 16). Sit quietly, empty your mind. Think of a vivid experience that took place when you were, say, five years old, not an important event in your biography, something random that happens to come to mind, a perception, scene, or feeling. Notice the setting, the characters, the time of day or season. Now think of another such experience when you were, say, ten years old, and then fifteen. Imagine then that these experiences (possibly experiences you had not remembered until now) and others like them constitute your actual biography. That the story you have been telling yourself all these years is a fake, a fabrication, a false, or at least a far less saliently true version. Something like this is I think what Emerson has in mind. It is these odd pulses and fits that do not seem to matter, and that we have entirely forgotten, that provide the poetry, the wisdom, the virtue, that make our lives not only bearable but even bountiful, delightful. Our lives—especially our collective, social lives—may be nonsensical and frustrating, but there's a kernel of experience (however vague and unreliable it may be) that renders them meaningful. There's a Power that speaks through, a music that sounds through, our lives, and this makes humanity's impossibility—in Emerson's words—a "golden impossibility."

> Divinity is behind our failures and follies also. The plays of children are nonsense, but very educative nonsense. So it is with the largest and solemnest things, with commerce, government, church, marriage, and so with the history of every man's bread, and the ways by which he is to come by it. Like a bird which alights nowhere, but hops perpetually from bough to bough, is the Power which abides in no man and in no woman, but for a moment speaks from this one, and for another moment from that one . . . underneath the inharmonious and trivial particulars, is a musical perfection. . . . (p. 477)

Emerson's essay ends on a rousing note. We may be alienated by our temperaments, doomed to nonsensical lives, our intellects incapable of truth, our hearts too distant for human contact, yet we are powerful because an "ineffable cause," a "Power," hovers round us. Isolation is also solitude, and solitude is the province of the soul, the source of those "fitful saltatory undulations" that take place outside time and yet bleed into our temporal lives to make them inspiring, despite the ridicule and the defeat. "Up again, old heart!" Emerson calls out to himself in the essay's final stirring paragraph, which finishes with the idealistic panache of a political speech:

> We must be very suspicious of the deceptions of the element of time. It takes a good deal of time to eat or to sleep, or to earn a hundred dollars, and a very little time to entertain a hope and an insight which becomes the light of our life. . . .
> We dress our garden, eat our dinners, discuss the household with our

wives, and these things make no impression, are forgotten next week; but, in the solitude to which every man is always returning, he has a sanity and revelations which in his passage into new worlds he will carry with him. Never mind the ridicule, never mind the defeat; up again, old heart!—it seems to say,—there is victory yet for all justice; and the true romance which the world exists to realize will be the transformation of genius into practical power. (p. 492)

## II. Deranged Experience

Science accumulates data. Since the machines can produce it, they do, and each new fact throws off shards and threads and new avenues of pursuit of further knowledge at an exponential rate. In the arts and humanities, this explosion of knowledge has been matched by an increasingly nuanced elaboration of subjectivity—as if the sense of being a person in all its angles and aspects must somehow match the endless articulation of the outer world of facts and things (including the insight that the inner and outer worlds cannot be separated and may not be fundamentally different). Writing in the 1840s, Emerson's appreciation of the secret folds of the inner life was already fairly developed. How much more now, post Freud, Marx, Heidegger, Wittgenstein, Derrida, Lacan, Merleau-Ponty, Foucault—to name only a few of the hundreds of essential theoreticians. Analysis and investigation of experience in intimate detail abounds and problematizes (a typical word!) the idea of, and the possibility of, experience. Language is an issue. Is there "pure" experience prior to and more pristine than our descriptions of experience after the fact? Possibly not. And if so, let's discover it; let's locate the ways in which our close experience of language distorts this pristine Edenic experience—if it exists. Culture, politics, economics is an issue. Is there any experience that isn't determined by political and cultural controls? Isn't the way I pass through my days, the texture of my thought and emotion, determined by my socioeconomic status? And cognitive science gets into the act. Surprisingly well funded in this underfunded age, it shows that (just as Emerson intimates) we are not actually having the experiences we tell ourselves we are having. Among many other studies, for instance, Daniel M. Wenger points out in *The Illusion of Conscious Will* that events register in our brains and nervous systems sometime before we decide to carry them out or have conscious experience of them. This means that our lives literally happen before we experience them, so that what we think of as experience is a nostalgic story about something now gone, that we did not notice while it was happening. The world as we actually live in it and the world as we describe it to ourselves are certainly two different things. And doubtless the closer we look at our experiences, the uncannier they seem to be. Did they actually happen? Were they real? And if so, then what? Where did today go when it became yesterday? And where is yesterday now that I am thinking about it today? Though thinking about yesterday happens only today, still, today's memory of yesterday is something different from seeing or hearing something today. But different how? And what about the tomorrow I envision today? Prospect and retrospect turn out to be certainly involved with the experience of experience, which takes place in time. But they seem dubious and self-contradictory at best. Indeed, exactly as Emerson says, we seem to be standing midway on a flight of stairs without any idea of how we got here, how far we have come, how far there is yet to go. (Though we would all appear to be in this world, there is no human being who actually has had the experience of entering this world or leaving it—our entering and leaving the world can be objectively corroborated but can never be subjective experiences.) Issues of memory, time, and immediacy have been much discussed and analyzed in the 175 years since Emerson wrote, making our experience of experience more known and at the same time more confusing than ever.

The following is "Story 171" in Dogen's collection of *300 Zen Stories* (called in Japanese *Mana Shobogenzo* and translated into English under the title *The True Dharma Eye* by John Daido Loori and Kazuaki Tanahashi, Shambhala, 2005, p. 229):

FAYAN'S NOT KNOWING

Fayan of Quinglian Monastery had a profound experience and gave up worldly affairs. He assembled a group of people and traveled away from the lake region. On their way they were caught by a rainstorm, and the valley stream swelled up, so they temporarily stayed at Dizang Monastery. While there Fayan asked Abbot Dizang Guichen for instructions.

Dizang said, "Where are you going, Reverend?"

Fayan said, "I am wandering on pilgrimage."

Dizang said, "What is the purpose of your pilgrimage?"
Fayan said, "I don't know."
Dizang said, "Ah! Not knowing is most intimate."
Straightway, Fayan had a great realization.

This is an interesting tale about experience. Fayan "had an experience." The experience is not described in the story, possibly because this is a sketchy story, but also possibly because the experience is essentially indescribable. In any case, the importance of the experience is not its nature or description but its effects: something, whatever it was, happened to (in?) Fayan that caused him to act differently. He does two things. He "gives up worldly affairs." And he assembles a group of people. Since Fayan was already a monastic, it is odd to say that after his experience he gives up worldly affairs, unless what this means is that having had the experience he starts off fresh, letting go of his previous domicile and way of life, and goes forth. The fact that he assembles a group of people to travel with him (why would he necessarily do this?) seems to tell us something else important about the experience, or as I am extrapolating, about experience in general: it is communicated. Having had an experience, we are then compelled to share it with others (since, being alive, we will inevitably interact with others, and having had an experience, how could we not inevitably share something of it with others through those interactions?). So experience is possibly unknown and yet has effects; and those effects are shared.

Fayan and his traveling group are then suddenly beset by something unexpected that changes their travel plan. A torrential rainstorm forces them to seek shelter at Dizang's Monastery, where Dizang and Fayan have the dialogue that constitutes the main burden of the story. (It is here worth noting, first, that Zen stories are almost always dialogical: the teaching only appears in interaction; and second, that they are understood as "case law," that is, as necessarily particular applications of universal principles that remain inert until they become concretized in the actual case.) "Pilgrimage" could be life, the undulatory, saltatory, and fitful wandering about that we rationalize as an ordinary lifetime. "What is the purpose of your pilgrimage?" Dizang asks. Fayan says he doesn't know and Dizang praises this not knowing as "most intimate."

This is only sensible and seems to be in accord with discussions of language and the contemporary psychology/physiology/politics of experience. We don't know our experience. Or to be more precise, what we know of our experience, what we have to go on, isn't the whole story, or the true story, or the most basic foundational aspect of the story.

We don't know our experience. How could we? To know something is to stand beside it so as to scrutinize it. We say "we have an experience." So the experience isn't us, we're not it. This fact makes the experience—as we understand experience—possible, which means that all scrutiny, all experience, must include a gap, a separation, a space, a vacancy, an alienation. This basic fact doesn't require a century and a half of discussion to appreciate—that when we have an experience, we are removing ourself from the fact we seem to be experiencing. And this removal of ourself from the fact—the fact of our life—turns out to be a removal of ourself from ourself. We *are* experience. We don't *have* experience. This must be how consciousness works—to be conscious of something is necessarily to be at some remove from it, so as to grasp hold of it. Experience requires alienation. Emerson, in writing his essay, possibly under the influence of his recent loss, feels this alienation most acutely. Yet in the very process of his thinking through how he is feeling, in the meandering expression of his essay, he seems to run unexpectedly into something else, something more intimate, something that, appearing as if from nowhere, gives him, by the end of the essay, hope, and even faith. Not knowing needn't be frustrating and dark. It may, in fact, be as Dizang suggests "most intimate," close and warm.

❧

In *I and Thou*, Martin Buber discusses the basic alienating quality of experience quite directly:

> We are told that man [*sic*] experiences his world. What does this mean?
> Man goes over the surface of things and experiences them. He brings back from them some knowledge of their condition—an experience. He experiences what there is to things.
> But it is not experiences alone that bring the world to man.
> For what they bring to him is only a world that consists of It and It and It, of He and He and She and She and It.
> I experience something.
> All this is not changed by adding "inner" experiences to the "external" ones, in line with the noneternal distinction that is born of mankind's craving to take the edge off the mystery of death. Inner things like external things, things among things!

I experience something.

All this is not changed by adding "mysterious" experiences to "manifest" ones, self-confident in the wisdom that recognizes a secret compartment in things, reserved for the initiated, and holds the key. O mysteriousness without mystery, O piling up of information! It,it,it!

Those who experience do not participate in the world. For the experience is "in them" and not between them and the world. (Scribner, 1970, pp. 54–56)

This is preceded by the statement "Whoever says You (ie Thou) does not have something; he has nothing. But he stands in relation." And later, "All real living is meeting" (p. 62). A footnote by the translator, Walter Kaufmann, points out that in German the word for experience is related to the verb "to drive" as in driving over the surface on a road, as a tourist would, to see the sights. Buber puts scare quotes around the phrase "in them" because there is, in fact, no "them" in which experience resides. Experience is exactly superficial—it doesn't go into anything; it stays on the surface.

This sense of experience as tourism is central to Buber's point. For Buber, authentic encounter—the meeting of I and You, in which both sides are put ultimately at risk, so as to truly touch one another—is beyond experience, which is precisely not that. Experience exists in a world of "its," not "yous." A world of materiality and instrumentality, of apparently fixed identity and separation. We use one another, we use ourselves, we use the world. This kind of living can't be avoided. It is the price of, and the nature of, living in a material world among others. Buber explicitly acknowledges this. Yet if this is all there were, we couldn't survive the world's pain. Life would be crushingly dark. We need "I-you" living as antidote and foundation, as home to which to return.

❧

Kinds of experiences. Outer experiences, inner experiences. But wait, which is which? Is a perception of the world "out there" an outer or an inner experience? Seeing happens inside, in the brain stimulated by the eye, which is stimulated by . . . we don't really know what. Probably the argument over whether there is anything out there or not (an argument engaged by brilliant minds) is pointless, but if there is something, whatever it is, we can't be sure what it is. So though we may know we are perceiving, we can't know what we are perceiving—and to what extend we're constructing what we perceive. Or to what extent the object of our perception is affected by our perceiving (as in quantum mechanics), so that perceiving is an interactive event. (Even light may be influenced by our looking at it, according to James Turrell, who has read the science.) Other people? To what extent do we understand them or know them at all? Anyone who has been in a deeply emotional communication bind with a significant other knows that mutual understanding, if it is even possible, only becomes more elusive the further we attempt to honestly explain or listen to explanations. Thoughts, feelings, moods? More and more slippery the closer we come. The more I examine my thought, the more I realize that I am thinking the opposite of what I think I'm thinking. As if the thrust of each thought eventually leads me, through the smooth surfaces of its contours, to its opposite, which will lead me onward either backward or forward to other thoughts that bubble up in mind—from where? Some unknown abyss that is not particular to myself (I think in a language that others have spoken and do speak, all my thoughts shaped by that language and by my past experiences, thoughts, and words as well as the thoughts, words, and experiences of others). This is true of my feelings as well. In fact, I can't tell the difference between thought and feeling. I never have a thought not accompanied by some feeling, and my feelings are constantly either producing thoughts, or are being explained to me by my thoughts. (By now the idea of "I" having "a thought" seems suspect.) There are sensations in my body. But the closer I look, the more difficult it is to pin them down. I am not sure of the connection between the words I use to describe my sensation and the sensations themselves. Sometimes when I describe the pain to my doctor, it goes away. Or maybe just being with her makes it go away. Or simply being intimately aware of the pain makes it go away. Or a particular thought produces a sensation in my body. Moods? I am not sure what a mood is or how long it lasts. Do moods flit across my mind (body?) instantaneously, one replacing the next with such speed I can't keep track of them? Or do I remain in a funk, a depression, a joyful fit of inspiration, for days and months on end? And there could be thousands more categories of experience for me to be confused about (and here I become aware of the crudeness of language— or at least my language—how could it possibly parse these matters?). The stairs I am standing on seem to be an escalator—although it appears I am not moving, not going up or down—yet at the same time everything seems to be moving. I am in the position of Augustine, who when asked about the nature of time, said: "I know well enough what it is provided no one asks me; but if I am asked what it is and try to explain I do not know" (Augustine, *Confession* XI 14. Cited in John Sallis, *Force of Imagination*, Indiana University Press, 2000, p. 189).

## III. RELIGIOUS EXPERIENCE

Maybe the problem is there is so much going on and I'm so caught up in it. Too much something, not enough nothing. If only there were more space. If only I could find a little peace in midst of all this noise. . . .

Religious life is meant to provide that, or at any rate, contemplative life—which is and has always been associated with the silent depths of our experience. The quiet of a cathedral. The peaceful corridors of a monastery.

In his landmark essay "Experience" (in *Critical Terms in Religious Studies*, edited by Mark C. Taylor, University of Chicago Press, 1998, pp. 94–116), which is specifically about religious experience, Buddhist scholar Robert Sharf begins by attempting to define the word "experience." He quickly realizes there's a problem. "It resists definition by design," he explains because the concept of experience is used heuristically by scholars and practitioners of religion to refute the authority of the objective and the empirical. The objective, the empirical, can be defined, measured, corroborated. But experience is impervious to empirical critique, because experience is subjective. It cannot be defined externally and need not be proven. It is personal, immediate, indubitable.

Sharf points out that the concept of experience is not as self-evident as religious scholars and practitioners (and the rest of us) would like to believe it is. In fact, it is a rather recently invented notion, one that goes hand in hand with the development of the concept of the free and autonomous (and atomized) individual who votes and makes consumer choices. Sharf details the history of the idea of experience as applied to religion. It was first advanced by the German theologian Frederich Schleiermacher (1768–1834), who argued that religion is more than a set of doctrines beliefs and practices. Its essence is a feeling of the infinite, "consciousness of absolute dependence." Religion is a universal human need; religious experience is a basic human experience that takes different forms in different religious traditions. In saying all this, Schleiermacher was defending his religion

against the new scientific critique, so powerful in his time, that was re-
ducing religion to an outdated ideology incompatible with contemporary
enlightened discourse. His defense was daring, modern, compelling, and
successful. Soon many other scholars interested in religion (among them
most notably William James, and then later Aldous Huxley with his famous
"perennial philosophy") adopted his "hermeneutics of experience," which
became so popular that today there seems to be no other possible idea of
what religion is—although, as Sharf points out, prior to Scheliermacher,
religion was simply not understood in this way. People did not imagine
themselves as having private religious experiences. Religion was more or
less understood as exactly a system of doctrines, beliefs, and practices,
taken, of course, to be absolutely true—in other worlds, a life one lived
within a cultural and theological matrix, rather than an experience one ac-
cessed and could discuss and report. A fifteenth-century Christian, Jew, or
Moslem was not having experiences—he or she was living a religious life.

Schleirmacher's brilliant new idea was developed around the same time
Europe was beginning to become aware of the religions of the East, which
were radically different from the European religions in that they were generally not theistic, certainly not monotheistic. Nor did they propose defen-
sible truths. (That is, they did not subscribe to Western binary logic, that
something is either true or not.) So it was quite persuasive to argue that
Buddhism, in particular, based, as it appears to be, on systematic meditation practice—is and has always been "experiential." Sharf takes this argument apart with devastating precision in his paper, showing that Buddhism
never understood itself in that way, and that, moreover, quite astonishingly,
the great Asian Buddhist pundits who first brought the practices of ageless
Asian wisdom to the West were, in fact, not bringing that at all, but were
instead bringing their own Western-inflected versions of Asian spirituality
(all of them having been educated in Western ways, and wanting to be successful in the West). True, Buddhist texts do seem to describe transcendent
experiences that seem to be the goal of the practice. But under analysis
such descriptions prove to be subject to much interpretation and debate
(thus undermining the notion that they are somehow precise, identifiable
psycho-physical experiences) and more a matter of literary production than
anthropological or autobiographical description.

Most devastating of all, Sharf chooses to use, as the coup de grâce of
his deconstruction of the notion of religious experience, the example of

alien abduction. (Abductees call themselves, and are called, in the not inconsiderable literature about them, "the experiencers.") With his tongue perhaps visibly in his cheek, and yet with all seriousness, Sharf reviews the literature and finds that there is clear similarity with these experiences—small thin androgynous bald beings wearing form-fitting blue-gray tunics who communicate telepathically as they abduct their subjects in order to study them (especially their reproductive systems), after which they disgorge them from their extensive spaceships near the places where they were originally seized, leaving them with a dim if indelible memory of the event. As Sharf argues, the issue is not whether these people have had these experiences—they seem to be quite sincere about them, and after all, if someone reports an experience they are sure they have had, and they seem not to be lying, who is to say they have not had the experience? The point rather is, what is the nature of the experience, how do we describe and understand it—and what do we do about it? Most researchers do not believe that the experiencers were actually abducted by aliens—though a few do. Most seek other explanations for the phenomenon. Likewise, Sharf argues, no one questions the experiences of meditators and practitioners of other religious techniques—only their claims that the experiences source from absolute unmediated religious truth. Such claims may be true—but only maybe. I have noticed, in my many years of contact with various forms of Buddhist practice in the West, that Vipassana Buddhists have Vipassana enlightenment experiences, satori-seeking Zen Buddhists have classical satori experiences, Tibetan Buddhists have colorful Tibetan Buddhist awakening experiences, and Soto Zen practitioners (the form of Zen that I practice) have the fuzzy, vague nonevents (that may or may not have occurred) that are cheerfully promised (or not) by that school. And Christians have emotionally powerful visionary experiences of Jesus. This alone is enough to give one pause to reflect that it is likely these experiences are not absolute but are mediated by cultural bias—however profoundly absolute they may feel to the one experiencing them at the time. Sharf, it probably goes without saying, has been roundly vilified by Buddhist practitioners and some scholars for his paper. He had already probably lost them even before the aliens, which appear toward the end of the paper.

Like Sharf, I am not interested in denying anyone's subjective experience: that would be impossible. There are all kinds of experiences—we have experiences of all sorts every day—and all of them are doubtful, all of them profound. Religious experiences are certainly valuable—we do need more silence, more nothing, more wonder, and to contemplate ultimate questions, to muse and be awestruck. But like all experiences, religious experiences pass. The point is not that we have or don't have experiences, but rather that we have or don't have a life of significance that is firm and kind and sustainable. Such a life does not come as a result of this or that particular experience, religious or otherwise. It comes from a lifetime of passing experiences and of encounters (in the Buberian sense of I-and-You) that are not merely memories or snapshots, but that, as with Fayan in the Zen story, prompt further actions, questions, and connections.

## IV. LANGUAGE

Experience is awareness (if I am not aware of an experience, I'm not "having" it); awareness involves naming. I know something because I can name it—even if the naming is vague, impressionistic, and problematic. Naming is language. "Pure" experience beyond or outside language is impossible.

Wittgenstein's *Tractatus Logic-Philosophicus* is the best analysis that I know of language's ability to confront our deepest experiences/encounters. Though I don't have enough technical knowledge to fully appreciate the *Tractatus*'s arguments, its conclusions seem plain enough. The world is a problem for us because we are confused about language, which so convincingly leads us to the vain and frustrating hope that we will be able to understand what we will never be able to understand. Wittgenstein proposes to clear all that up for us by strictly delineating (and proving without a shadow of a doubt that this delineation is necessarily built into what language actually is) what language can and cannot distinguish.

> 6.4321 The facts all contribute to setting the problem, not to its solution.
> 6.44 It is not how things are in the world that is mystical, but that it exists.
> . . .
> 6.5 When the answer cannot be put into words neither can the question be put into words. The riddle does not exist. If a question can be framed at all, it is also possible to answer it.
> . . .

6.522 There are, indeed, things that cannot be put into words. They make themselves manifest. They are what is mystical.

Language, in other words, is clear and scientific, if limited in what it can do. All our existential and philosophical problems come from the misguided hope that we can figure out who and what we are and what we are experiencing—which is to say, that we can hold these things somehow in language. But language doesn't do that. While the practical effect of the *Tractatus* has been to convince philosophers who follow Wittgenstein that speaking of metaphysics, or even of deep subjective experience—and certainly religious experience—at all is nonsense and should be avoided, because such experiences are themselves nonsensical, this misses Wittgenstein's own sense that just because such things are nonsense doesn't mean they are not significant. Quite the contrary—they are what is most significant.

The *Tractatus* ends with this:

6.54 My propositions are elucidatory in this way: he who understands me finally recognizes them as senseless, when he has climbed out through them, on them, over them. (He must so, so to speak, throw away the ladder, after he has climbed up on it). He must transcend these propositions, and then he will see the world aright.

This is the conclusion to the sixth chapter. The seventh and final chapter, in its entirely:

7. What we cannot speak about we must pass over in silence.

As is well known, Wittgenstein changed his mind about language although precisely how or why is less clear—by design. In fact, as I read in his later works, there's above all an abandoning of any sense of system, certainty, and rigorous step-by-step logical proof, in favor of a meandering circular methodology that had more to do with exploration, questioning, musing, conversation, and doubt than worked-out philosophy. (The *Tractatus* is the only book Wittgenstein ever actually wrote; all his other works are patchworks, put together mostly by others after his death.) In other words, Wittgenstein seems to have felt that despite the truth of what he'd presented as a young man, there was more. Language was a living thing, a "game," an almost infinite series of games, in which the rules keep changing, an analog of, if not a reflection of, or a form of, life, rather than the keen instrument, however limited (though in terms of "facts," and natural science, it was not at all limited), that Wittgenstein had previously taken it to be. So for the rest of his life Wittgenstein ruminated—living his language as speaking, listening, dialogue, relationality—engaged within a shared practice of language—rather than standing back, as he had done earlier, looking at language in front of him as an object of study, and figuring it out.

In *On Certainty* (edited by G. E. M. Anscombe and G. H. Von Wright, Harper Torchbooks, 1969, p. 73e.), Wittgenstein writes:

> 559. You must bear in mind that the language-game is so to say something unpredictable. I mean it is not based on grounds. It is not reasonable (or unreasonable).
> It is there—like our life.

And this from his 1929 "Lecture on Ethics":

> Now I am tempted to say that the right expression in language for the miracle of the existence of the world, though it is not any proposition in language, is the existence of language itself. But what then does it mean to be aware of this miracle at some times and not at other times? For all I have said by shifting the expression of the miraculous from an expression by means of language to the expression by the existence of language, all I have said is again that we cannot express what we want to express and that all we can say about the absolute miraculous remains nonsense. . . .

> That is to say: I see now that these nonsensical expressions were not nonsensical because I had not yet found the correct expressions, but that their nonsensicality was their very essence. For all I wanted to do with them was just to go beyond the world and that is to say beyond significant language. My whole tendency and, I believe, the tendency of all men [*sic*] who ever tried to write or talk Ethics or Religion was to run against the boundaries of language.

This running against the walls of our cage is perfectly, absolutely hopeless. Ethics so far as it springs from the desire to say something about the ultimate meaning of life, the absolute good, the absolute valuable, can be no science. What it says does not add to our knowledge in any sense. But it is a document of a tendency in the human mind which I personally cannot help respecting deeply and I would not for my life ridicule it.

⁓

As a modern scientific-minded person trying to work out the limits of knowledge, Wittgenstein couldn't help feeling the hopelessness of our ever being able to fully understand our experience. And as an essentially religious person, he also couldn't help respecting the effort to continue to try to do so, nonsensical though it may be. Eihei Dogen (1200–1253), the Japanese Buddhist priest who brought Zen to Japan from China, held a view of language quite similar to Wittgenstein's, it seems, but contextualized in a completely different set of circumstances and preconceptions. As a committed religious person, he was engaged with a set of procedures, doctrines, and emotions that gave him a way to successfully grapple with the impossibility Wittgenstein so clearly saw. Dogen also saw the limitations of language, the cage it makes for us, and the suffering caused by our perennial hope to be liberated from that cage. But Dogen believed that we could be liberated from it—not by escaping, but by seeing and embracing the cage completely. For Dogen religious practice wasn't the means to this end—it was already that end, the ongoing process of being in/seeing through the cage.

One of his essays, "Gabyo" ["Painting of a Rice Cake"], is built around the common Zen phrase, "You can't eat a painting of a rice cake." This phrase has always been taken to mean, "You need real religious experience; you can't just read about it in books." Dogen claims that although it is certainly true that language can't explain, describe, substitute for, or dominate experience, language is itself a profoundly liberating experience. As such, Dogen holds, language is essentially nonsense, because language is never doing what it proposes to do—explain, fix, or control things. The various instrumental uses of language mask language's truest purpose—to call us forth into our innermost being. To dwell truly within language is to plunge into the wonder of experience, thought, and consciousness, without the illusion that one has explained or grasped anything. Language doesn't grasp.

It encounters, embraces. So, Dogen concludes, you *can* eat a painting of a rice cake. In fact, only a painted rice cake can assuage your hunger—which is a painted hunger:

> The paints for painting rice cakes are the same as those used for painting mountains and waters. For painting mountains and waters, blue and red paints are used; for painting rice cakes rice flour is used. Thus, they are painted in the same way and they are examined in the same way.
>
> Accordingly, painted rice cake spoken of here means that sesame rice cakes, herb rice cakes, milk rice cakes, toasted rice cakes, millet rice cakes and the like are all actualized in the painting. Thus understand that a painting is all-inclusive, a rice cake is all-inclusive, things are all-inclusive. In this way, all rice cakes actualized right now are nothing but a painted rice cake. . . .
>
> Since this is so, there is no remedy for satisfying hunger other than a painted rice cake. Without painted hunger, you never become a true person. There is no understanding other than painted satisfaction. In fact, satisfying hunger, satisfying beyond hunger, not satisfying hunger and not satisfying beyond hunger cannot be attained or spoken of without painted hunger. For now, study all these as a painted rice cake.
>
> —From "Gabyo," in *Dogen, Treasury of the True Dharma Eye*, Volume 1, edited and translated by Kabuki Tanahashi (Shambhala, 2010), pp. 445–46, 449.

☙

Which brings us finally to writing. For me, writing is exactly the sort of intimate engagement with language—and therefore beyond language—Dogen is speaking of. In writing there's no explaining something thought or known beforehand. There's no prior thinking, no effort to communicate *something*, only the encountering of self and other in past and future within the very words held in mouth and mind, in dread or awe of entering a procedure that covers everything with doubt. Writing is a profound confrontation with time: the time of writing, of pondering, of reading, the fact that a word written lives long after the writing hand is gone, can lie dormant for centuries and come alive again in completely new ways, utterly different while remaining the same. Writing can be open to and open up immense streams of further language gushing across centuries.

So writing is essentially religious, always evoking nonsensical encounters throughout space and time in which nothing is exchanged, nothing takes place, though everything is risked and called forth. In my own practice of writing (including writing this essay) there's always an intense timeless feeling of not knowing what I am doing (sometimes uncomfortable, sometimes joyful) propelled by some urgent human impulse that I not only can't prevent, but want to give myself to. Although writing can sometimes make a wreck of my life, without writing I become crabby, narrow, and confused.

Though probably most people (even most writers) would not subscribe to this, there's nevertheless a common view of the writer as hierophant. We see it in the cult of the author, whose bestseller (or maybe academically respected work) causes him or her to become suddenly a highly sought-after commentator, sage, and all-round attractive and powerful individual. This persists even though writing is much less important than it once was. And it goes beyond our general worship of knowledge and fame. We still seem to believe that engagement with, grappling with, language per se is a kind of mysterious superpower. One engages it alone, in unspeakable interiority, in mystery. This seems to most people scary, which is why they hold writers in awe (or consider them essentially weird). Yet this grappling with language in our being mesmerized by it is a superpower we all share equally. It is the power of our essential humanness. I agree with Dogen that there are no special experiences outside language—that language itself is a special experience, Heidegger's "house of being." Now I am tempted to say that the right expression in language for the miracle of the existence of the world, though it is not any proposition in language, is the existence of language itself.